MY SECRETS FOR BETTER COOKING

MADAME BENOIT

MY SECRETS FOR BETTER COOKING

Les éditions
Héritage inc.

PRODUCTION
Director: Bernard Benoit
Assistant: Ginette Guétat
Editorial consultant: Michelle Robertson

ART AND DESIGN
Director: Dufour et Fille, Design
Illustrations: Christine Dufour

PHOTOGRAPHY
Director: Paul Casavant

Canadian Cataloguing in Publication Data

Benoit, Jehane, 1904-1987

My secrets for better cooking

Issued also in French under title:
Mes secrets de la bonne cuisine

ISBN 2-7625-6058-6 (v. 2)

1. Cookery.   I. Benoit, Bernard   II. Guétat, Ginette.
III. Robertson, Michelle.   IV. Title.

TX651.B4613   1991   641.5   C90-096619-X

Legal deposit: 2nd quarter 1991
National Library of Canada

ISBN: 2-7625-6058-6   Printed in Canada

LES ÉDITIONS HÉRITAGE INC.
300, Arran, Saint-Lambert, Québec J4R 1K5
(514) 875-0327

Contents

CHAPTER 9

Meat: the real staff of life

MEAT has so much going against it these days that one might expect to see it driven entirely out of our diet. Can we do without it? Not easily. Millenia of meat-eating have confirmed it as our most satisfying food. This is especially true of the Western world, particularly North America.

A quick look backward reminds us that meat was the main food available to the early settlers; when meat became scarce, they grew weak and demoralized and were often decimated by disease. As the population grew, meat consumption decreased because other food was cultivated. A well-balanced agriculture provided a variety of foods, resulting in a better-balanced diet. The importance of meat has diminished somewhat, but it has by no means disappeared.

Vegetables now have an equal place on our tables, and they will be discussed at length in a later chapter. For the moment, conjure up in your mind the thought of a crispy-brown, nutty-flavoured roast of beef, or a sizzling, juicy T-bone steak. For many of us, a well-cooked piece of meat transcends almost any other food we can think of in terms of aroma.

Fortunately, buying and cooking meat is relatively simple if we learn a few fundamental meat secrets. We must study the basic cuts and, when we have made our choice, we must apply the right type of cooking to each one.

BUYING MEAT

Good cooking begins at the market for most of the food we eat. This is particularly true with meat.

Butchers and general meat merchants are well aware that the average shopper can identify only a few of the most familiar cuts. Your butcher may suggest an unnecessarily higher-priced cut, or one that is the most profitable for him to sell. Of course, not all butchers are unscrupulously waiting to pounce on gullible and unwary customers, but they are in business to make a profit. You will want to get the best value for your money.

Supermarkets, where meats are on display, ready-cut and packaged in clear plastic, with price, weight and name of the cut on the label, may seem to be the answer. But they still leave you with the problem of knowing which cut to choose for your particular need.

Personally, I always feel a certain sense of pride — as I am sure you will — when I can ask for a specific cut of meat, rather than just "a nice roast" or "a tender steak."

A large part of every food dollar goes for meat, and it is important to know everything you can about this essential food. Buying meat is inseparable from cooking meat. If you buy the wrong cut for your purpose, the meal will not be successful. And remember, even the best cut can be spoiled by bad cooking.

My daughter was only 12 years old when I began to give her a certain amount of responsibility in the buying of meat. I could have taken her with me and taught her how to shop at the meat counter, but I knew that children are only half attentive when they can rely on someone else. So I began to send her alone to make her own selection, for which she assumed full responsibility.

I would give her a sum of money and tell her to choose the meat, keeping in mind what she intended to do with it when she brought it home. I was truly amazed at how few mistakes she made — and these were more than compensated for by the number of bargains she found.

Having bought the meat herself, she was always interested in the effect cooking had on it, and she quickly learned to enjoy new cuts she had previously not wanted to taste. She often had bought these in a conscientious effort to get the most for her money.

Now, as a wife and mother with an extremely busy household, buying and preparing meat are second nature to her and require no special fuss, worry or waste of valuable time.

I have related this personal experience with my daughter in the hope that it might encourage other mothers to try my method. I highly recommend it.

Learn to recognize the many cuts of meat from the following illustrations and charts. Keep in mind, however, that cuts can vary from one butcher to another and from one supermarket to the next. Study the cuts from one area of the animal at a time, trying to identify them the next time you are at the meat counter.

A word about hams

Bacon and ham are the most familiar kind of cured pork, but there are also salt pork, smoked pork shoulders and various kinds of sausages.

Whole hams. A whole ham weighs between 10 and 16 pounds (4.5 to 7.25 kilograms), but these often are cut into portions. Shank halves contain part of the leg bone. Although they cost less per unit of weight than butt, they have a higher proportion of meat. The butt end actually has more bone in proportion to lean meat, but the meat is a little more tender than the shank end. It is also more expensive.

Ham slices. The best slices are cut out of the centre of a whole ham in thicknesses of 1 to 3 inches (2.5 to 7.5 cm). Slowly baked, these are delicious. They can also be braised. Ham slices, particularly thick ones, are expensive bought as such. For economy, have one or two slices cut off when you are buying a half ham.

Cured shoulder. The picnic ham, which is available in 4- to 8-pound (1.8 to 3.6 kg) pieces, is cut from the shoulder. The shoulder roll, or butt, weighs from 2 to 4 pounds (1 to 1.8 kg). Both cuts are economical, but both are fairly fat.

Country-style hams. These are dark-brown, crusted, maple-smoked hams, or hams that have been smoked many times. They are especially delicious and as easy to cook as any other ham. However, people often find them too smoky.

Very few Canadian country hams have to be soaked. Nevertheless, ask your butcher whether the one you buy should be; he "or she" will know. If it should be soaked, leave it in cold water, just enough to cover, for 8 to 12 hours.

Nothing on a ham should be wasted. Chunks, strips, assorted bits, even shreds of leftover ham, all can be used in any number of ways. Even bone and fat need not be wasted.

Ham generally can be divided into two groups — ham that must be cooked before eating, and ham that comes fully cooked. Cook-before-eating ham includes regular hams, whole, shank and butt halves, and slices. Cuts of cured pork are available in cook-before-eating forms.

Fully cooked hams include whole hams, leg bone in, which weigh from 8 to 12 pounds (3.6 to 5.4 kg) and rolled boneless ham. Fully cooked ham requires no cooking, but I think even these can be improved by cooking, as you will see later.

It is important to find out when buying any cured pork just how much cooking is required. These meat products are sold under various names, such as tenderized, pre-cooked and mild-cured. Since all pork should be well cooked, read the labels or tags, or ask your butch-er to be sure what you are buying. Even if you are entirely familiar with the cut, you can't guess at the style of processing the packer used.

TENDERNESS

Here is a chart of bone shapes that will help you identify cuts of meat and predict tenderness.

Here is a simple explanation to help you remember which cuts are more tender and which are less tender.

The legs and neck of an animal carry weight, work hard and move a great deal. As a result, these parts develop strong muscles and become tough and gristly. Careful, slow cooking with moisture for long periods is required to soften and tenderize such cuts. Since these cuts come mostly from mature animals, they are usually full of flavour and are by far the best for making stews, casseroles and minced-meat dishes. They are also much cheaper than cuts used for roasting and frying because they are not nearly so much in demand. Most shoppers prefer meat that can be cooked quickly.

The middle parts of the animal — the loin, and the organs, such as kidneys — are protected by the back of the animal and do little work. These are less muscular and will be tender without lengthy cooking. Because these are the cuts in greatest demand, the price tends to be high.

	TENDER			LESS TENDER	
	T-bone	Rib bone	Wedge bone	Round bone	Blade bone
Beef					
Veal					
Pork					
Lamb					

Young animals are more tender, even in their legs and neck. In fact, a properly cooked leg of lamb can be more tender than lamb chops. Milk-fed veal, which is pinkinsh-white, is rather scarce. Grain-fed veal, which is more plentiful, is a more deeply coloured meat; the lighter it is, the better. The same goes for lamb, which is classified as red meat. A dark red is the sign of an older lamb.

STORING MEATS

Meat is at its very best when cooked as soon as possible after it is bought. Often, however, that is not possible.

As all meats are perishable, it is important that you refrigerate them immediately upon arriving home. Put them in the coldest part of your refrigerator. If your refrigerator has a meat drawer, that is where the coldest part is.

Whether the meat should be refrigerated wrapped or unwrapped depends on what it is wrapped in when you bring it home. When the meat is wrapped only in butcher paper, it should be unwrapped, transferred to a clean platter or tray, and covered loosely with waxed paper. The transparent wrap on packaged meats is designed for refrigerator storage, both in the meat case and at home. This special wrap allows some oxygen to enter the package and controls moisture loss, thus maintaining the good colour of fresh meat. It's a good idea to remove the trays on which packaged meat rests and then rewrap it with its own transparent wrapping, but this is not necessary if the meat is to be cooked within 48 hours following purchase.

How long can fresh meat be stored in the refrigerator before use? In general, large cuts of meat can be kept in the refrigerator longer than small cuts. The important factor is the proportion of cut surface to the total piece of meat. For instance, a fair-sized standing rib roast of beef could be stored successfully for 5 to 8 days, but ground meats should be used within 2 days of purchase. All chops can stand 3 to 4 days of storage, but be careful with variety meats such as liver, heart, kidneys, sweetbreads and brains; these should be cooked within 2 days to assure freshness.

Whenever you buy sweetbreads or brains, soak the brains and pre-cook them or sweetbreads on the day they are purchased. This will allow you to keep them 3 to 4 days longer.

To keep liver for more than 2 days place the slices in a glass dish and cover them with milk or butter milk. This keeps liver fresh for 3 to 5 days longer, while making it very tender and creamy when cooked.

What about rewrapping cured meats such as frankfurters, bacon, ham and cold cuts once they have been unwrapped? Should they be rewrapped before being refrigerated? Yes, but it is sufficient to rewrap them in the package they were purchased in. Overwrap them only if they cannot be completely wrapped in their own packaging after they have been opened.

Many people worry about how they can recognize spoilage in meat. First, there is usually a change in the colour, from bright red in the case of beef, pink in the case of pork or veal, to a dull grey. Also, you will discover that an off-odour develops. If the meat has been kept in unopened packages, a slippery surface may also develop, and you will notice an unnatural softness, a certain lack of resilience to the meat. When meat has reached any of these stages, spoilage has taken place. If such meat is not always unsafe to eat, it is certainly unpleasant, to say the least.

However, mold on the surface of cured and ready-cooked ham does not necessarily mean that the meat is spoiled. Simply trim off the mold; it will not have affected the flavour or goodness of the meat. If cured meat has really spoiled, it will have an off-odour.

How should meats cooked for future use, or meat leftovers be kept? They should be covered and quickly cooled in the refrigerator, or in a cool room with good air circulation, then refrigerated. Many people believe cooked meats cannot be refrigerated while still hot. They most certainly can be, and this hastens the cooling — but it may not be ideal for the other food in the refrigerator. The heat of the cooked meat may lower the temperature in the refrigerator and, if not covered, will add excess humidity. However, it is the best thing to do with the meat.

Hot cooked meat can also be left for 2 hours before being placed in the refrigerator; this is about the length of time it will take a fair-sized piece of meat to reach room temperature. It should not be left longer than this, because bacteria, which can cause food poisoning, thrives at temperatures between 60° and 110°F (15° and 26°C). Since room temperatures is within this range, it is wise to put the meat in the refrigerator as soon as possible after this point has been reached.

When cooked meat like chicken or turkey is stuffed, remove the stuffing and refrigerate it separately from the meat.

For maximum eating enjoyment, cooked meat can be refrigerated for no more than about 4 days. Smoked or corned meats can be kept for approximately 2 weeks.

Remember: ☞ Lightly cover raw meats. Tightly cover cooked meats.

Butchers, nutritionists and home economists all frown on the practice of washing uncooked meat before storage and so they should, for running water does not remove bacteria. Besides, water washes away much of the flavour and even some of the food value. If you feel you absolutely must clean meat, the best way to do it is to dip a cloth or a piece of absorbent paper into vinegar or brandy, then rub it over the meat. This will clean the meat without affecting the flavour or food value.

BASIC TECHNIQUES OF COOKING MEAT

Once you have mastered the art of buying and cooking meat, you will be able to transform economy cuts into tasty, interesting dishes. First learn the cooking techniques applicable to the various cuts of meat. When you master the art of roasting a piece of meat of one kind, you will be able to apply the same technique to other roasts. You will likewise discover that braising a piece of beef is much like braising a piece of veal or lamb, and so on.

There are 10 basic methods of cooking meat, each related to a specific type of heat.

COOKING METHOD	TYPE OF HEAT USED
Roasting	Trapped heat, in an oven
Broiling or grilling	Radiation, usually from an overhead broiler
Barbecuing	Radiation, direct or indirect, usually from a barbecue below the meat
Panbroiling	Contact with hot metal, usually in a heavy metal frying pan
Panfrying	Contact with hot fat in a heavy metal pan
Sautéing	Contact with very little fat in a hot metal pan
Braising and pot-roasting	Contact with hot fat, then with moist heat in a closed cooking pot
Stewing	Immersion in hot liquid
Poaching or simmering	Cooking in more or less liquid
Fricasseeing	Contact with hot fat, then with liquid or sauce

Most of the basic methods of cooking meat can be achieved in a microwave oven. Roasting, braising, stewing, poaching or simmering, and fricasseeing are done in simple microwave-safe utensils. Panbroiling, however, requires a special utensil called a browning dish.

Microwave ovens equipped with broiler and convection heating devices allow for broiling and roasting in the conventional manner or in combination with microwave cooking.

This is a good place to remind you about marinating. Any meat can be marinated to flavour and tenderize it before cooking, no matter what cooking method you are using. But it's more important with less-tender cuts.

Roasting
There are four classic methods of roasting meat, and you will no doubt find that one will suit your need better than another at various times and with different types of meat. No matter which method you use, follow these general rules:

Place any cut of meat in a shallow roasting pan.

Do not put flour on top of the meat.

Do not cover the roasting pan.

Do not baste while roasting.

FIRST METHOD

Preheat oven at 450°F (230°C); this will take about 15 minutes. Make sure there is a natural coating of fat on top of the roast; add a thin layer of chopped fat if the meat is lean. Roast for exactly 15 minutes to seal the outside pores of the meat and preserve the natural juices. Reduce temperature to 325°F (160°C) for the balance of the time required.

SECOND METHOD

Reverse the above temperature. Preheat the oven to 325°F (160°C) and roast the meat for 15 minutes, then raise the temperature to 450°F (230°C) for the balance of the roasting time. This method is the best to use with fatty cuts of meat.

THIRD METHOD

Preheat oven to 325°F (160°C). Roast at this temperature for the whole period required. The fat on top will not get as crusty brown as with either of the first two methods. To brown the surface fat, at the end of the cooking raise the oven heat to 425°F (220°C) and roast for

another 10 minutes. This is the most economical of the methods, because there is less meat shrinkage. However, the top of the roast lacks crustiness.

FOURTH METHOD

Preheat oven to 350°F (180°C) and roast the meat at this temperature for the entire time. This is the easiest method. The shrinkage, as in the third method, is less than in the first or second. The meat is always tender and the top is crusty brown.

TIMETABLE FOR ROASTING BEEF

FIRST METHOD, beef roast with bones

Weight: 6 to 8 pounds (2.7 to 3.6 kg)
Oven temperature: 450°F (230°C) for 15 minutes, then reduce to 325°F (160°C) for balance of roasting time

	Interior Temp. on therm.	Minutes of cooking time
Rare	140°F (42°C)	15 to 18/lb (30 to 40/kg)
Medium	160°F (53°C)	20 to 22/lb (45 to 50/kg)
Well done	170°F (60°C)	25 to 27/lb (55 to 60/kg)

NOTE: For rolled roasts or other roasts without bones, add 10 minutes per pound (20 minutes/kg)

SECOND METHOD, beef roast with bones

Weight: 6 to 8 pounds (2.7 to 3.6 kg)
Oven temperature: 325°F (160°C) for 15 minutes, then raise to 450°F (230°C) for balance of roasting time.

	Interior temp. on therm.	Minutes of cooking time
Rare	140°F (42°C)	15 to 18/lb (30 to 40/kg)
Medium	160°F (53°C)	20 to 22/lb (45 to 50/kg)
Well done	170°F (60°C)	25 to 27/lb (55 to 60/kg)

NOTE: For rolled roasts or other roasts without bones, add 10 minutes per pound (20 minutes/kg).

THIRD METHOD, beef roast with bones

Weight: 6 to 8 pounds (2.7 to 3.6 kg)
Oven temperature: 325°F (160°C) for entire roasting time

	Interior temp. on therm.	Minutes of cooking time
Rare	140°F (42°C)	15 to 18/lb (30 to 40/kg)
Medium	160°F (53°C)	20 to 22/lb (45 to 50/kg)
Well done	170°F (60°C)	25 to 27/lb (55 to 60/kg)

Rolled roast or other roasts without bones

Weight: 6 to 8 pounds (2.7 to 3.6 kg)
Oven temperature: 325°F (160°C) for entire roasting time

	Interior temp. on therm.	Minutes of cooking time
Rare	140°F (42°C)	25 to 30/lb (55 to 65/kg)
Medium	160°F (53°C)	33 to 35/lb (75 to 80/kg)
Well done	170°F (60°C)	40 to 45/lb (90 to 100/kg)

FOURTH METHOD, beef roast with bones

Weight: 6 to 8 pounds (2.7 to 3.6 kg)
Oven temperature: 350°F (180°C) for entire roasting time

	Interior temp. on therm.	Minutes of cooking time
Rare	130°F (37°C)	10 to 13/lb (20 to 30/kg)
Medium	140°F to 150°F (42 to 48°C)	15 to 17/lb (30 to 35/kg)
Well done	160°F to 170°F (53 to 60°C)	20 to 22/lb (45 to 50/kg)

Rolled roast or other roasts without bones

Weight: 6 to 8 pounds (2.7 to 3.6 kg)
Oven temperature: 350°F (180°C) for entire roasting time

	Interior temp. on therm.	Minutes of cooking time
Rare	140°F (42°C)	20 to 25/lb (44 to 55/kg)
Medium	160°F (53°C)	28 to 30/lb (60 to 65/kg)
Well done	170°F (60°C)	35 to 40/lb (80 to 90/kg)

Meat thermometer

To roast any type of meat or poultry exactly as one wishes without the help of a meat thermometer requires a great deal of experience and a complete understanding of one's oven. Only a meat thermometer can give an accurate measurement of the degree to which roasted meat is done. When this is coupled with a reliable roasting timetable, it is always possible to get good results. When the meat reaches the interior temperature indicated on the timetable, it is done to the degree indicated.

A good meat thermometer is designed so that the reading gauge is placed on the top, for easy visibility, while the tip is of pointed stainless steel, so it can be inserted easily into the meat.

For the best results, and to make things easier for yourself, make a hole with a metal skewer in the centre of the thickest part of the roast. Then insert the

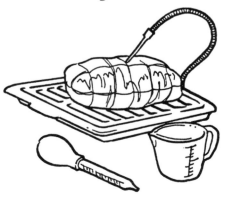

thermometer until the tip reaches the centre of the meat. Be sure it is not in contact with the bone or heavy fat. This is easy to determine because you will feel the bone instantly and the softer fat will allow an easier penetration of the tip than the muscle part of the meat.

Kitchen scales help you determine the accurate weight of the meat or poultry you cook. Not that the weight given on the package is innacurate, but many changes occur in a piece of meat from the time it is originally cut and weighed to the time it is ready for roasting.

CUTS FOR ROASTING

When you choose a cut of meat to roast, evaluate its cost in relation to its bone and fat content. The fat, incidentally, is not to be scorned, because it adds juiciness and flavour. When you are looking for a steak or a fine roast, therefore, make sure to choose a cut with streaks of fat running through the lean. The butcher refers to a cut of meat thus fatted as "well marbled". Remember, a good covering of fat is an indication that you are getting high-quality meat.

Beef

Beef has two hindquarters and two forequarters. Any cut from the hindquarters is more expensive than from forequarters.

The roasting pieces from the hindquarters are as follows:

Round. A 4-inch steak from the top round can be successfully roasted by following the Third Method. You can identify the cut by the small round bone through the centre. It is a semi-economical cut.

Sirloin tip. This is a thick, triangular wedge of boneless meat that is the tip of the round. This is a tender and economical cut. It can be roasted successfully by the Third Method.

Rump. A superb roast for flavour, this is a large even piece of meat, found just above the round. The whole rump weighs from 10 to 15 pounds (4.5 to 6.8 kg). It is expensive as a whole roast unless many portions are required. It is mostly sold cut into smaller roasts, either with or without bones. It is best cooked by either the First or Fourth Methods.

Loin. This is a large section of the beef, located between the ribs at one end and the round at the other. The loin end is recognized by its wedge-shaped bone. The T-bone of the short loin provides the choice cuts — the sirloin roast, the porterhouse roast and the tenderloin. All of these are luxury cuts and are best roasted by either the First or Fourth Methods.

Flank. This is coarse grained, boneless and almost fat free. It adjoins the short loin of the beef. It is often overlooked, but it should not be, because it is not only economical but tender and tasty. It will cook to perfection by the Third Method.

The roasting pieces of the forequarter are as follows:

Rib. You have a choice here between a standing rib roast and a rolled rib roast. The standing rib has more flavour because of the bones. The rolled rib is more economical in a top-quality piece, because it is boneless. The term "prime rib" refers to grade or quality of meat. The best piece is cut from the section nearest the loin and is referred to as "first rib roast".

A 3-rib piece, weighing 3¼ to 4 pounds (1.5 to 1.8 kg) is more economical than a 2-rib piece and will roast better. Use the First or Third Methods.

Lamb

Because almost all lamb in North America comes from young animals, rarely over one year old, all cuts except perhaps the shank are tender. Genuine spring lamb is only 2 to 3 months old. Although more tender than the one year-old lamb, it has less flavour.

Lamb is a red meat and should be roasted the same as beef. The choice cuts of lamb for roasting are the leg and the loin. These are best roasted by the First or Fourth Methods.

A boned and rolled lamb shoulder is economical, tender, and makes an excellent roast. Unless the bones are removed, however, it is not a successful roast because carving it is too difficult. The best methods of cooking the un-rolled shoulder are broiling or poaching. For roasting rolled shoulder, use the Third Method.

For roasting lamb by the First, Second and Fourth Methods, use the same temperature per unit of weight as for beef. The interior temperatures should read the same as given in the table below for the Third Method.

TIMETABLE FOR ROASTING LAMB

Leg and loin

Weight: 5 to 8 pounds (2.2 to 3.6 kg)
Constant oven temperature: 325°F (160°C)

	Interior temp. on therm.	Minutes of cooking time
Medium rare	140° to 150°F (42° to 48°C)	15 to 20/lb (30 to 45/kg)
Well done	175° to 180°F (62° to 65°C)	25 to 30/lb (55 to 65/kg)

Boned rolled roast

Weight: 3 to 5 pounds (1.3 to 2.2 kg)
Constant oven temperature: 325°F (160°C)

	Interior temp. on therm.	Minutes of cooking time
Medium rare	140° to 150°F (42° to 48°C)	20 to 25/lb (45 to 55/kg)
Well done	175° to 180°F (62° to 65°C)	30 to 35/lb (65 to 80/kg)

Shoulder

Weight: 4 to 6 pounds (1.8 to 2.7 kg)
Constant oven temperature: 325°F (160°C)

	Interior temp. on therm.	Minutes of cooking time
Medium rare	140° to 150°F (42° to 48°C)	15 to 20/lb (30 to 45/kg)
Well done	175° to 180°F (62° to 65°C)	25 to 30/lb (55 to 65/kg)

Veal

The loin with kidney attached is the most delicate and delicious cut to roast, but it is also the least economical since there are so many bones. Roast by either the First or Fourth Methods for beef.

The rib is also a good cut. To roast, use the Timetable for Veal. (see chart).

The leg, either whole or half, is also excellent. You will find it easy to carve and full of meat. To roast, use the Timetable for Veal.

Regardless of the cut, veal, because of its blandness, requires more seasoning than other meats. Garlic, onion, or herbs such as tarragon, thyme and bay leaf help greatly to bring out the very fine flavour.

When roasting veal by the First, Second or Fourth Methods, use the same temperature per unit of weight as for beef. Specifications for the Third Method are given below:

TIMETABLE FOR ROASTING VEAL

THIRD METHOD

	Weight	Constant oven temp. therm.	Interior temp. on time	Minutes of cooking
Leg with bone in	5 to 8 lb (2.2 to 3.6 kg)	325°F (160°C)	170°F (60°C)	20 to 25/lb (45 to 55/kg)
Leg boned and rolled	4 to 6 lb (1.8 to 2.7 kg)	325°F (160°C)	170°F (60°C)	35 to 40/lb (80 to 90/kg)
Loin	4 to 6 lb (1.8 to 2.7 kg)	325°F (160°C)	170°F (60°C)	25 to 30/lb (55 to 65/kg)
Ribs	3 to 5 lb (1.3 to 2.2 kg	325°F (160°C)	170°F (60°C)	25 to 30/lb (55 to 65/kg)
Shoulder	5 to 8 lb (2.2 to 3.6 kg)	325°F (160°C)	170°F (60°C)	20 to 25/lb (45 to 55/kg)

Pork, fresh

Pork is rich, fat and succulent when well done. For a top-quality roast, choose a cut with fine-grained flesh, firm white fat and bones that have a pinkish colour.

As with veal, the best pork cut for roasting is the loin. Pork loin is more economical than veal, because pork has more meat in relation to the bones.

The loin of pork with the attached tenderloin is more expensive than the loin without the tenderloin, but both are choice pieces. If you buy the loin with the tenderloin, you can quite easily detach it from the roast before cooking and use it for a separate meal.

A fresh pork leg (called a ham when smoked), either whole of half, is economical to roast and easy to carve.

Roast all cuts of pork by the Fourth Method only.

TIMETABLE FOR ROASTING VEAL

FOURTH METHOD

	Weight	Constant oven temp. therm.	Interior temp. on time	Minutes of cooking
Whole pork leg	10 to 12 lb (4.5 to 5.4 kg)	350°F (180°C)	185°F (67°C)	30 to 35/lb (65 to 80/kg)
Loin centre with tenderloin	3 to 5 lb (1.3 to 2.2 kg)	350°F (180°C)	185°F (67°C)	35 to 40/lb (80 to 90/kg)
Half of loin	5 to 7 lb (2.2 to 3.1 kg)	350°F (180°C)	185°F (67°C)	40 to 45/lb (90 to 100/kg)
Shoulder boned and rolled	4 to 6 lb (1.8 to 2.7 kg)	350°F (180°C)	185°F (67°C)	40 to 45/lb (90 to 100/kg)
Cushion	3 to 5 lb (1.3 to 2.2 kg)	350°F (180°C)	185°F (67°C)	35 to 40/lb (80 to 90/kg)

Pork, cured

Ham is the kind of cured pork we most often roast, although we usually call it "baking" when we speak of ham. There is relatively little you need to know about this because it will cook without being watched. A simple glaze will give it a certain glamour and enhance the flavour, but it can be equally delicious without.

Whole hams, halves — either butt or shank end — and ham slices can be roasted, as can the shoulder butt or picnic shoulder.

Put the meat, fat side up, on a rack in an open roasting pan.

Insert a meat thermometer into the centre of the thickest part. Make a gash in the thick skin to facilitate penetration. Do not let the thermometer touch the bone. Do not cover the meat; do not wrap in foil; do not add water. Bake in a 325°F (160°C) oven for the length of time indicated on the timetable.

Even fully cooked ham is improved by baking. If you allow 20 minutes per pound in a 325°F oven (45 minutes per kilogram in a 160°C oven), you will improve both the flavour and the texture greatly. This really requires little effort. The ham will also keep better refrigerated when cooked in this way. If you want to give it a beautiful appearance, glaze it. This certainly does something to a ham. (See page 213).

TIMETABLE FOR BAKING HAM AT 325°F (160°C)

Type	Weight	Interior temp.	Approx. cooking time in hours
FULLY COOKED HAM			
bone-in whole ham	8 to 12 lb (3.6 to 5.4 kg)	130°F (37°C)	2¼ to 2¾
bone-in whole ham	14 to 18 lb (6.3 to 8.1 kg)	130°F (37°C)	3 to 3½
bone-in half ham	6 to 8 lb (2.7 to 3.6 kg)	130°F (37°C)	2 to 2¼
boneless whole ham	8 to 10 lb (3.6 to 4.5 kg)	130°F (37°C)	2½ to 3
boneless quarter or half ham	2.5 to 5 lb (1.1 to 2.2 kg)	130°F (37°C)	1½ to 1¾
picnic shoulder bone in	3 to 5 lb (1.3 to 2.2 kg)	130°F (37°C)	1½ to 2
picnic shoulder bone-in	7 to 9 lb (3.1 to 4 kg)	130°F (37°C)	2½ to 3
COOK-BEFORE-EATING HAM			
bone-in whole ham	8 to 12 lb (3.6 to 5.4 kg)	155°F (50°C)	2¾ to 3¼
bone-in whole ham	14 to 18 lb (6.3 to 8.1 kg)	155°F (50°C)	3½ to 4
bone-in half ham	6 to 8 lb (2.7 to 3.6 kg)	155°F (50°C)	2 to 2½
picnic shoulder bone-in	4 to 6 lb (1.8 to 2.7 kg)	170°F (60°C)	2½ to 3
picnic shoulder bone-in	8 to 10 lb (3.6 to 4.5 kg)	170°F (60°C)	4 to 4½

Standing rib roast with Yorkshire pudding

A three-rib standing roast usually weighs 5 to 7 pounds (2.2 to 3.1 kg). Do not use a boned and rolled piece of the ribs for this recipe.

5 to 7 lb (2.2 to 3.1 kg) standing ribs of beef

1 tsp (5 ml) dry mustard

Salt and freshly ground pepper

3 tbsp (50 ml) chopped beef fat

Remove the roast from the refrigerator an hour or two before roasting. Place the meat in a roasting pan 2 to 4 inches (5 to 10 cm) deep (enameled cast iron is best) with bones down, fat on top. Do not use a rack.

Rub the mustard on the red part of the meat. Sprinkle with salt and pepper. Then spread the chopped beef fat around the meat. Do not add water, as meat prepared in this manner is self-basting. Do not cover; — this would steam the meat instead of roasting it.

Insert a meat thermometer in the centre of the thickest portion of the meat, but avoid touching bone or fat. Roast according to the Second Method.

The roast is cooked, rare, when the thermomether registers 140°F (42°C), medium when it registers 160°F (53°C) and well done when it registers 170°F (60°C).

Yorkshire pudding

1 cup (250 ml) flour

½ tsp (2 ml) salt

1 cup (250 ml) milk

2 eggs

Sift flour and the salt together in a bowl. Add the milk and beat the mixture with a wire whisk or a hand beater until it has about the thickness of cream. Beat the eggs until thick and pale yellow, then add to the flour mixture. Beat hard for another 2 to 3 minutes.

If you wish to cook the Yorkshire pudding in the roasting pan, in the English way, remove ½ cup (125 ml) of the drippings for gravy and set aside. Pour the pudding mixture around the roast, then raise the heat to 400°F (200°C) and cook for 15 minutes. Lower heat to 350°F (180°C) and bake for another 10 minutes.

If you have a hot tray or a warming oven, the roast can be first cooked completely and the pudding batter cooked in the roasting pan after the meat has been removed along with the ½ cup (125 ml) of drippings. Bake at the same temperature and for the same length of time as described above.

The Yorkshire pudding should be well browned and crusty around the edges. It should also be all puffed up and slightly moist in the centre.

½ cup (125 ml) roast drippings

3 tbsp (50 ml) flour

1½ cups (375 ml) water, consommé or vegetable water

¼ tsp (1 ml) ground thyme

or 2 tbsp (30 ml) Madeira wine

or 1 tbsp (15 ml) H.P. or Worcestershire sauce

or 2 tbsp (30 ml) chutney or chutney sauce

Heat the drippings in a cast-iron frying pan and add the flour. Stir constantly until smooth, well blended and lightly browned. Add the water, consommé or vegetable water. Simmer for at least 5 minutes, stirring most of the time. For a velvety smooth sauce, beat it with a wire whisk. Adjust seasoning. Also add, to taste, ground thyme, Madeira wine, H.P. or Worcestershire sauce, chutney or chutney sauce. Simmer for 2 minutes and serve.

Brown gravy with flour

½ cup (125 ml) roast drippings

1 10-oz (284 ml) can beef consommé

Heat the drippings to a rolling boil. Add the undiluted condensed beef consommé. Heat together, but do not boil. Serve in a sauceboat.

English gravy with horseradish

Add 2 to 3 tablespoons (30 to 50 ml) prepared horseradish to the French Gravy when it is hot.

French gravy without flour

2 flat beef rib bones

4.5 to 5 lb (2 to 2.2 kg) rolled rib roast

1 garlic clove (optional)

⅓ cup (80 ml) melted butter or salad oil

1 tsp (5 ml) salt

½ tsp (2 ml) pepper

¼ tsp (1 ml) dry mustard

½ tsp (2 ml) sugar

1 tbsp (15 ml) brown gravy maker or soy sauce

Place the flat beef bones, which you can obtain from your butcher, in the bottom of roasting pan. Set the meat on the bones, with the fattest side up, on top of the meat. Cut the garlic clove in two. Make slits with a pointed knife at each end of the meat and push the garlic into the slits.

Mix together the melted butter or salad oil, the salt, pepper, mustard, sugar and brown gravy maker or soy sauce. Rub all over the meat.

Roast, following the Fourth Method. Insert the meat thermometer and roast until the interior temperature registers 140°F (42°C) or 160°F (53°C) or 170°F (60°C), whether you want the meat rare, medium or well done.

Roast rolled ribs of beef

Pan-browned potatoes

Place whole peeled medium-sized potatoes in a bowl and pour boiling water over them. Cover and let stand on the kitchen counter for about 20 minutes. Drain and place around the roast after the roast has been in the oven about 25 minutes. Roll the potatoes in the drippings. Continue to roast the meat, turning the potatoes once or twice more in the drippings.

Make gravy just as you would for a standing rib roast.

Roast tenderloin of beef with Madeira mushroom sauce

2 flat beef bones

4.5 to 6 lb (2 to 2.7 kg) whole beef tenderloin

1 tsp (5 ml) salt

½ tsp (2 ml) coarse-grained pepper

¼ tsp (1 ml) dry mustard

2 tbsp (30 ml) chutney

4 tbsp (60 ml) soft butter

1 cup (250 ml) thinly sliced fresh mushrooms

½ cup (125 ml) undiluted condensed canned beef consommé

3 tbsp (50 ml) Madeira wine

The technique for roasting this costly cut of beef varies slightly from the usual. Its tenderness, lack of fat, and long narrow shape make it necessary for it to be cooked quickly at a high temperature. It is important to use a shallow roasting pan 1½ to 2 inches (3.75 to 5 cm) deep when roasting beef tenderloin.

Place the meat on 2 flat beef bones, which you can obtain from your butcher. Placing the meat on the bones is es-

pecially important because the meat should not touch the metal of the roasting pan.

Mix together the salt, pepper, mustard, chutney and 2 tablespoons (30 ml) of the butter. Rub the top of the tenderloin with this mixture.

Preheat the oven to 450°F (230°C). Insert the thermometer. Roast the beef for 20 to 40 minutes, or until the thermometer registers 140°F (42°C) for rare or 160°F (53°C) for medium. Never change the oven temperature. The meat is at its best when the thermometer registers 140°F (42°C), because beef tenderloin should be served rare. (A thermometer is almost indispensable for consistently excellent results with beef tenderloin.)

When the roast is ready, remove it to a hot platter, reserving the drippings in the roasting pan. Keep on a hot tray or in a warm place until ready to serve.

Add the sliced mushrooms and consommé to the drippings in the pan. Stir over high heat, scraping the bottom of the pan. Boil for 1 minute. Then add the Madeira and the remaining 2 tablespoons (30 ml) butter. Simmer for about 30 seconds. Pour into a warm sauceboat. Makes 8 servings.

6 tbsp (90 ml) butter

1 lb (500 gr) mushrooms, minced

8 to 10 green onions, minced

¼ cup (60 ml) minced parsley

1¼ cups (310 ml) undiluted canned condensed consommé

1 envelope unflavoured gelatin

½ cup (125 ml) red wine or port or Madeira

Salt and pepper

4.5 to 6 lb (2 to 2.7 kg) whole beef tenderloin

5 to 7 oz (140 to 200 gr) paté de fois gras

2 boxes ready-mixed pie pastry, or pie pastry of your choice

2 tbsp (30 ml) cold water

1 egg, slightly beaten

Heat 4 tablespoons (60 ml) of the butter until brown. Add the mushrooms, green onions and parsley and cook over medium heat, stirring often, until the moisture disappears. Let cool.

Measure ¼ cup (60 ml) of the consommé, add the gelatin to it, and let stand for 5 minutes. Heat together the remaining cup (250 ml) of consommé with the wine of your choice.. Add the soaked gelatin and stir over low heat until dissolved. Season with salt and pepper to taste and pour into an 8-inch-square (20 by 20 cm) cake pan. Refrigerate until ready to use.

Sprinkle the beef tenderloin with salt and pepper. The shape of a tenderloin tapers at one end to a point; fold this pointed tip partly back on the meat, so you have two broad ends of more or less equal width. Tie the doubled-over piece around so it will hold securely.

Heat the remaining 2 tablespoons (30 ml) butter in a large, heavy metal frying pan. When very hot, sear the beef tenderloin all over, then set it aside on a platter.

Add the pâté de fois gras to the cooled mushroom mixture, mixing it thoroughly.

Prepare the pastry and roll it out in one piece about 16 to 9 inches (40 by 23 cm) and ¼ inch (6 mm) thick. It should be large enough to wrap the meat in one piece. Spread the mushroom mixture over the pastry, leaving an uncovered border along the outside edge. Place the meat face down in the middle of the pastry. Fold the pastry over the meat and seal the seams at the top and ends by rubbing with a little of the cold water and egg beaten together. Then transfer to a baking sheet, placing it seam-side down. Brush the top and sides of the pastry with the remaining mixture of cold water and egg. Prick the dough in a crisscross design with the tines of a fork.

Preheat the oven to 400°F (200°C) for 15 minutes. Place the tenderloin in the oven and bake for 30 to 40 minutes, or until the pastry is deep brown. The first searing of the tenderloin and the 30 to 40 minutes of baking are sufficient to cook it.

When done, cool by placing the baking sheet on a cake rack, then store in a cool place. Do not refrigerate. It can be prepared 4 to 5 hours ahead of serving, or it can be served hot as soon as it is ready.

If you are serving it cold, set the tenderloin on a platter and place around it wine jelly cut into small dice. If you are serving it hot, pass diced jelly in a separate dish.

In either instance, slice the beef very thinly, as this dish is very rich. Each slice will have a layer of the mushroom and pâté mixture surrounding it, then a circle of crust. Makes 8 servings.

Beef tenderloin Wellington

Rolled chuck roast, garnished

A low-cost cut, rolled chuck roast can be very tasty, even tender, when cooked with the proper technique. Choose a roast that will be 5 to 6 inches (13 to 15 cm) thick at the end of the meat roll.

4 to 5 lb (1.8 to 2.2 kg) rolled chuck

2 flat beef bones

1 tsp (5 ml) meat tenderizer

Juice of 1 lemon

6 medium-sized potatoes

12 medium-sized carrots

½ tsp (2 ml) crumbled dried savory or sage

Place the meat on the bones in a shallow roasting pan. Thoroughly moisten each side of the meat, patting cold water on it with the fingers.

Mix together the meat tenderizer and the lemon juice. Pierce the meat deeply with a sharp fork at ½-inch (1.25 cm) intervals. Pour the lemon-juice mixture on top and pierce a second time. Cover the roast with waxed paper and let it stand for 1 hour. Remove the paper and roast, following the Third Method, for 25 minutes per pound (500 gr), or until the thermometer registers 140°F (42°C) for rare or 160°F (53°C) for medium rare.

While the roast is cooking, peel the potatoes and carrots and place them in a bowl. Pour rapidly boiling water on top of them and let them soak for 30 to 40 minutes. Drain the vegetables and place them around the roast about 1 hour before you expect it to be done. Sprinkle them with the savory or sage. Baste vegetables 2 to 3 times with the drippings as they cook.

To serve, remove the roast from the pan and place it on a platter with the vegetables around it. Make gravy, according to your taste. Makes 8 servings.

Cold beef salad

You can make a good main-course salad, fine for a lunch or supper, with leftover roast beef. This salad originates in Greece, although variations of it are served by the French, Italians and Mexicans.

1 to 2 lb (500 gr to 1 kg) cold beef, sliced thin

1 mild onion, sliced thin

2 tbsp (30 ml) capers

3 tbsp (45 ml) minced parsley

½ tsp (2 ml) crumbled dried marjoram

¼ cup (60 ml) salad oil

2 tbsp (30 ml) cider vinegar

1 tsp (5 ml) prepared mustard

½ tsp (2 ml) salt

Place the sliced beef on a deep platter. Break the onion slices into rings and place on top of the meat. Sprinkle the onion with the capers. Mix the parsley and marjoram and sprinkle over.

Mix together the remaining ingredients. Shake well and pour over the salad. Cover loosely and let stand for 3 hours, then refrigerate if you are not ready to serve. Garnish with lettuce or watercress. Makes 3 to 6 servings.

Lamb takes to glazes and sauces as well as ham does.

4 to 5 lb (1.8 to 2.2 kg) leg of lamb

1 tsp (5 ml) crumbled dried basil

1 tsp (5 ml) salt

¼ tsp (1 ml) pepper

¼ cup (60 ml) Dijon or German mustard

¼ cup (60 ml) honey

2 tbsp (30 ml) soft butter

Rub the leg of lamb with the basil, salt and pepper. Place on a rack in a shallow roasting pan. Roast medium rare, by using the Third Method (p. 193), or until thermometer registers 150°F (48°C) (approximately 15 to 20 minutes per pound; 30 to 45 minutes per kilogram).

Combine the mustard, honey and soft butter. Spread on the meat about 20 minutes before it is done. Raise heat to 400°F (200°C) and continue to roast until the meat is nicely glazed, basting a few times. It should take 15 to 20 minutes.

To make the sauce, remove the meat to a platter and place the roasting pan over direct heat. Add 1 cup (250 ml) cold consommé (homemade or undiluted canned) to the drippings and stir, scraping the bottom of the pan. Just bring to a boil and then pour into a hot sauce bowl.

Serve with baked potatoes, cooked while roasting the lamb. Makes 6 to 8 servings.

This recipe is easy to prepare when fresh chives are available on the market or in your garden.

4 to 5 lb (1.8 to 2.2 kg) leg of lamb

1 tsp (5 ml) salt

½ tsp (2 ml) pepper

½ tsp (2 ml) crumbled dried rosemary

¼ cup (60 ml) chopped chives

½ cup (125 ml) fresh lemon juice

2 tbsp (30 ml) Dijon mustard

Rub the leg of lamb all over with the salt, pepper and rosemary. Place on a rack in a roasting pan. Roast by the Third Method for roasting lamb (p. 193) until thermometer registers 150°F (48°C) (15 to 20 minutes per pound; 30 to 45 minutes per kilogram).

Combine the chives, lemon juice and mustard. Pour over the lamb and roast for another 20 to 25 minutes. Serve with boiled rice, stirred with butter and chopped chives and mixed with cooked green peas. Makes 6 to 8 servings.

Roasted rack of lamb à la Française

Nothing equals a rack of young lamb, roasted to perfection. The rack comes just before the loin (see illustration) and consists of all the rib chops in one piece. The French chef always removes the layer of meat that covers the end of the bones.

1 rack of lamb (about 3 lb; 1.3 kg)

1 tsp (5 ml) salt

¼ tsp (1 ml) pepper

½ tsp (2 ml) crumbled dried basil

½ tsp (2 ml) paprika

3 tbsp (50 ml) salad oil

Place the rack standing up on the back bones, directly touching the bottom of the roasting pan. Sprinkle with the salt, pepper, basil and paprika. Pour the salad oil on top. Roast by the Second Method for roasting beef (p. 193), until the thermometer registers 160°F (53°C) or for 20 minutes per pound; 45 minutes per kilogram.

Serve with plain gravy, parsleyed boiled potatoes, and a green salad. Makes 4 servings.

Leg or shoulder of lamb à la Grecque

The Greeks use lots of fresh lemon with their food. It is particularly effective with lamb. They combine it with garlic to heighten and perk up the mild lamb flavour.

4 to 5 lb (1.8 to 2.2 kg) leg of lamb, or 1 rolled shoulder of lamb (about 3 lb/1.3 kg)

1 tbsp (15 ml) salt

1 tsp (5 ml) crumbled dried thyme

¼ tsp (1 ml) pepper

½ cup (125 ml) flour

2 garlic cloves, crushed or minced

Grated rind of 1 lemon

Juice of 1 lemon

¼ to ⅓ cup (60 to 80 ml) cider, apple juice, or Italian red wine

With the point of a sharp knife, make slashes about 2 inches (5 cm) apart over the surface of the meat. Cut each slash about ½ inch (1.25 cm) deep and 1 inch (2.5 cm) long.

Combine in a bowl the salt, thyme, pepper, flour, garlic and lemon rind. Gradually blend in enough lemon juice to form a smooth paste, not too thick. Then rub the paste over the entire roast, especially inside each of the slash-openings, pushing it in with the fingers.

1. Make slashes ½ inch (1.25 cm) deep and 1 inch (2.5 cm) long — 2 inches (5 cm) apart.

2. Rub lemon-garlic paste over entire roast, pushing it into slash openings with fingers.

In a shallow roasting pan, place a double thickness of aluminum foil, approximately 18 by 30 inches (46 by 76 cm). Place the prepared roast on this and bring the narrow edges up, then the other sides, leaving just the top of the roast exposed.

Roast by the Second Method for roasting beef (p. 193), until the thermometer registers 160°F (53°C) or 20 minutes per pound (45 minutes per kilogram). Then turn back the aluminum foil to allow for browning, which should take another 20 to 30 minutes.

Skim off excess fat from the drippings and add the cider, apple juice or wine. Stir together and serve with the lamb. Mashed potatoes and sliced tomatoes are excellent accompaniments. Makes 6 to 8 servings.

Rolled shoulder of lamb, Texas style

The tart barbecue sauce used on this roasted shoulder of lamb need not be limited to this cut. Use it also with winter lamb, which is somewhat drier and heavier than spring lamb.

3 to 4 lb (1.3 to 1.8 kg) lamb shoulder, boned and rolled

½ cup (125 ml) butter or bacon fat

½ cup (125 ml) cider vinegar or lemon juice

1 tsp (5 ml) salt

½ tsp (2 ml) pepper

½ tsp (2 ml) crumbled dried thyme, basil or rosemary

½ tsp (2 ml) dry mustard

Place the meat on a rack in a shallow roasting pan, just as it is or stuffed with a few pieces of garlic to taste. Roast by the Third Method for roasting lamb (p. 193) for 2 hours, or until the thermometer registers 170°F (60°C) or for 35 minutes per pound (1 hour, 20 minutes per kilogram).

Bring to a boil the butter or bacon fat, cider vinegar or lemon juice, salt and pepper, whichever herb you are using, and the mustard. Use this to baste the roast every 15 minutes. When the sauce is used up, use the juices in the pan to continue basting until the meat is cooked. Serve with baked potatoes, glazed onions or buttered lima beans, and barbecue sauce. Serves 8.

Rolled lamb shoulder Oriental

Don't worry about the use of 4 garlic cloves; the way they are used actually imparts only a light flavour to the meat. The finished roast should have a deep brown glaze.

4 garlic cloves, crushed or minced

½ cup (125 ml) boiling water

⅓ cup (80 ml) honey

1 cup (250 ml) soy sauce

1 rolled or cushion shoulder of lamb (about 3½ lb; 1.8 kg)

Juice of 1 orange

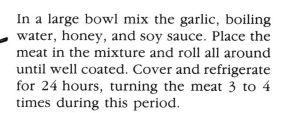

In a large bowl mix the garlic, boiling water, honey, and soy sauce. Place the meat in the mixture and roll all around until well coated. Cover and refrigerate for 24 hours, turning the meat 3 to 4 times during this period.

To roast, remove the meat from the marinating mixture and place it in the roasting pan. Pour ½ cup (125 ml) of the marinating mixture on top. Roast by the Third Method for roasting lamb (p. 193), until the thermometer registers between 165°F (55°C) and 175°F (62°C), or for 25 to 30 minutes per pound (55 minutes to 1 hour, 5 minutes per kilogram). This roast is served well done.

When the meat is cooked, skim off most of the fat and add the orange juice to the drippings. Boil for a few seconds while scraping the bottom of the pan.

Serve with fried or curried rice and blanched cauliflower. Makes 6 to 8 servings.

Roast loin of veal

This is a luxury cut greatly appreciated by French chefs, who refer to it as la rognonnade, *which means the loin of veal with the kidney and its fat attached.*

2 tbsp (30 ml) salad oil

1 medium-sized onion, diced

1 carrot, grated

1 celery rib, diced

4 to 5 lb (1.8 to 2.2 kg) loin of veal with kidney attached

1½ tsp (7 ml) salt

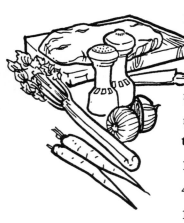

½ tsp (2 ml) pepper

½ tsp (2 ml) crumbled dried thyme

1 tsp (5 ml) paprika

4 tbsp (60 ml) soft butter

1 10-oz (284 ml) can condensed beef consommé, undiluted

Heat the salad oil in a frying pan. Add the onion, carrot and celery. Stir over low heat for 8 to 10 minutes. Place in the bottom of the roasting pan where the meat will be set.

Place the meat on the vegetables, with the fat of the kidney directly on the vegetables. Blend together the salt, pepper, thyme, paprika and soft butter. Spread on top of the meat. Roast by the Fourth Method for beef (p. 193) until the thermometer registers 170°F (60°C) or for 20 minutes per pound (45 minutes per kilogram).

Add the consommé to the roasting pan and boil hard for 2 minutes. Pass the mixture through a strainer or whirl in a blender.

Serve the roast and puréed vegetables with pan-browned potatoes and buttered green peas and mushrooms. Makes 8 servings.

The rib of veal is tender, but it is not as meaty as the loin, which has the tenderloin and kidney. This cut is the same as the rack of lamb and the rib roast of beef; of course, it is larger than the lamb and smaller than the beef. Also, this cut is leaner than the loin and requires more fat when it is roasting.

Roast rib of veal

3 to 4 lb (1.3 to 1.8 kg) rib roast of veal

3 tbsp (50 ml) salad oil

1 tbsp (15 ml) flour

½ tbsp (8 ml) paprika

¼ tsp (1 ml) grated nutmeg or ground sage

1 tsp (5 ml) salt

½ tsp (2 ml) pepper

½ cup (125 ml) diced fat salt pork

Place the meat on a rack in a roasting pan. Blend together the salad oil, flour, paprika, nutmeg or sage, salt and pepper. Spread on top of the meat. Cover with the diced salt pork.

Roast by the Third Method for veal (p. 193) until the thermometer reads 170°F (60°C) or for 25 minutes per pound (55 minutes per kilogram).

Serve with pan gravy, to which could be added a few tablespoons of dry sherry or Madeira, and with mashed potatoes and parsleyed carrots. Makes 6 to 8 servings.

This is a perfect recipe for half a leg of veal, rolled and tied. It is simple and tasty. It is also nice for a buffet dinner, as it is easy to slice and is equally good hot or cold.

Rolled leg of veal Anglaise

½ lb (250 gr) breakfast bacon

4 to 5 lb (1.8 to 2.2 kg) boned and rolled leg of veal

½ tsp (2 ml) salt

¼ tsp (1 ml) pepper

2 bay leaves

½ cup (125 ml) butter

½ cup (125 ml) white wine, or ¼ cup (60 ml) fresh lemon juice

½ cup (125 ml) commercial sour cream

Dice the bacon and place it in the bottom of a shallow roasting pan. Place the meat on top of this. Sprinkle with salt and pepper. Tuck the bay leaves under the meat. Roast by the Third Method for veal (p. 193) until the thermometer registers 170°F (60°C), or for 35 minutes per pound (1 hour, 20 minutes per kilogram).

Heat together the butter and white wine or lemon juice, and use this to baste the roast every 20 minutes during the roasting period, until none is left.

To make gravy, simply add the cold sour cream to the drippings. Stir fast with a wire whisk over low heat until hot and well blended, but not boiling.

Serve the roast with fine noodles and buttered broccoli, with the gravy on the side. Makes 8 to 10 servings.

Leg of veal Italiano

Certain fish, such as tuna and anchovies, go very well with veal. The Italian chefs are best at preparing veal with these fish.

6 to 8 lb (2.7 to 3.6 kg) leg of veal

½ cup (125 ml) salad oil

½ cup (125 ml) diced celery

1 medium-sized onion, diced

1 7-oz (200 ml) can white tuna, chopped

8 flat anchovy fillets, diced

1 cup (250 ml) chicken consommé

Salt and pepper

3 tbsp (50 ml) capers

Pat the veal as dry as possible with absorbent paper. Heat the oil in a large frying pan over medium heat and brown the meat all over. Then place it in a roasting pan with the celery, onion, tuna and anchovies. Add the chicken consommé. Sprinkle the meat lightly with salt and pepper. Then cover the roasting pan with aluminum foil.

Roast by the Third Method for veal (p. 193) until the thermometer registers 170°F (60°C) or for about 25 minutes per pound (55 minutes per kilogram). When done, remove the meat, strain the sauce, and add the capers to it.

To serve cold, place the meat in a deep dish and pour the caper gravy on top; it will cool into a clear jelly. Cover and refrigerate for 24 hours before serving.

This easy-to-carve roast is especially good served cold for a buffet dinner. Makes 10 or more servings.

Roasted stuffed shoulder of veal

The combination of lemon rind and parsley is one of the tastiest stuffings one can make for veal. The same stuffing can also be used for a boned shoulder of veal.

2 tbsp (30 ml) salad oil or melted bacon fat

1 tsp (5 ml) salt

¼ tsp (1 ml) pepper

¼ tsp (1 ml) grated nutmeg

3 cups (750 ml) soft fresh bread cubes

½ cup (125 ml) chopped parsley

Grated rind of 1 lemon

3 tbsp (50 ml) lemon juice

3 green onions, chopped

1 tbsp (15 ml) melted butter

3 to 4 lb (1.3 to 1.8 kg) shoulder of veal, boned or shaped into a cushion

Mix together the salad oil or melted bacon fat, the salt, pepper and nutmeg. Set aside. Combine the bread cubes with the parsley, lemon rind and lemon juice, green onions and butter. Add salt and pepper to taste. If using a boned shoulder, use the mixture to stuff it, then pour the oil mixture over the veal. If a cushion is used, pour the oil mixture over the cushion and pat the stuffing firmly on top of the meat.

Roast by the Third Method for veal (p. 193) until the thermometer registers 175°F (62°C) or for about 25 minutes per pound (55 minutes per kilogram).

Serve with the gravy and a green salad. Makes about 8 servings.

The loin of pork constitutes the entire rack. It is usually sold in one piece, or divided into rib end and loin end. The loin end has the tenderloin, so it is always slightly more expensive than the rib end.

Roast loin of pork gourmet

4 lb (1.8 kg) rib or loin end of pork,

or 5 to 6 lb (2.2 to 3.6 kg) rack of pork

2 garlic cloves

1 tsp (5 ml) salt

½ tsp (2 ml) pepper

½ tsp (2 ml) ground sage

Make incisions in the meat and stuff them with the garlic cloves cut into halves. Place the meat on a rack in a roasting pan. Sprinkle the top with salt, pepper and sage.

Roast by the Fourth Method for pork (p. 193) until the thermometer registers 185°F (67°C) or for 35 minutes per pound (1 hour, 20 minutes per kilogram).

To make all pork roast gravy, proceed in the following manner: remove the meat from the roasting pan. Place the pan over medium heat. If there is too much fat, remove some but keep at least ½ cup (125 ml). Add ½ cup (125 ml) flour and stir over medium heat for 10 minutes. This is important, as the flour must cook to lose its rawness. Add all at once 3 cups (750 ml) cold water, or 2 cups (500 ml) cold water with 1 cup (250 ml) red wine, cider or orange juice. Stir together until creamy and smooth. Season with salt and pepper to taste.

Serve with mashed potatoes and apple slices sautéed in some of the fat from the roast. Makes about 8 servings.

The leg of pork, or fresh ham as it is sometimes called, can be cooked either boned or with the bone in, the same as cured ham. It can be roasted whole or halved. The whole leg weighs about 12 pounds (5.4 kilograms) and is too large for most families, but either the butt or shank half makes a good roast.

Roast leg of pork

1 half leg of pork (about 6 lb (2.7 kg))

Salt and pepper

1 tsp (5 ml) ground sage

1 garlic clove, crushed

2 cups (500 ml) apple juice or strong cider

Rub the roast all over with salt, pepper and sage. Spread the garlic on top. Place on a rack in a roasting pan. Add the apple juice or cider.

Roast by the Fourth Method for pork (p. 193) until the thermometer reads 185°F (67°C) or for 35 minutes per pound (1 hour, 20 minutes per kilogram).

Make the gravy in the same way as for the loin of pork. Serve with buttered noodles, coleslaw and applesauce. Makes 8 servings.

Citrus dressing for stuffed roast pork

This citrus dressing is a wonderful complement to pork. It can be used for a crown roast of pork, or for a boned leg of pork. To serve with a roast loin of pork, bake the dressing separately.

¼ cup (60 ml) butter

1 cup (250 ml) diced celery

1 large onion, diced

2 medium-sized apples, peeled and chopped

6 cups (1.5 L) diced bread

1 tsp (5 ml) ground sage

¼ tsp (1 ml) ground marjoram

1 8-oz (220 ml) can whole cranberry sauce

¼ cup (60 ml) brown sugar

1 tsp (5 ml) salt

Grated rind of 1 orange

½ cup (125 ml) fresh orange juice

Melt the butter in a frying pan and add the celery, onion and apples. Stir over medium-low heat until softened, but do not brown. Add the diced bread, sage and marjoram. Place in a saucepan the cranberry sauce, brown sugar, salt and orange rind. Stir together over low heat until the sugar is dissolved. Add to the bread mixture. Add the orange juice gradually, continuing to mix until the bread is moistened. It is now ready to use as a stuffing for any type of roast pork.

To bake separately, put in a baking dish and bake, covered, at 350°F (180°C) for 1 hour.

Roast stuffed pork tenderloin

A pork tenderloin is an ideal cut when a small roast is required. It is equally good hot or cold.

1¼ to 1½ lb (625 to 750 g) pork tenderloin

½ recipe for Citrus Dressing (above)

½ tsp (2 ml) salt

¼ tsp (1 ml) pepper

½ tsp (2 ml) curry powder

Beat the tenderloin with the flat side of a cleaver to flatten it, then slit into two without detaching the two pieces. Fill with dressing and tie securely.

Mix the salt, pepper and curry powder. Rub all over the stuffed tenderloin. Place on a well-oiled roasting pan without a rack. Roast by the Fourth Method for pork (p. 193) until the thermometer registers 185°F (67°C) or for 35 minutes per pound (1 hour, 20 minutes per kilogram).

Serve with browned potatoes and broccoli with butter and lemon juice. Makes about 4 servings.

Glazing a baked ham

About 30 minutes before the ham is done, remove it from the oven and take off the rind. Cut off the brown top fat and score the remaining fat in an S shape with a punch-type can opener, or in crisscross diamonds with a sharp knife.

Choose a glaze; if it is a clear glaze, spread it on the ham with a spoon; if it is a thick glaze, spread it on with your hands.

Return the ham to the oven and bake again at 375°F (190°C) until the ham has a good glaze. Baste it two or three times.

Simple glaze

Spoon onto the ham honey, maple syrup or corn syrup. On top of this pat on brown sugar.

Chef's favourite

Heat 1 cup (250 ml) of apricot jam with the grated rind of 1 orange, or 3 tablespoons (50 ml) rum, or ½ cup (125 ml) finely chopped walnuts. Spoon over ham. Heated jam by itself also makes a good glaze.

American favourite

Heat 1 tablespoon (15 ml) prepared mustard with 1 cup (250 ml) red-currant jelly, ½ teaspoon (2 ml) ground cloves, ½ teaspoon (2 ml) ground cinnamon and ½ cup (125 ml) firmly packed brown sugar. Spoon over ham.

Scotch glaze

Heat 1 cup (250 ml) bitter orange marmalade with 3 tablespoons (50 ml) orange juice or Scotch whisky and ½ cup (125 ml) firmly packed brown sugar. Spoon over ham.

Buffet-style glaze

Heat together 1 cup (250 ml) apricot preserves, 3 tablespoons (50 ml) cider vinegar, ¼ cup (60 ml) corn syrup and 1 teaspoon (5 ml) ground ginger. Spoon over ham.

Western-Canadian favourite

Stir 1 cup (250 ml) honey with the grated rinds of 1 orange and 1 lemon. Spoon over ham.

Delicatessen special

Heat together 1 cup (250 ml) firmly packed brown sugar and ½ cup (125 ml) liquid from sweet pickles or ¼ cup (60 ml) ginger ale or cola. Spoon over ham.

German glaze

Mix 1 cup (250 ml) firmly packed brown sugar, 2 tablespoons (30 ml) German-style prepared mustard and enough beer to moisten. Spread over ham.

Finnish glaze

Spread the fat with a generous coating of prepared mustard, German or Finnish style. Then pat on a generous layer of fine bread crumbs. Top with a thick layer of brown sugar, which should be patted on with the hands.

Broiling

To broil or to grill, the meat is placed some distance from the source of heat. It is the red-hot heat radiating on the food, but not touching it, that does the cooking.

A certain amount of shrinkage occurs in meat when it is cooked, no matter what technique is used. It is caused by the natural juices of the meat seeping through the surface. These juices become part of the cooking liquid or gravy, depending on how the meat is cooked.

In broiling, however, the juices extracted from the meat are evaporated almost immediately by the heat radiating overhead. This evaporation, or drying-off process, forms a brown crust on the top of the meat being broiled.

Since excess juices that fall into the pan under the grill are usually very fatty, or overcooked, they are indigestible and should be discarded.

Broiling is used on very tender cuts of meat, which should be cooked quickly to prevent hardening or drying of the muscle. To achieve this, the first heat penetrating the surface of the meat must be quick and hot so that the centre of the meat is raised quickly to cooking temperature.

This contrast between the degrees of doneness on the inside and outside of the meat distinguishes broiled meats from those cooked by other methods; the outside of the meat is cooked and browned a great deal more than the inside.

To sear the top of the meat, the broiler should be preheated for at least 15 minutes. Rub the meat vigorously with soft butter or oil and broil as close to the source of heat as can be managed without the fat catching on fire, from 2 to 4 minutes. This searing speeds the formation of the brown layer on the top and stops the juices from escaping. The broiling should then be finished about 3 to 4 inches (8 to 20 cm) away from the source of the heat.

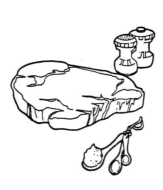

You will be able to tell when steaks and chops are cooked by the appearance of small drops of blood on the *uncooked* side of the meat. At that point, turn the meat and wait again for the juice to appear in small droplets, which is the signal that the meat is cooked.

☛ If yours is a gas broiler, broil with the door closed, because gas flames consume smoke and absorb moisture.

☛ If your broiler is electric, leave the door slightly ajar during the broiling period, to expel moisture from the oven.

Whether your broiler is gas or electric, make sure you have read the specific directions for your particular oven. There usually are special mechanical adjustments you will have to make to get the best broiling results.

Where to position the broiler pan in any type of oven depends upon the food being broiled. The following is a list of foods that, after the first few minutes of searing, should be placed so that they are 2 to 3 inches (5 to 8 cm) from the source of the heat:

meat to be cooked rare;
food requiring only brief cooking;
food to be heated or browned only on top.

The following should be placed 4 inches (10 cm) or more from the source of heat:

thick steaks, after the first minute of searing;
steaks and all other meats that are to be well done;
fish;
poultry (broil 5 to 6 inches (13 to 15 cm) from the source of heat)
foods that require long cooking.

Remember, for best results it is important always to choose tender cuts of meat. Use choice or prime grade when buying steaks; have them cut at least 1 inch (2.5 cm) thick and not more than 2 inches (5 cm) thick. You will find that steaks less than 1 inch (2.5 cm) thick are better panbroiled or pangrilled.

0—🗝 Slash edges of fat on steaks or chops in several places to prevent the meat from curling.

0—🗝 Brush all foods with oil, soft butter or margarine before broiling. You can also sprinkle with paprika to help browning. For extra flavour, add lemon juice to the oil or butter.

For crispiness, roll foods to be broiled — except for steaks and chops — in fine bread crumbs.

0—🗝 Sprinkle with pepper before broiling, but add salt only after broiling, because salt may draw the flavourful juices to the surface and slow the browning.

0—🗝 Have the meat at room temperature for 1 hour before broiling. This reduces the cooking time and gives a better brown top to the meat.

If an emergency requires that you broil frozen or very cold steaks or chops, broil them at a lower temperature, in other words, 4 to 5 inches (10 to 13 cm) away from the source of heat, and for a longer period. Frozen meat needs 25 to 50 per cent more time than meat at room temperature.

Always grease the broiler rack with salad oil before putting the meat on it. As the rack will be hot from preheating, spread the oil on with a brush.

0—🗝 Do not remove all the fat from steaks or chops when broiling, because fat gives extra flavour to the meat and to some extent helps to hold in the juices.

0—🗝 Do not use a fork to turn meat. Use tongs, or a wide, firm spatula. If meat is pricked with the tines of a fork, its juices will escape during cooking.

During the last 5 minutes of broiling, you can add to the rack well-oiled and well-seasoned halves of tomatoes, slices of mild onions or mushrooms cut into thick slices if they are large, left whole if they are button mushrooms.

Quadrillage or checkering

You can add a note of elegance to grilled meats by creating a beautiful checkered pattern on them.

The way to proceed is as follows: Brush the meat with oil while you heat the broiler rack red hot. Then place the meat on top of the rack. A sizzling sound will be heard and a bat of smoke appears, but don't worry about this. Leave the meat in this position for 2 minutes. Then give it a right-angle turn. The hot bars of the grill will mark a checkerboard pattern on the meat. After another 2 minutes, turn the meat over and repeat the same process, thus creating the pattern on both sides. 0—🗝 The secret to this is two-fold: first, the well-oiled meat (or fish or fowl); second, the red-hot grill.

CUTS FOR BROILING

BEEF: steaks — club, porterhouse, rib, sirloin, T-bone; flank; tenderloin; ground meat patties; beef frankfurthers.

LAMB: chops — loin, rib, shoulder; sirloin; ground meat patties; liver; kidneys, split in two.

VEAL: steaks; chops; cutlets; calf's liver.

PORK: bacon, sausages, ready-cooked ham slices.

TIMETABLE FOR BROILING MEAT
IN PREHEATED BROILER TOTAL BROILING TIME IN MINUTES

	Thickness	Rare	Medium	Well done
Steak	1 inch (2.5 cm)	12	15	20
	1½ inches (3.75 cm)	15	20	25
	2 inches (5 cm)	25	30	35
Flank steak (London broil)	7	9	12	
Lamb chops	1 inch (2.5 cm)	8	10	12
	1½ inches (3.75 cm)	12	15	18
Meat patties	2 inches (5 cm)	10	15	20
Liver	¾ to 1 inch (1.9 to 2.5 cm)	8	10	12
Kidney	8 to 10 minutes in all			
Bacon	2 to 3 minutes on each side			
Pork sausages	3 to 4 minutes on each side			

Broiled ham steaks

The centre-cut slices of ham 1½ to 2 inches (3.75 to 5 cm) thick are delicious broiled. Slash the fat around the edge with a sharp knife before cooking to prevent curling. Mix together 1 teaspoon (5 ml) each of brown or white sugar and prepared mustard. Brush one side of the ham steak with half the mixture, then brush it with melted butter. Broil according to timetable. Brush the second side with the remaining sugar and mustard mixture and butter.

TIMETABLE FOR BROILING HAM STEAKS

Thickness of slice	Distance from heat	Minutes of cooking time per side
Fully cooked ham		
½ inch (1.25 cm)	3 inches (8 cm)	3 to 5 (do not turn)
1 to 3 inches (2.5 to 8 cm)	4 inches (10 cm)	5
Cook-before-eating ham		
½ inch (1.25 cm)	3 inches (8 cm)	4
1 inch (2.5 cm)	4 inches (10 cm)	9
1½ inches (3.75 cm)	4 inches (10 cm)	10

A sirloin steak 1 to 1½ inches (2.5 to 3.75 cm) thick is a family-sized steak. It includes a large section of tenderloin, a large section of loin and a small amount of bone. It is cut from the loin of the beef, which is the most expensive of major beef cuts and the most tender.

If the steak has been frozen, it should be placed in the refrigerator for 9½ hours to thaw, or on the kitchen counter for 4 hours to reach room temperature.

Perfect broiled sirloin steak

1 sirloin steak (2 lb; 1 kg)

3 tbsp (50 ml) salad oil

1 tsp (5 ml) coarse-ground pepper

1 tsp (5 ml) MSG

4 bay leaves

Brush the steak on both sides with the salad oil. Sprinkle with the pepper and MSG.

Place on the grill of a preheated broiler. Broil 2 inches (5 cm) from the source of heat for 4 minutes, then turn and sear on the other side in the same manner. Continue cooking 3 to 4 inches (8 to 10 cm) from the source of heat for 5 minutes on each side for very rare, 6 minutes on each side for rare, and 10 minutes on each side for medium rare.

At 2 minutes before the meat is cooked, top with the bay leaves and allow them to scorch on top of the meat.

Serve with chive butter (melted butter and chives) and sliced tomatoes. Makes 4 servings.

Teriyaki is a Japanese word meaning coal (teri) broil (yaki). The marinating sauce makes it greatly different from other broiled meats. Club steak, top sirloin and rib lamb chop are my favourite cuts for teriyaki.

When it is served as an appetizer, it can make a party. Cut the meat into bite-size pieces, broil and serve with small bamboo sticks.

World-famous Hawaiian teriyaki

2 to 3 lb (1 to 1.3 kg) steak or chops

1½ cups (375 ml) soy sauce

⅓ cup (80 ml) sugar or honey

½ tsp (2 ml) crushed garlic

1 tbsp (15 ml) grated fresh gingerroot

1 tsp (5 ml) MSG

Place the meat in a single layer in a shallow dish. Heat together the soy sauce, sugar or honey, garlic, gingerroot and MSG. Cool. Pour the mixture over the meat and marinate for 1 to 3 hours. Remove meat from the marinade and broil.

VARIATIONS

Sesame-seed marinade for teriyaki

½ cup (125 ml) soy sauce
½ cup (125 ml) sesame oil
1 small onion, chopped
1 garlic clove, crushed
¼ to ½ cup (60 to 125 ml) sesame seeds

Mix together the first 4 ingredients and marinate the beef in it. At 2 minutes before it is cooked, spread the meat with the sesame seeds.

Sherry marinade for teriyaki

1 cup (250 ml) soy sauce
¼ cup (60 ml) sherry
1 garlic clove, halved
1 tsp (5 ml) sugar

Use the mixture to baste steak as often as possible during the broiling period.

My family lambburger

Use any lamb cut that is low in cost. Grind this two or three times in a meat grinder, or ask your butcher to do it for you.

1.5 to 2 lb (750 gr to 1 kg) ground lamb

½ tsp (2 ml) onion or garlic salt

½ cup (125 ml) chopped green onions

4 tbsp (60 ml) sherry or fresh lemon juice

1 tsp (5 ml) salt

½ tsp (2 ml) sugar

½ tsp (2 ml) ground basil or thyme

¼ tsp (1 ml) pepper

Blend and mix everything together thoroughly. Gently shape, without packing, into patties. Broil in a preheated broiler 3 inches (8 cm) from the source of heat for 6 to 8 minutes on each side. These patties are at their best when cooked on the rare side. This should make 6 to 8 servings.

PANBROILING

Panbroiling is cooking in a shallow open container, over the heat source, instead of by overhead radiation. Though you use a heavy metal frying pan heated from below, the final result of panbroiling is entirely different from panfrying and much more like oven broiling. Panbroiling is by far the best way to deal with slices of meat such as chops or steaks less than 1 inch (2.5 cm) thick, or when only small portions are required. Broiling these cuts would dry them out and they would get hard and be overdone.

In order to panbroil with success, remember the following points: ⊶ The meat should be dry. Pat it with absorbent paper before cooking. The meat can be marinated or tenderized, but be sure to pat it dry before you start to cook it.

⊶ The pan should be very hot. To check the heat, place a square of newspaper in the middle of the frying pan and wait until it gets brown. When this happens, the pan is ready to use.

A heavy metal electric frying pan, preheated to 400°F (200°C) can be used. Keep it at the same temperature throughout the panbroiling period.

When the pan is hot, rub it lightly with the fatty part of a chop or steak, or with a small piece of bacon. Place the meat in the prepared hot pan and cook over high heat until crusty brown on one side. Then turn the meat, sprinkle the cooked side with salt and pepper, and cook the other side. For timing, use the broiling timetable (p. 216) but cut the given time in half. For example, 8 minutes on each side in oven broiling is reduced to 4 minutes on each side in panbroiling.

When chops and steaks are quite thick and the fat looks pale, turn the meat on end and hold it there to let the sides brown.

○━┳ A little secret for crisper, darker rims on chops is to brush them with brown gravy maker and cook them for 1 to 2 minutes longer.

○━┳ Pour off any fat that accumulates in the frying pan as the meat is being cooked. Otherwise you will be frying and not panbroiling.

Broiling with a Swedish iron skillet

A Swedish grill skillet is a heavy iron skillet with a grid formed in the bottom. This pan is perfect for panbroiling, as it does away with the need to pour off the fat, which collects in the grooves and does not come close to the chops or steaks. The bottom is greased and the pan is preheated the same as an ordinary frying pan. With this skillet, it is easy to do continental checkering, or *quadrillage*. Heat the pan; then press the meat against the hot grid for 30 seconds. Turn the meat so the lines cross and press for another 30 seconds. Turn and repeat the operation. Then take 2 minutes off the total cooking time.

Salt broiling

This is very old method of panbroiling, used for steaks and chops 1 inch (2.5 cm) thick. Heat a heavy black iron frying pan, or heat an electric frying pan to 400°F (200°C). Pour in coarse salt to a depth of about ½ a inch (1.25 cm). Let the salt get very hot, right to the top. It is easy to feel with the tips of the fingers.

Place the meat on the hot salt and cook over medium high heat, turning only once. For rare, cook for 3 to 4 minutes on each side.

Do not fear that the meat will taste salty. The salt will absorb the drippings and should be thrown away once it has cooled.

BRAISING AND POT-ROASTING

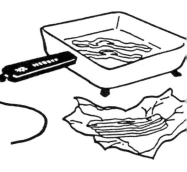

In both braising and pot-roasting, the roast is first browned in fat, but in braising no liquid is added after the browning; the meat cooks in the hot fat and natural juices. In pot-roasting, liquid is added after the meat is browned.

The suitable cuts for braising are included in the timetable on page XX. Smaller cuts can be either panfried or sautéed.

Braised roasts are economical and give you the most flavour for your meat dollar. A well-braised roast ends up as an accumulation of delicious flavours, with no single one predominating. To obtain the best results, the meat must be cooked slowly over low heat. But it cooks by itself and requires no attention once it has been prepared. Braising has the added advantage of making its own rich gravy, which can be served with the roast. With oven-roasted or pot-roasted meats, the gravy has to be made by the cook.

A braised roast will also be even more delicious if it is refrigerated overnight. To serve it the next day, warm it up in exactly the way it was originally cooked — covered and over very low heat. A word of warning: If the roast is to be kept overnight, use a stainless-steel, enameled cast-iron, flameproof glass or ceramic pan.

Braising can be done on top of the stove or in the oven, as you will see in the timetable. The oven temperature may range from 250° to 350° (130° to 180°C). At the lower temperature it will take longer to cook. I prefer 250°F (130°C) slow cooking.

Whether the braising is done on top of the stove or in the oven, the technique is the same:

Braised roast

Use 1 to 3 pounds (500 gr to 1.3 kg) of boned meat, or 1 to 5 pounds (500 gr to 2.2 kg) of meat with bones.

Warm some fat in a heavy metal pan with a good cover. For the fat use 2 to 4 tablespoons (30 to 60 ml) drippings, fat cut away from the meat, bacon fat, cubed fat salt pork, salad oil, olive oil or butter. Each will give a different flavour to the meat. Only when the fat is hot should the meat be placed in the pan.

Brown the meat evenly all over, over medium-low heat. The slow, even browning is important. You can brush the meat with a browning aid such as soy sauce before browning.

When you have browned the meat evenly, remove it to a plate and prepare a bed of flavouring vegetables or 1 or 2 flat beef bones for it to sit on. This is done so that the meat will not touch the bottom of the pan while being braised.

Use ½ cup (125 ml) of sliced or diced flavouring vegetables for each pound (500 gr) of meat. Choose from one to three of the following: onions, carrots, celery, tomatoes, mushrooms or leeks. No matter what your choice, you will find the final flavour subtly different each time.

Add the prepared vegetables to the fat in the pan and cook over low heat, stirring, for 5 minutes, or until they are softened and have developed their flavour. Then spread them evenly in the bottom of the pan and place the meat on top of them.

Next comes the seasoning. Here again the choice is wide: salt, pepper, parsley, bay leaves — these are the obvious; but many herbs or spices can be used to vary the flavour. Browsing through the chapter on herbs and spices in vol. I will give you many ideas. The quantity to use is

TIMETABLE FOR BRAISING

Over low heat on top of stove, or in the oven at 250° to 350°F (130° to 180°C)

CUT	APPROXIMATE TIME
Beef	
Brisket, chuck, flank, round, rump, sirloin tip, short rib	Whole: 2½ to 3½ hours Small, or cut small: 1½ to 2½ hours
Veal	
Blade, breast, neck, round, shoulder, flank	Whole: 45 minutes to 1½ hours Small, or cut small: 45 minutes to 1¼ hours
Lamb	
Breast, neck, shank, shoulder	Rolled or whole: 1 to 1¾ hours
Pork	
Shoulder chop, tenderloin, cubed shoulder, spareribs	1 to 1¾ hours
Variety Meats	
All kidneys, sliced thin	10 to 20 minutes
Liver, in one piece (1 to 2 pounds; 500 gr to 1 kg)	45 minutes to 1 hour
Heart, whole	1 to 3 hours

Braised lamb

On top of stove

	Weight	Time in hours
Shoulder roast, boned and rolled	3 lb (1.3 kg) 5 lb (2.2 kg)	1¾ 2¾
Shank	¾ to 1¼ lb (375 gr to 625 gr)	2
Shoulder chops (½ inch thick)		½
Heart	¼ to ½ lb (125 to 250 gr)	1¾
Shoulder, neck (cut into 1½ inch cubes)		2
Breast	1½ to 2 lb (750 gr to 1 kg)	2

very much the same as with salt and pepper — a matter of personal taste. Start with ¼ teaspoon (1 ml) for each 2 pounds (1 kg) of meat and experiment with more later.

After the meat has been well browned, placed on the fragrant vegetable bed and seasoned, cover the pan with a tight-fitting lid. No liquid whatever is added. Place over low heat or in the oven and cook according to the timetable. There is no need to watch, stir, or turn the meat when the heat is low. The roast will form its own gravy and cook to a perfect tenderness while you attend to other things.

When done, remove the meat from the pan and put the final touch on the gravy by passing the vegetables and juice through a food mill or sieve. Heat and serve.

Braised chuck roast

This is a versatile recipe. Without liquid it is braised beef; with liquid it becomes a beef pot roast. Both are interesting, but quite different. Cook a large piece, since it is excellent to serve cold, sliced thin.

4 tbsp (60 ml) flour

1 tsp (5 ml) salt

½ tsp (2 ml) pepper

1 tsp (5 ml) paprika

**1 tsp (5 ml) crumbled dried savory
or ½ tsp (2 ml) crumbled dried thyme**

1 tsp (5 ml) ground ginger

4 to 5 lb (1.8 to 2.2 kg) beef chuck or shoulder

4 tbsp (60 ml) fat or oil of your choice

2 onions, chopped fine

1 large carrot, grated

½ cup (125 ml) minced celery leaves

Blend together the flour, salt, pepper, paprika, savory or thyme, and ginger. Roll the meat in the mixture and pound in as much of the seasoning as you can.

Heat the fat or oil in the braising pan and brown the meat all over, over medium heat. When the meat is browned, remove from the pan. Add the chopped onions, grated carrot and minced celery leaves to the pan. Stir them in the fat until they are well softened. Place the meat on top. Cover and simmer for 1½ to 3 hours over low heat or in a 300°F (150°C) oven until the meat has become tender. Makes about 10 servings.

To make a pot roast proceed as above, but add 1½ cups (375 ml) tomato juice or beef consommé and ½ teaspoon (2 ml) sugar. Simmer until meat is tender. For the last 30 minutes of cooking, add whole or diced carrots and medium-sized potatoes.

Braised short ribs

Beef short ribs are a medium-priced cut that braises perfectly. Choose them as meaty and as thick as possible.

2 lb (1 kg) beef short ribs

2 tbsp (30 ml) flour

1 tsp (5 ml) salt

¼ tsp (1 ml) pepper

¼ tsp (1 ml) ground thyme

2 bay leaves, crushed

¼ tsp (1 ml) curry powder

2 tbsp (30 ml) drippings or salad oil

1 large onion, sliced

Leafy tops of 3 celery ribs, chopped

Leave the ribs in 1 piece, or cut into 4 serving pieces. Blend together the flour, salt, pepper, thyme, bay leaves and curry powder. Roll the meat all over in this mixture.

Heat the drippings or salad oil in a heavy metal frying pan or a Dutch oven. Brown the meat on all sides over medium heat. Add the onion slices and celery leaves. Stir the meat to coat with some of the fat. Cover tightly. Simmer over low heat, or in a 300°F (150°C) oven for 1½ to 2 hours, or until meat is tender. Makes about 4 servings.

To pot roast proceed as above until ready to cover. Add 1 cup (250 ml) water, tomato sauce, onion soup or red wine. Cook in the same manner. When ready to serve, the gravy can be thickened, if you choose, with 2 tablespoons (30 ml) flour mixed with a few spoonfuls of cold water.

Braised veal shoulder à la Française

French cuisine offers numerous ways to cook veal, a meat that is often difficult to cook properly. This recipe is an example of the perfection that can be achieved with an economical rolled shoulder of veal.

2.5 to 3 lb (1.125 to 1.3 kg) veal shoulder, boned and rolled

1 garlic clove, quartered (optional)

2 tbsp (30 ml) salad oil

1 tbsp (15 ml) butter

1 tsp (5 ml) salt

½ tsp (2 ml) freshly ground pepper

¼ tsp (1 ml) ground mace

1 pinch ground thyme

1 lemon, unpeeled and sliced thin

½ cup (125 ml) diced fresh tomatoes

¼ tsp (1 ml) sugar

If you are using the garlic, make 4 incisions in the meat and push a piece of garlic into each.

Heat the salad oil and butter in a Dutch oven.

Blend the salt, pepper, mace and thyme. Rub all over the meat thoroughly. Place the roast in the hot oil and butter and brown over medium heat until well browned all over. Place the lemon slices on top of the meat. Mix the tomatoes with the sugar and place around the veal. Cover tightly and simmer over low heat for 1¼ to 1½ hours, or until the meat is tender. Beware of overcooking, which makes veal stringy.

Remove the lemon slices and meat from the pan. Add ¼ cup (60 ml) cold water to the juice and beat with a whisk over medium heat until the sauce is creamy and hot. Makes 6 servings.

NOTE: A rolled shoulder of lamb can be braised in the same manner. Replace the thyme with basil.

Braised ham steak

Slash the fat around the edges of the steak. Heat 1 to 2 tablespoons (15 to 30 ml) butter or salad oil in a large frying pan. Sauté the ham on both sides over high heat until lightly browned on both sides. Cover and simmer over very low heat, turning once, for 20 to 30 minutes. A 2-pound (1 kg) ham steak should give you 4 to 6 servings.

Variation: After the ham is browned; add ¼ to ½ cup (60 to 125 ml) cider, red wine or orange juice. Cover and cook for the same time as above.

SAUTEING AND PANFRYING

Sautéing is a very quick cooking process in which meat is tossed in very little butter or fat in a sauté pan or frying pan over fairly high heat. This method is used for any meat that requires a sharp heat and quick cooking. The pan used for this is called in French a *sautoir*. It is a shallow, thin-bottomed pan, usually fairly large, so the food can be easily sautéed and quickly turned over.

Panfrying is done in a small amount of fat in a shallow frying pan. It is used for food that requires a certain amount of cooking after being browned, such as chops.

How to sauté

Use a large frying pan of good quality, because it is important to have even heat distribution.

Beware of using too much fat. The best combination is 1 teaspoon (5 ml) salad oil to 2 teaspoons (10 ml) butter for each pound (500 gr) of meat. **O➤** Butter is always combined with oil, since butter alone cannot be heated to the proper high temperature without burning.

Make sure the fat is hot enough before adding the meat or other food being sautéed.

Food to be sautéed must be as dry as possible, because dampness prevents successful browning and searing. This is especially important with fish and meat. **O➤** Wrap these tightly in absorbent paper for 2 minutes before sautéing.

As soon as the fat is hot, add the meat immediately. The browning must be done in a matter of minutes. Of course, the rest of the meal should be ready to be served. Sautéed foods are instant foods and do not wait.

One last word of caution: **O➤** Be very careful not to overcrowd your pan, because a lack of space between the pieces will cause the meat to steam rather than brown and the juices will be lost. This is one of the reasons a large frying pan is recommended for sautéing.

Coatings

Many sautéed or panfried foods are coated to help the browning process. Some of these coatings are flour, egg and bread crumbs, and batter. The pieces of meat or other foods are rolled in or dipped into the coatings.

Flour — During the cooking period, the starch bursts and the flour gluten sets, giving a light coating to the food.

Egg and bread crumbs — The egg sets with the application of heat and holds the bread crumbs. If you use egg only, you will have a light coating. With bread crumbs added to the egg, the coating is stronger and also looks better.

Batter — This is a coating used less for sautéing than for deep-frying, although it is often used for sautéing seafood such as scallops and oysters. A batter is composed of flour, milk and eggs. The effect of hot fat on batter is similar to the effect on flour coating.

How to panfry

Use a heavy cast-iron or enameled cast-iron frying pan to panfry successfully.

Use enough fat to cover the bottom of the frying pan. When the fat is quite hot, add the meat and sear on both sides to brown. This part is done over high heat. When the meat is browned, lower the heat to a more moderate level. Do not cover the pan.

Season the meat with pepper but no salt. When herbs are used, add them at this stage. Cook, usually for 4 to 6 minutes per side, turning only once, after the searing is done. This timing, incidentally, applies to most foods that are panfried, not just to meat.

When the food is done, remove it from the pan and serve immediately. Never leave panfried food standing in the pan, because water will accumulate and steam the food as well as give it an unattractive colour.

To make gravy: After the food has been removed from the pan, add to the hot drippings a few spoonfuls of cold water, tea, wine, tomato juice, consommé or cream. Stir this over medium heat, scraping the pan for any of the brown meat juices that have stuck to it. This takes only a minute or so.

COOKING IN LIQUID

These next cooking methods are based on the principle of cooking in liquid and both for the same reasons — to extract flavour from the vegetables and to tenderize the meat. While this process is going on, the liquid becomes richer as it absorbs the flavour of both meat and vegetables.

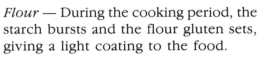 Meat that is cooked in liquid must never boil. Boiling will toughen even the most tender piece of meat and make it fibrous. It is the slow cooking, or simmering, that makes the meat tender.

To understand the difference between boiling and simmering, let us look at the thermometer: Water boils when the temperature reaches 212°F (100°C); it is at this point that bubbles rise constantly and break at the surface. When water simmers, the thermometer registers between 185° and 190°F (67° and 70°C); at this stage bubbles form slowly and collapse below the surface. When they reach the surface and break there, the boiling point has been reached again.

Of course, you do not need to check the water with a thermometer every time you cook food in it, but if you watch the water carefully as it comes to a boil, you will easily see the difference between simmering and boiling.

Stewing

How to stew

For a stew, meat is usually cut into 1 to 2-inch (2.5 to 5 cm) cubes, as uniform as possible, not only for the sake of appearance, but for even cooking as well.

Roll the meat in seasoned flour. Mix 3 tablespoons (50 ml) flour, 1 teaspoon (5 ml) each of salt and paprika, ½ teaspoon (2 ml) pepper and ¼ teaspoon (1 ml) herb or spice for each pound (500 gr) of meat. Here is where your own personality enters: vary the spices and herbs and the finished product will be quite different each time. ⌐ The small quantity of paprika suggested helps to brown the meat and give a rich brown colour to the liquid; it is not used to flavour the meat, since more than this is needed for flavour. Put the mixture on a large plate and roll the meat in it; or put the flour mixture in a paper bag, add the meat and shake until the meat is coated.

Next, brown the meat. Use a Dutch oven, an enameled cast-iron pan or a heavy stainless-steel saucepan. Use 3 tablespoons (50 ml) fat per pound (500 gr) of meat. As to the fat, you have a choice: bacon fat, drippings, margarine, butter, oil, prepared dressing, melted meat fat or diced salt pork. Each fat gives a different flavour to the finished product. Heat the fat until it is hot, then add the meat, just enough at a time to cover the bottom of the pan. If there is too much, the meat will steam and stay whitish, instead of browning. Brown over fairly high heat. Remove the meat to a plate as it is browned and continue with the other pieces until all are done. After the browning is complete, return the entire lot to the pan.

Now comes the addition of the liquid. The liquid used can be water, half water, half wine or all wine; canned tomatoes, tomato juice, vegetable juice or the cooking water from vegetables. You can also use water with the juice and rind of citrus fruit: 1 cup (250 ml) for each 3 cups (750 ml) of water. Again, each chosen liquid will give a different flavour to the stew.

⌐ What counts most is that the liquid must also sear the meat, so it must be boiling rapidly just before it is poured in.

Now add the vegetables; onion, garlic and all root vegetables can be used. In general, use 2 cups (500 ml) or 1 pound (500 gr) vegetables per pound (500 gr) of meat. The vegetables can be left whole or diced, quartered or cut into thick or thin slices. And have no fear that they will be broken up or will disappear in the sauce if they are cooked for the same length of time as the meat. They won't if you keep the stew at a constant simmer; it is boiling that disintegrates vegetables.

Cover the pan tightly and simmer over low heat until the meat is tender. ⌐ I cannot repeat often enough, *do not boil*, because the whole secret of a good stew is the long, slow cooking in a tightly covered pan.

The meat you use, the spices, the fat and the liquid in turn will each influence the final flavour. So you will be able to make hundreds of different kinds of stews by using your imagination, without having a specific recipe for each one.

For length of cooking time, refer to the timetable on page ... for stewing and poaching.

POACHING OR SIMMERING

Poaching is one of the most useful cooking operations, especially with meat and poultry. Many cooks either overlook, or altogether fail to realize, that the tougher the meat, the more flavourful it is. ⚋🗝 Tougher cuts cost less and yet they have more flavour than more expensive tender cuts. If fast cooking concentrates the elusive flavour of tender meat, poaching tenderizes and brings out the full flavour of tougher meats.

⚋🗝 The liquids used to poach food are often acidulated with fresh lemon juice, cider vinegar, dry wine or even beer, especially stale beer, which, besides its tenderizing effect gives added flavour. For example, the world-famous Belgian *carbonnade,* which is a simple beef stew, is slowly cooked or poached in beer as part of the liquid. Each acidulated liquid that is used will give a different final flavour to the dish.

How to poach

Choose the meat; consult the timetable for stewing and poaching for meat cuts that are especially good cooked this way. Stainless-steel, flameproof glass or ceramic or enameled cast-iron saucepans are best for poaching. The size is also important; the saucepan or pot must contain the meat comfortably with enough space for the liquid.

In poaching as well as in stewing, the meat can be browned slowly all over before the liquid is added, especially when there is a need to improve the colour and the flavour of the meat. However, do not coat with seasoned flour as you would for stew. The type of fat used and the proportions are the same as those used in stewing.

When the meat is not browned, simply melt the fat over medium heat and roll the meat in it until the meat is well coated with the fat. This is done to close the pores of the meat so it will retain most of its natural juice. Then season with salt, pepper, spices and herbs to taste, as for stewing. Vegetables such as carrots, onions, leeks, garlic, parsnip, celery are also added—whole, sliced or diced — to be served with the poached meat or to be used as a flavouring.

⚋🗝 Cover the meat next with cold liquid, contrary to the method used in stewing, where you use boiling liquid. In poaching it is important to use just enough water to barely cover the meat. The more water you use, the less flavourful the meat will taste. Of course, the liquid can be all water or a combination of the liquids mentioned before. Bring the water to the boiling point over medium-low heat, not over high heat. Do not bring to a fast rolling boil, but just to the point where you see a quivering of the surface of the liquid and the formation of scum around the edge. Remove the scum. Then, turn the heat very low. Cover tightly and poach or simmer very gently until the meat is tender.

At no time during the cooking process should the liquid boil. Also, be careful not to overcook the meat. The timetable that follows will give you a fair idea of the approximate time required for the different cuts of meat.

Here is a secret that gives all poached meat that is to be served cold a perfect flavour, tenderness and juiciness. ⚋🗝 Cook the meat for 20 to 30 minutes less than you would to serve it hot, then cool the meat in its own liquid, in a cool place but not in the refrigerator. The hot liquid will continue the cooking process without the help of the heat from the stove.

To serve hot, remove the meat from its cooking liquid only when ready to serve, at the end of its full cooking period. This will prevent the meat from drying on top, which is what happens when it becomes exposed to air or stands for any length of time.

TIMETABLE FOR STEWING AND POACHING

On the top of the stove, or in a 250° to 300°F (130° to 180°C) oven	
CUT	**APPROX. TIME**
Beef brisket, flank, plate, rump	3 hours
Beef cut into 1-inch (2.5 cm) squares: flank, rump, shin, short ribs	2 hours
Veal cut into 1-inch (2.5 cm) squares: breast, shoulder, flank, neck	1½ to 2 hours
Lamb cut into 1-inch (2.5 cm) squares: breast, shoulder, flank, neck	1½ to 2 hours

Pork, fresh shoulder, pig's feet or knuckles	2 to 3 hours
Pork, cured smoked ham 10 to 12 pounds (4.5 to 5.4 kg)	25 minutes/lb 55 minutes/kg
over 12 pounds (5.4 kg)	20 minutes/lb 45 minutes/kg
half ham	30 minutes/lb 65 minutes/kg
picnic shoulder	45 minutes/lb 100 minutes/kg
fully cooked ham	20 minutes/lb 45 minutes/kg
Variety Meats heart	1½ to 2½ hours
tongue	3 hours

Poached beef brisket

Fresh brisket can be delicious when cooked the right way. The right way is to poach it, instead of, as a dear old friend of mine in Calgary used to say, "boiling it to death". It was this friend who showed me how to cook a brisket to perfection; the meat is not stringy and there is almost no shrinkage. When cold, it is moist, tasty and can be sliced paper-thin.

3 lb (1.3 kg) boneless beef brisket

Salt and pepper

1 tsp (5 ml) dry mustard

1 onion, chopped

1 celery rib with leaves, chopped

1 bay leaf

1 tsp (5 ml) brown sugar

Sprinkle the brisket with salt, pepper and mustard. Spread these all over the meat with your hands. Place the onion, celery, bay leaf and brown sugar in the bottom of a casserole. Add only ¼ cup (60 ml) cold water. Mix well. Place the meat on top. Cover tightly and poach in a 300°F (150°C) oven for 3½ hours, or until the meat is tender. Makes about 6 servings.

To serve cold, keep covered, allow to cool, then refrigerate until cold.

This is the way my friend in Calgary served it the first time I ever ate it, sitting in her garden, on a superb summer evening. She put small new potatoes (in the winter you could use potatoes cut into 2-inch/5 cm squares) in an earthenware casserole with ½ cup (125 ml) water, and she completely covered the potatoes with chopped parsley. The casserole was covered and the potatoes were baked in the 300°F (150°C) oven with the beef for 1 hour, the last hour the meat was poaching. The water disappears and parsley gives a delicious taste to the tender potatoes. There is no need for salt.

The mustard sauce my friend served was the crowning glory of the meal. She blended 1 tablespoon (15 ml) dry mustard with a bit of cold water and cider vinegar and mixed this together until it had the consistency of heavy cream. This was then refrigerated for 1 hour. It was then stirred into ½ cup (125 ml) thick sour cream with a little vinegar and salt to taste. She placed this in a bowl and sprinkled the top with freshly ground black pepper. It was marvelous.

Belgian beef carbonnade

This family dish is world renowned. The combination of beer, brown sugar and thyme blends into one delicate, pleasant flavour. Since the stew is twice as good reheated over low heat, make it for the family in a large quantity. It also freezes exceptionally well.

4 tbsp (60 ml) flour

2 tsp (10 ml) salt

1 tsp (5 ml) pepper

1 tsp (5 ml) paprika

½ cup (125 ml) butter or margarine

6 large onions, sliced

3 lb (1.3 kg) round steak or chuck, cut into 1-inch (2.5 cm) cubes

1 garlic clove, halved

1 bay leaf

¼ tsp (1 ml) dried thyme

½ cup (125 ml) chopped celery leaves

¼ cup (50 ml) chopped parsley

3 tbsp (50 ml) brown sugar

2½ cups (625 ml) beer

2 tbsp (30 ml) cider or malt vinegar

Blend together the flour, salt, pepper and paprika. Roll the meat cubes in this mixture until they are well coated. Melt the butter or margarine in a large heavy metal saucepan. Add the onions, and sauté over medium heat until they are softened and tender, being careful not to brown them. Remove from the pan with a perforated spoon, pressing out as much fat as possible.

Place the same pan over high heat and in it sear the cubes of meat, a few at a time. This operation will give colour to the finished *carbonnade.* Return to the pan the onions and all the meat. Set pan over low heat.

Tie together in a square of cheesecloth the garlic, bay leaf, thyme and celery leaves. Add to the meat, sprinkle the parsley on top, and add the sugar and beer. Bring to a simmer, while stirring, then cover tightly and poach over low heat until the meat is tender, about 1½ hours.

Discard the *bouquet garni,* or cheesecloth bag of seasonings. Add the vinegar. Simmer for 5 minutes.

Serve with a dish of boiled floury potatoes and a beet salad or pickled beets. Makes about 6 servings.

Our Nanny's "Honest Irish Stew"

Clara, who was our nanny when we were children, was French, but she had an Irish mother. She cared very little for cooking, no doubt because she had her hands full with her boisterous charges, but every now and then a spark of interest would flare up and she would make one of her mother's "famous" Irish dishes. The mother had brought from Ireland as part of her dowry a very special little book, which contained recipes meticulously written out by her grandmother, who had passed it on to her mother. Eventually the book was given to her as the eldest daughter when, as Clara put it, her mother had "left this world to live in glory with the angels."

Whenever any of us had a cold, Clara insisted that eating "Honest Irish Stew" was the only thing that would cure us. Here is the recipe.

3 lb (1.3 kg) neck of lamb

12 medium even-sized potatoes

4 large onions, sliced thick

Salt and pepper

½ tsp (2 ml) ground thyme

2 cups (500 ml) cold water

The neck is a low-priced cut. Ask your butcher to reserve 3 pounds (1.3 kg) of lamb neck in advance; it's worth the trouble. But other inexpensive lamb cuts will do.

Remove excess fat from the meat, if necessary, and then cut into sections through the bones. Your butcher can also do this for you, but do not let him or her remove the bones as they are necessary for flavour.

Peel the potatoes and cut four of them into thin slices, as for scalloped potatoes. Leave the rest whole.

In the bottom of a heavy metal saucepan or casserole, place the sliced potatoes, then half of the sliced onions, and top this with the pieces of lamb. Season generously with salt and pepper. Sprinkle the rest of the onions with the thyme and place them on top of the lamb. Surround them with the remainder of the potatoes, left whole. Pour the cold water on top. Cover tightly. Poach in 350°F (180°C) oven for 2½ hours, or simmer over very low heat for the same length of time. The sliced potatoes thicken the juice and the top ones, left whole, will retain their shape and will be cooked just right. Makes 6 servings.

Clara used to serve capers, homemade mustard and chopped parsley with her Irish stew. In the summer you can replace the parsley with chives.

Our Nanny's "Honest Irish Stew"

Poached lamb shank Niçoise à la Nice

It is too bad we don't make more use of lamb shanks. They are low in cost, high in flavour, and superb in texture, with gelatinous meat. The Indians use them to make superb curry; the Scots poach and braise them; the French, along the Mediterranean, poach them with green peppers, olives and tomatoes.

4 to 6 meaty lamb shanks

2 tbsp (30 ml) lemon juice

1 tsp (5 ml) salt

¼ tsp (1 ml) pepper

Grated rind of 1 lemon

3 tbsp (50 ml) olive or salad oil

½ tsp (2 ml) dried basil or rosemary

1 garlic clove, minced

1 onion, quartered

2 green peppers, cored and quartered

¼ cup (60 ml) black olives, pitted

4 tomatoes, peeled and sliced

½ cup (125 ml) hot consommé, water or white wine.

Ask your butcher to give you the whole lamb shanks without cracking the joints. They are most attractive that way. Rub lemon juice all over the meat. Mix together the salt, pepper and lemon rind and roll the meat in it.

In a heavy metal saucepan heat the oil and brown the shanks over high heat. Lower the heat and sprinkle with the basil or rosemary and the garlic. If any lemon juice is left, pour it on top. Arrange the onion over the meat. Add the green peppers, black olives, tomatoes and consommé, water or wine. Bring the whole to a simmer. Cover tightly and poach in a 325°F (160°C) oven for 2½ hours, or until the meat is tender. Serve with rice or lentils. Makes 4 to 6 servings.

The art of boiling ham is almost lost, because so many pre-cooked or fully cooked hams are available. This should really be called "poached ham," because at no time should it boil. Nothing can replace a poached ham to take on a picnic, to make sandwiches, or simply to serve as cold cuts on a hot summer day.

This is a good basic recipe that is easily varied. You can replace the molasses with corn or maple syrup, sweet pickle syrup, apple juice or beer. Your imagination will, no doubt, supply other variations once you have experimented with it. A word of caution here: A ham that is ready-to-eat should not be poached.

Boiled ham

8 cups (2 L) cold water

8 cups (2L) beer, apple juice, red wine or cider

3 carrots, quartered

4 onions, quartered

1 garlic clove, halved

4 celery ribs with leaves

8 peppercorns

1 tbsp (15 ml) dry mustard

6 whole cloves

10 to 18 lb (4.5 to 8 kg) cook-before-eating ham

Place all the ingredients except the ham into a large saucepan. Bring to a fast, rolling boil. Lower the heat, then simmer for 30 minutes. This flavours the water.

Lower the ham into the simmering water. Cover and keep simmering over low heat for 25 to 30 minutes per pound (500 gr); 30 minutes per pound (500 gr) when the ham is to be served hot; 25 minutes per pound (500 gr) when it is to be served cold. In the latter case, remove the pan from the heat when the cooking period is up and place it in a cool place. Let the ham cool in the cooking liquid.

Remove the skin from the ham while it is hot.

If you want, a poached ham can be glazed in the same way as ready-to-serve ham.

Without a glaze, the ham, either hot or cold, can be covered with minced parsley. A 10-pound (4.5 kg) ham will make 12 to 14 servings.

FRICASSEEING

Fricasseeing combines two basic techniques — browning lightly, which is contact with hot fat; and cooking in liquid or sauce, which is poaching.

In a sense, a fricassee is a thick stew, usually made with pieces of chicken, rabbit, lamb, or veal, poached in a seasoned bouillon and finished in a *sauce velouté* made with the cooking liquid.

Fricassee of veal

This recipe is a good basic example of a fricasseed meat. Later you will find a recipe for fricassee of chicken (p. 248), which probably is the meat most frequently cooked this way, but the method works well for meats too.

First make a veal stock; of course, you can vary the flavour by adding other herbs, or by adding other vegetables such as onions.

VEAL STOCK

1 lb (500 gr) veal shank

6 cups (1.5 L) water

1 celery rib

1 carrot, sliced

1 bay leaf

½ tsp (2 ml) salt

Put the veal shank in a deep pot and add the water. Bring to a boil and cook for a few minutes. Then remove the scum and add the celery, carrot, bay leaf and salt. Reduce to a simmer and cook for 2½ hours. Cool and strain. You can do this the day before if you wish.

5 tbsp (75 ml) butter

2 lb (1 kg) veal, cut into 1-inch (2.5 cm) cubes

Salt and pepper

Pinch or two of grated nutmeg

1 small onion, minced

1 cup (250 ml) milk

2 cups (500 ml) veal stock

4 tbsp (60 ml) flour

Mushrooms (optional)

Paprika, or minced parsley

Melt 2 tablespoons (30 ml) of the butter in a heavy saucepan and add the veal cubes. Cook them over medium heat until browned on all sides. Then sprinkle with salt, pepper and nutmeg. Add the onion. Pour the milk on top. Bring to a simmer, cover tightly, and simmer over low heat, or cook in a 250°F (130°C) oven for 2 hours.

Measure the veal stock. If it is more than 2 cups (500 ml), reduce it until you have 2 cups (500 ml).

Melt the rest of the butter and add the flour; stir and blend together over low heat until the flour is cooked, but do not let the roux brown. Strain the milk from the veal into the cooked roux and beat with a whisk to blend. Then add the stock, whisking all the time over medium heat until you have a smooth velvety sauce. Adjust seasoning if necessary.

You can add sliced fresh mushrooms to the sauce when you add the stock; the mushrooms will cook in the sauce. Or add drained canned mushrooms at the very last minute.

Pour the sauce over the veal, sprinkle with paprika or minced parsley, and serve. Makes about 4 servings.

ORGAN MEATS

Internal meats, which are often completely overlooked, provide healthy variety in the diet. These include the liver, kidneys, heart, sweetbreads, tripe, tongue and brains. They are all well worth learning how to prepare, for they can provide many delicious and economical dishes. These meats are sometimes called "variety meats." Each has a distinctive flavour, texture and shape. All are considered delicacies, yet they can be classified as economical family fare, because they all have special food value and are high in vitamins A, B, C and G. Liver in particular is especially high in iron, vitamin A, riboflavin and niacin.

Another quality of variety meats is that they are boneless and waste free. As a general rule, you can count on 4 servings per pound (500 gr).

These meats are cooked by the same methods, as muscle meats — braising, cooking in water, panfrying, sautéing, broiling and baking. Those that are tender, like brains, sweetbreads, liver and kidneys, cook quickly. Overcooking or cooking at too high heat will toughen them. The less tender benefit from long slow cooking like any other meat.

Pork liver is the richest in vitamins and minerals and has the strongest flavour. Beef liver is less strong, but the flavour is still a hearty one. Lamb liver is delicate, but has an unfortunate tendency to be a little dry. Livers of veal (young animal usually not more than 3 months old) and calf (from 3 to 9 months old) are the most delicate and are creamy and tender in texture.

Calf and veal livers are more expensive as a consequence of supply and demand. The popularity of these tender livers of young animals is great, increasing demand and causing the price to be higher.

Make sure you actually get calf or veal liver when you ask for it. Veal liver is from a very young calf, but its colour is darker than calf's liver and its texture a little coarser. Calf's liver is pinker and has a very smooth, close texture.

Basic preparation and cooking of variety meats

LIVER
Preparation: Do not soak or scald. Precook liver only when it is to be ground.
Cooking: Panfry or broil veal or lamb liver. Braise pork or beef liver. Liver can be baked with bacon, or ground for use in loaves and patties.

KIDNEYS
Preparation: Broil veal and lamb kidneys. Braise pork and beef kidneys. Grind, slice or chop for patties, loaves or kidney pie.

HEARTS
Heart is a lean muscle meat.

Preparation: Do not soak or pre-cook. Trim out fibres on top (easy to do with kitchen shears). Wash thoroughly in cold water.
Cooking: Cook heart in water until it's tender, then grind or dice for hash, meat pies or casseroles. Beef or veal heart can be stuffed and braised. Pork and lamb heart can be braised whole or in slices. All are good sliced thin and served cold.

BRAINS

Tender, soft and very delicate in flavour. *Preparation:* Soak in salted cold water for 15 minutes. Remove membrane. Pre-cook in simmering water for 15 minutes, then prepare for desired serving.

Cooking: Cooked brains can be diced for use in scrambled eggs or creamed dishes. They can also be sliced, dipped into egg batter and breaded, then fried in deep fat or panfried.

SWEETBREADS

These are the thymus gland of the animals. They are tender, with a delicate flavour. *Pork sweetbreads* are not used. *Veal sweetbreads* are the gourmet's preference.

Preparation: Do not soak. Pre-cook in simmering water for 15 minutes. Remove loose membrane and prepare for desired cooking and serving.

Cooking: Cooked sweetbreads can be braised, panfried, broiled or baked whole. Use pre-cooked sweetbreads diced in salads or creamed dishes. Can also be sliced, dipped into egg batter, rolled in crumbs and fried.

TONGUE

Available fresh, smoked, canned or pickled. *Pork* and *lamb tongues,* being small, are usually canned whole. The larger size of *beef* and *veal tongues* makes them better for home use.

Preparation: Simmer fresh tongue in seasoned salted water until tender. Then remove outer skin. Omit salt in cooking smoked tongue.

Cooking: Slice and serve hot or cold. Can be diced and used in casseroles or salads.

TRIPE

This is the first and second stomachs of beef only. *Plain tripe* is mostly canned. *Honeycomb tripe* is sold as "fresh", even though it is always pre-cooked before being sold. It also comes pickled and corned.

Preparation: Fresh or pickled honey-comb tripe is pre-cooked, ready for final cooking.

Cooking: When pre-cooked, brush with melted fat, then broil on each side for 5 minutes. Tripe can also be panfried, braised or served in sauce.

This is a rare delicacy. Prepared with calf's liver, it is a choice dish indeed, but you can use young steer liver, which is equally tender and flavourful, if a little less delicate in texture. It is superb when served cold and sliced paper-thin. Although a true braised meat, liver is always cooked with a certain amount of liquid to prevent dryness.

Braised whole liver

2 to 2.5 lb (1 to 1.25 kg) liver, in 1 piece

2 tbsp (30 ml) flour

¼ lb (125 gr) fat salt pork

1 tsp (5 ml) butter

2 medium-sized onions, sliced

2 carrots, sliced

1 celery rib and leaves, diced

¼ cup (60 ml) chopped parsley

1 bay leaf, crushed

½ tsp (2 ml) crumbled dried thyme

1 tbsp (15 ml) brown sugar

Salt and pepper

1 cup (250 ml) red wine or apple juice

Grated rind of 1 lemon

Roll the liver in the flour. Dice the salt pork and place it in a Dutch oven with the butter. Cook over low heat until the salt pork is melted and browned. Add the liver and sear on both sides in the hot fat over high heat. Remove the liver and add the onions, carrots, celery, parsley, bay leaf, thyme and sugar. Stir over medium heat until the vegetables are well coated with the fat, about 3 minutes. Place the liver over the vegetables. Sprinkle with salt and pepper.

Add the red wine or apple juice and the lemon rind. Cover tightly and cook in a 350°F (180°C) oven for 45 minutes to 1 hour, or until the liver is tender.

Remove the liver from the liquid. Boil the liquid, uncovered, over high heat until slightly reduced. Pass through a sieve to purée as much of the vegetables as possible; use as gravy. Makes about 8 servings.

Calf's-brain salad

If you have never eaten brains, this is an excellent introduction.

2 pairs calf's brains

2 tbsp (30 ml) vinegar

2 thick unpeeled slices of lemon

1 tsp (5 ml) salt

3 tbsp (50 ml) salad oil

1 tbsp (15 ml) lemon juice

2 tbsp (30 ml) minced fresh dill

Salt and pepper

Lettuce

Cover the brains with lukewarm water and add the vinegar. Let stand for 1 hour. To clean, remove the small membranes on top; these will have been darkened by the vinegar so they will be easy to find. Place the brains in a saucepan with the lemon slices and the salt. Add enough water to cover. Simmer, uncovered, for 30 minutes. Drain and set on absorbent paper to drain further. Place in a bowl and refrigerate, covered, until ready to use.

When ready to serve, slice the brains. Mix the oil, lemon juice and dill and add to the brains. Season with salt and pepper to taste. Toss gently. Serve each portion on lettuce leaves or shredded lettuce. Makes about 6 servings.

CHAPTER 10

All's fair with fowl

A CHICKEN in every pot is no longer the remote dream it once seemed. Far from it! Chicken is in plentiful supply year round and it is one of the most economical of protein foods. The trick is to learn how to serve it in a variety of ways so that the appetizing flavour of the bird is accentuated.

The nutritive value of chicken is almost equal to that of red meat. However, it does not have as full-bodied a flavour and it contains much less iron.

☐━☞ One of the first secrets to learn is how to choose the best bird for the type of cooking you are going to use. Knowing the kind of chicken that responds best to various cooking methods will pay off with two dividends — a more flavourful chicken dish and a more economical meal. For example, do not purchase a roasting chicken to make soup. This would be the same as buying beef tenderloin to make hash. Also, if a 5-pound (2.2 kg) roasting chicken costs more than twice as much per pound (500 gr) as a 3-pound (1.3 kg) bird, two smaller chickens will be, in the long run, a better buy and will yield more roasted white meat and more favourite pieces than will the one larger bird.

TYPES OF CHICKEN

Squab is a young pigeon that has never flown. The flavour is similar to chicken, and squabs are cooked by the same methods. These weigh about 1 pound (500 gr) and are served roasted whole, one to a person. They are a luxury item available at specialized dealers and are usually served only at elaborate dinners.

Broiler-fryers are young, all-purpose birds, weighing from 2 to 4 pounds (1. to 1.8 kg). They are called "all-purpose" because they can be roasted, broiled, sautéed, panfried or deep-fried. In some places, birds weighing up to 2½ pounds (1.25 kg) are called broilers and those from 2½ to 4 pounds (1.25 to 1.8 kg) fryers.

Stewing chickens or fowl are mature females, less tender and less expensive than roasters, but generally heavier. To be at their best they should weigh at least 5 pounds (2.2 kg). They are good poached for cold sliced chicken, salads or casserole dishes. They are simmered for soups and are usually kept whole for greater flavour, tenderness and succulence.

Capons are castrated cocks, usually weighing from 6 to 7 pounds (2.7 to 3.1 kg). These are good to use when a large roasting bird is needed. The flavour, however, is somewhat bland compared to that of a nice fat roasting hen.

Eviscerated oven-ready or ready-to-cook chickens have been completely cleaned, with the entrails taken out, and are ready for the oven. The heart, liver, gizzard and neck are wrapped in paper and returned to the cavity of the bird and are added to the final weight. This eviseration of chickens has contributed greatly to the increase in chicken consumption, since most women rebel at having to do this work themselves.

Dressed poultry is a bird that has been slaughtered, bled and had its feathers plucked, but still has its feet, head and viscera. At farmers' markets, fresh poultry is mostly sold dressed.

PREPARING CHICKEN FOR COOKING

Even when a chicken is sold eviscerated, check it for pinfeathers. These are easily removed with tweezers. Also, feel the inside to make sure the lungs have been removed, and cut out the little oil sac above the tail piece if this has not been done (most of the time it has been removed).

0— *Do not wash poultry before cooking.* Running cold water over the bird does not really clean it; all this does is help destroy *the flavour. Certainly it does not in any way sterilize it. To do that you would have to use boiling water, not cold water, and this would change the texture of the meat completely.

Most poultry for sale in our markets has been carefully packaged, and needs only to be wiped off with a damp paper towel. Or use this method. Put 2 to 3 tablespoons (30 to 50 ml) fresh lemon juice, brandy or whisky inside the chicken and swish it around with your fingers or with absorben paper.

Flavouring chicken
Whole poultry that is to be roasted or poached should be flavoured on the inside. First sprinkle salt and pepper inside the neck and body cavities. Then rub inside and out with the cut side of a lemon. Sprinkle a few pinches of thyme or tarragon into the cavity, then add a sprig or two of parsley and 1 tablespoon (15 ml) of butter. Then either stuff the bird or truss it if you are cooking it unstuffed.

Stuffing poultry
A bird can be stuffed with countless fillings. To make the bird look more handsome and fatter, stuff both the neck and the body cavity. To do this, first spoon some of the stuffing in the neck, push it right in and pull the neck skin under the bird. Spoon the remainder of the stuffing into the body cavity. **0—** On top, right at the opening, put a crust or thick slice of stale bread, lightly buttered and rubbed with onion or garlic, placed buttered side out. The slice of bread acts as a kind of door, preventing the stuffing from oozing out during roasting. The bread becomes crisp and roasted on the outside and soft inside and has a very special flavour. Use a needle and thread to fasten the opening or fasten with poultry pins. Do not stuff any poultry until just before cooking because the stuffing will spoil if allowed to stand.

How to truss a chicken
Use a soft white string, cut about 20 inches (50 cm) long. Place the chicken on a flat surface, with its feet toward you. Push the legs back close to the body of the chicken. Put the centre of the string across the end of the legs and bring it around and up between the legs, forming a figure 8. Then put the string between the legs and the breast, turn the chicken over, and put the string through the wings. Make sure the neck is pulled over the vent and tie the string over it. **0—** Chickens cooked whole, whether roasted or poached, should always be tied to keep them in a neat shape.

How to cut up poultry
All you need is a sharp knife.

To remove wings (1), pull the wings out from the body and slash the skin between body and wing. Cut around the shoulder joint to separate the wing from the breast, leaving as much white meat on the breast as possible. If you wish, you can cut off the wing tips. (They can be reserved for making stock).

To remove legs, drumsticks and thighs (2), slash the skin between the body and the thigh, then press down and out on the leg until the hip joint pushes out of its socket. Cut through the hip joint, separating the thigh from the body of the bird. If you wish, you can cut the drumstick away from the thigh through the knee joint. Repeat for the other leg.

Note how the "oyster" (a fleshy, oyster-shaped piece) pulls away from the spoon-shaped hollow of the backbone of a chicken. In turkeys the thigh tendon must be cut before the oyster will pull away from the backbone.

To remove neck and backbone (3), starting at the tail, cut through the ribs slightly to the right of the backbone, all the way to the neck. Repeat on the left side of the backbone. Remove the backbone and neck in one piece by cutting the skin around the neck.

To separate a breast from back (4), insert your knife in the wing socket and cut through the rib joints to the back of the bird. This separates the back from the breast, leaving part of the ribs on each part.

To divide the breast (5,6), spread the bird open and cut the pearl-like cartilage on either side of the keel bone in the neck region. Hold the bird firmly and press from underneath, forcing the keel bone to spring up so that it can be removed easily. Cut the breast lengthwise into halves.

To cut broilers into halves, remove neck and backbone and divide the breast as described above. For quarters, cut each half crosswise into two pieces.

Wipe cut-up birds with a damp cloth; dry thoroughly. Wrap loosely in wax paper and store in the refrigerator until time for cooking.

BASIC WAYS TO COOK POULTRY

Chicken and all other poultry can be roasted or baked, broiled, barbecued, sautéed, deep-fried, stewed, poached or fricasseed, in the same ways that meat is cooked. All the rules that apply to meat regarding each basic method are applicable to poultry. The cooking time for most methods can be based, with some slight differences, on the timetable for roasting chicken.

Because poultry is a protein, the most important rule that applies to it, as to all meat, is to use the lowest possible heat for the basic method you follow and *do not overcook*. If you must err, let your poultry be a little underdone rather than overdone. And don't worry about the pink colour next to the bone in a completely cooked bird. This is caused by the same chemical reaction that produces redness in ham. It does not indicate undercooking, nor does it affect the flavour.

Roasting chicken

Roast all chickens at an even temperature of 350°F (180°C), placing them in a preheated oven. **O—⊶** The chicken should always be at room temperature when it is placed in the oven.

Contrary to the procedure with red meats, a thermometer to test chicken doneness is not necessary; in any case, it is difficult to insert it far enough into the flesh of a bird without touching a bone.

A satisfactory test that is always accurate is to test the drumstick. With a folded piece of cloth or paper towelling to protect your fingers, take hold of the drumstick. The meat should feel soft and the bone should move easily in its socket.

Another way is to prick the thickest part of the leg with a fork. Juices should run clear yellow without a trace of pink.

Two chickens in a pan

It is often more economical to buy two smaller chickens than one large one. It is also more economical to roast two chickens at a time. If you do roast two, roast them in a pan generous enough for them to have elbow room. Also use a higher heat than normal, say around 360° to 375°F (182° to 190°C) otherwise they will stew or poach in their own juices instead of roasting. One bird can be served cold on another day.

TIMETABLE FOR ROASTING CHICKEN

Constant oven temperature at 350°F (180°C)	
Ready-to-cook weight	**Approximate total cooking time**
¾ to 1 lb (375 to 500 gr)	30 to 40 minutes
1½ lb (750 gr)	40 to 50 minutes
3 lb (1.3 kg)	50 to 60 minutes
4 lb (1.8 kg)	1 hour, 10 to 20 minutes
4½ lb (2.05 kg)	1 hour, 15 to 20 minutes
5 to 6 lb (2.2 to 2.7 kg)	1 hour, 30 to 45 minutes

French roasted chicken

This is a very good, reliable recipe for roasting a chicken, stuffed or unstuffed. It is a fine way to prepare a bird to serve cold with mayonnaise.

1 chicken (4 to 5 lb; 1.8 to 2.2 kg)

1 tsp (5 ml) salt

½ tsp (2 ml) pepper

Giblets of the chicken

1 small garlic clove

¼ tsp (1 ml) ground thyme

2 tbsp (30 ml) soft butter

1 tsp (5 ml) dry mustard

1 cup (250 ml) cold liquid

Remove any extra fat from the chicken. Dice the fat and place it in a little pile in the middle of the roasting pan.

Sprinkle part of the salt inside the chicken, then use the rest to rub on the outside. Sprinkle the pepper inside only. Place the cleaned liver, heart, cut-up gizzard and the garlic and thyme inside the cavity. This gives a delicious flavour to the chicken. You can, however, omit this and fill the cavity with a big bunch of unchopped fresh parsley. Truss the chicken.

Blend the soft butter and dry mustard. Spread this mixture on the breast of the chicken. Sit the chicken on the little pile of chicken fat.

Do not sear. Do not add water. Do not cover. Roast in an oven preheated to 350°F (180°C) for 1½ to 2 hours, depending on the tenderness of the chicken. To make sure it is cooked, use the drumstick test.

Remove the chicken from the pan. Place the pan over direct heat. When the pan drippings are bubbling hot, add the cold liquid to the contents; this liquid could be water, chicken bouillon, white wine, orange juice or cream. Stir, scraping the bottom of the pan. Bring to a boil, strain, and serve. This chicken can be served with English Bread Sauce (see page 133, Volume 1). Makes 6 servings.

I think this is one of the best stuffings I know.

Bread and lemon stuffing

3 cups (750 ml) soft fine bread crumbs

3 tbsp (50 ml) fresh lemon juice

Grated rind of ½ lemon

¼ cup (50 ml) minced fresh parsley

½ tsp (2 ml) salt

¼ tsp (1 ml) pepper

Use only the white part of fresh white bread, cut up fine. Combine all ingredients in a bowl. Mix thoroughly and use to stuff chicken. Makes enough to stuff 1 roasting chicken.

Sausage-meat stuffing

If you plan to serve your roast stuffed chicken cold, remove the stuffing, which comes out in one piece. Cut the stuffing into thin slices and place it around the chicken.

2 tbsp (30 ml) melted chicken fat or butter

1 large onion, chopped fine

¼ to ½ lb (125 to 250 gr) fresh mushrooms, chopped fine

½ lb (250 gr) sausage meat

½ lb (250 gr) very lean pork, minced

5 chicken livers, chopped

2 tbsp (30 ml) chopped parsley

¼ tsp (1 ml) dried thyme or tarragon

2 slices of bread with crusts, diced

1 tsp (5 ml) salt

¼ tsp (1 ml) pepper

Cut the chicken fat into small pieces and melt it in a frying pan, or use butter. Add the onion and mushrooms and stir over medium heat for about 5 minutes. With a slotted spoon transfer them to a bowl, pressing out all the fat you can.

Add the sausage meat and minced pork to the bowl. Sauté the chicken livers in the fat left in the frying pan over high heat for 1 minute. Add to the first mixture, along with the parsley, thyme or tarragon, bread cubes, salt and pepper. Mix thoroughly and use.

VARIATION: For a chestnut stuffing, replace the sausage meat with 2 cups (500 ml) cooked chestnuts broken into coarse pieces. The best to use are the water-packed chestnuts imported from France.

Golden baked chicken

Use this when you wish to serve a crispy brown chicken cut into serving pieces. It is not fried, and it is not as fat as roasted chicken. Baking chicken in this manner combines the roasting and poaching methods, because it is cooked covered and a higher heat is required. This is a picnic favourite.

1 egg

2 tbsp (30 ml) water

2 tsp (10 ml) salt

½ tsp (2 ml) pepper

½ tsp (2 ml) crumbled dried basil

1 frying chicken (3 lb; 1.3 kg), cut into pieces

½ cup (125 ml wheat germ or fine bread crumbs

2 tbsp (30 ml) butter

Chopped parsley (optional)

Break the egg into a bowl and beat with the water, salt, pepper and basil. Drop each chicken piece into this and stir around until well coated.

Roll each piece in the wheat germ or bread crumbs. Place in a buttered (optional) shallow baking pan and dot with the butter. Cover and bake in a 400°F (200°C) oven for 1 hour, or until the chicken is tender. Sprinkle with parsley and serve. Makes 4 servings.

My favourite broiled chicken

1 broiler (2½ to 3 lb; 1.25 to 1.3 kg)

Salt and pepper

3 tbsp (50 ml) salad oil

1 tsp (5 ml) paprika

½ tsp (2 ml) crumbled dried tarragon, basil or savory or ¼ tsp (1 ml) ground thyme or sage

Separate the chicken into halves with poultry shears or a pair of good kitchen scissors. Start by cutting down the back first, then turn and cut through the breast bone. Remove the backbone and the neck and use these for chicken stock. Twist the wing joints in their sockets so the pieces will lie flat.

Place the bird skin side down directly on the broiler pan, not on a rack. Sprinkle the top with salt and pepper, pour the salad oil on top, and sprinkle with paprika. If you like herbs, sprinkle on the herb of your choice.

Place the broiler pan in the lowest part of the preheated broiler, as far as possible from the source of heat. Broil on one side for 30 minutes, or until the skin is crisped and golden brown. After 15 minutes, decrease the heat if the skin is browning too rapidly.

The chicken is now ready to serve. It is so good that it needs only a large bowl of crisp cool green salad and a bottle of chutney as accompaniments. Makes 4 servings.

This dish is very nice served cold, but it is even better when it has not been refrigerated first.

The Scandinavians are masters of the art of using sugar with food. This broiled chicken is an excellent example. It is the combination of sugar and lemon juice that gives the special tang and crust to the broiled chicken.

Scandinavian broiled chicken

1 lemon

2 plump 2½ lb (1.1 kg) broilers split

or one 3 to 3½ lb (1.3 to 1.5 kg) broiler quartered

1 tbsp (15 ml) salt (no error here)

½ tsp (2 ml) freshly ground pepper

1 tsp (5 ml) paprika

½ cup (125 ml) melted butter

or ¼ cup (60 ml) melted butter and ¼ cup (60 ml) chicken fat (better)

2 tbsp (30 ml) sugar

Grate the rind of the lemon, then cut it into halves.

Place the small broilers or the quarters in the bottom of the broiling pan. Rub them all over with the cut lemon halves, squeezing as you go, so that the juice runs over the chicken. Blend the salt, pepper and paprika and sprinkle ithe mixture on top of the chicken. Coat each side of each piece with the melted butter or mixed butter and chicken fat, using a brush. Arrange the pieces, skin side down, and sprinkle with half the sugar.

Broil as for My Favourite Broiled Chicken (above). When the chicken is turned, baste with the remaining butter and sprinkle with the rest of the sugar. Serve with broiled tomatoes and parsleyed rice. Makes 4 servings.

The Chinese part of this recipe is the blanching trick used before broiling. Use this recipe when broiling chicken breasts or a large cut-up broiler.

Chinese deviled chicken

2 lb (1 kg) chicken breasts, or 1 chicken (3½ to 4 lb; 1.5 to 1.8 kg), quartered

4 tbsp (60 ml) butter or peanut oil

1 tbsp (15 ml) cider or wine vinegar

½ tsp (2 ml) crumbled dried tarragon

1 tsp (5 ml) dry English mustard

1 tsp (5 ml) sugar

Salt and pepper

Fill a bowl with boiling water and drop the pieces of chicken into it, letting them stand for about 5 minutes, with no additional heat. Drain, then pat the pieces dry with absorbent paper or a clean towel.

Heat the butter or peanut oil and add the vinegar, tarragon and mustard. Brush the chicken pieces on both sides with this mixture. Sprinkle with the sugar. Place skin side down on the rack of the broiler. Broil the same as for My Favourite Broiled Chicken (above), but remember the total broiling time may be 15 minutes less because of the hot dip at the beginning. When ready, place on a hot dish. Sprinkle salt and pepper on each piece, and serve. Makes 4 servings.

Poached chicken

This is the classic poached chicken known as bonne femme. Many fresh vegetables besides potatoes can be added. With a little imagination this recipe can undergo many transformations. It is the best way to poach all poultry.

1 chicken (3 to 4 lb; 1.3 to 1.8 kg)

2 tbsp (30 ml) flour

1 tsp (5 ml) salt

¼ tsp (1 ml) pepper

¼ tsp (1 ml) ground thyme or curry powder

⅓ cup (80 ml) drippings, butter, chicken fat, or salad oil

2 garlic cloves or 1 onion minced

8 to 10 small potatoes, peeled

1 cup (250 ml) chicken bouillon or water

Cut the chicken into seving pieces. Place the flour, salt, pepper and thyme or curry powder in a paper bag. Put the chicken in the bag with this mixture and shake until each piece is lightly coated; do each piece separately.

Heat the fat in a large saucepan with a cover; add the garlic or onion and the chicken pieces. Add only a few pieces at a time if the saucepan is not large enough to hold them all in one layer. Brown the chicken on all sides, then drain on paper towels and return all the chicken pieces to the pan with the potatoes placed in it here and there. Pour the chicken bouillon or water on top. Cover tightly and poach over low heat until the chicken is tender, 40 to 50 minutes.

Remove the chicken and potatoes and place on a hot platter. Boil the liquid, uncovered, over high heat until slightly reduced; then pour it over the chicken. Makes 4 servings.

Poached chicken, my way

In France, this recipe is called poule à la ficelle. Ficelle means string, and when you read the recipe, you will see how this name applies. A nice thing about this recipe is that it gives you not only a perfectly poached chicken, but a delicate and tasty soup, and chicken-flavoured fat, which you can use to cook with another time.

1 capon (4 to 6 lb; 1.8 to 2.7 kg) or
1 large stewing chicken

¼ lb (125 gr) salt pork, diced

2 tbsp (30 ml) butter

2 tbsp (30 ml) olive or salad oil

6 to 8 green onions, chopped

½ lb (250 gr) fresh mushrooms, diced

¼ cup (50 ml) chopped fresh parsley

½ tsp (2 ml) dried thyme

1 bay leaf

1 tbsp (15 ml) salt

½ tsp (2 ml) pepper

1 garlic clove, crushed

5 cups (1.25 L) boiling water

Choose a heavy metal saucepan with a good cover, deep enough to hold the chicken standing up. Tie the chicken legs together with a string long enough to tie also to the handle of the saucepan.

Melt the salt pork with the butter and oil over medium heat until the diced pork is all golden. Brown the chicken lightly all over in the fat, then add the onions, both the green and white parts.

Stir to coat them with fat. Remove the saucepan from the source of heat.

Tie the chicken to the side of the handle of the saucepan so the bird will stand up, head down, against the side of the saucepan. Add the mushrooms, parsley, thyme, bay leaf, salt, pepper and garlic. Pour the boiling water over all. Cover the pan tightly. Since only about a quarter of the bottom part of the chicken is actually in the water, this might be called steaming rather than poaching. Cook the chicken for about 2 hours, but check and continue to cook longer, if necessary, until the chicken is tender.

When the bird is done, untie it and place it, breast side down, in the bouillon. Cover and leave until cold. Then if you wish to serve it hot, warm it up.

When the bird is cool, remove it. Add 3 to 4 cups (750 ml to 1 L) hot water to the bouillon remaining in the pan. Taste and add more seasoning if necessary. Bring to a boil and add ½ cup (125 ml) very fine noodles. Simmer for 20 minutes and your soup is ready to serve.

Make a *sauce velouté* to serve with thin slices of the chicken along with a dish of parsleyed rice. Makes about 8 servings.

OTHER POULTRY

Other kinds of poultry can be cooked by the same methods as chicken. Turkeys, ducks, geese and tender game birds are commonly roasted. Turkeys are usually stuffed, but sometimes fatty birds like ducks and geese are filled loosely with celery and onions, or with apples. While turkeys and game birds usually need to be basted, or to have strips of salt pork wrapped over the legs and breast, or to be well buttered, ducks or geese have a layer of fat beneath the skin and they will be self-basted. In fact, you may need to pour off some of the fat as it accumulates.

Truss these other kinds of poultry just as you would truss chickens, and if you are cutting them up, the directions for cutting up chicken can be used for other poultry too.

Other poultry can also be broiled. Baby turkeys can be split or quartered. Breast of duckling and squab halves are good broiled. Brush turkeys and squab with butter or oil, but duck does not need this because of its natural fat.

Squab can be sautéed, and cut-up turkey can be panfried.

TIMETABLE FOR ROASTING STUFFED TURKEY

constant oven temperature at 325°F (160°C)
interior temperature on thermometer 180°F (65°C)

Drawn weight stuffed in pounds and (kilograms)	Approximate roasting time in hours
6 to 8 (2.7 to 3.6)	3¾ to 4
8 to 10 (3.6 to 4.5)	4 to 4½
10 to 12 (4.5 to 5.4)	4½ to 5
12 to 14 (5.4 to 6.3)	5 to 5½
14 to 16 (6.3 to 7.25)	5½ to 6
16 to 18 (7.25 to 8.1)	6 to 6½
18 to 20 (8.1 to 9)	6½ to 7½
10 to 24 (9 to 10.8)	7½ to 9
Over 24 (over 10.8)	Add 15 minutes additional per pound (500 gr)

NOTE: Without stuffing, deduct 5 minutes per pound (500 gr) from the time given for stuffed turkey.

Duck and turkey, cut into serving pieces, are good braised or pot-roasted. Braising is the perfect way to cook game that is no longer young and tender.

Fricassee of chicken

This recipe is very like the recipe for Fricassee of Veal (p. 286), but the chicken cooks in less time than the veal, and it takes less time to make the chicken bouillon than it does to make veal stock.

1 chicken (3 ¼ to 4 lb; 1.4 to 1.8 kg)

4 tbsp (60 ml) butter

Salt and pepper

Pinch or two of grated nutmeg

1 small onion, chopped fine

1 cup (250 ml) milk

1 celery rib

1 carrot, sliced

1 bay leaf

1 tsp (5 ml) salt

3 cups (750 ml) water

1 tsp (5 ml) diced chicken fat

4 tbsp (60 ml) flour

2 to 3 tbsp (30 to 50 ml) heavy cream

With a sharp pointed knife, remove all the meat from the chicken. Save the carcass. Cut the boned meat into 1- or 2-inch (2.5 to 5 cm) pieces.

Melt 2 tablespoons (30 ml) of the butter in a saucepan. When the butter is golden brown, add the pieces of chicken and brown them on all sides over medium heat. Sprinkle with salt and pepper and add the nutmeg and the onion. Pour the milk on top. Bring to a simmer, cover tightly, and simmer over very low heat, or cook in a 250°F (130°C) oven, for 1 hour.

While the meat of the chicken cooks, place the carcass in a saucepan with the celery, carrot, bay leaf, salt and water. Bring to a boil, cover, and boil gently over low heat for 1 hour. Pass through a fine strainer, and measure. If there are more than 2 cups (500 ml) bouillon, return the whole to the rinsed saucepan and boil fast, uncovered, until reduced to 2 cups (500 ml).

Make a *sauce velouté*. Melt the remaining 2 tablespoons (30 ml) butter and the chicken fat. When the fat is melted, add the flour; then stir and blend together for 3 minutes over low heat as the flour and butter must not be browned. The cooking and stirring is important as this partly cooks the flour and prevents a starchy flavour in the finished sauce. Strain the milk from poaching the chicken into the cooked butter-flour mixture. Beat with a whisk to blend, and add the 2 cups (500 ml) bouillon. Beat and stir over medium heat until smooth and creamy.

Pour the sauce over the chicken. Simmer together for a minute, while stirring gently. Adjust seasoning. ⟞⟶ At this point the French chef has a secret, which is to add the cream, whipped stiff. This is stirred into the sauce just when the chicken is ready to serve. Do not cook after adding the cream. Makes 4 to 6 servings.

CHAPTER 11

Fish and shellfish

PEOPLE who live near the sea are especially blessed; they can often enjoy fish caught, cooked and eaten in less than 24 hours. People who live inland, on the other hand, may never know the special flavour of a fish that has flipped out of the water into the frying pan. Many younger people today know only the taste of frozen fish.

Mind you, you can certainly enjoy fish without knowing its history. The important thing is to cook and eat it often, because it occupies a most important place among the foods essential to a properly balanced diet. Eat a lot of fish and you'll live longer.

Some nutritionists and doctors recommend that fish be eaten as often as four times a week. It is very low in that bugbear, cholesterol fat, and it is one of the most easily digestible of high-protein foods. Another excellent reason for eating fish is that it is always tender — whether large, small, strong, weak, saltwater or freshwater. Fish can be cooked, with only slight variations, in the same way you cook very tender cuts of meat. But there is one important difference: Fish is cooked to develop flavour, while meat is cooked to make it tender.

What are the main things to know about buying fish? The amount depends on what you are buying. Fish fillets are entirely edible and fish steaks are about 85% edible, so ½ pound (250 gr) per person will do nicely. Dressed fish is about 45% edible, so plan on as much as 1 pound (500 gr) per person. There is obviously no argument about fillets being the best buy, even though you may pay more per unit of weight.

○━┳ Look for fish that are plump for their type, bright-eyed, red-gilled, smooth-skinned, with all their scales adhering to firm flesh, and the overall colour shimmering and clear. Take a good look at the eyes, and make sure they are bright, full and clear. If they have a hazy white look, the fish is not fresh.

○━┳ If you touch the flesh of a scaled fish and find that no impression of your fingers remains, this is a sign of freshness. A less-fresh fish will retain an impression because the flesh has gone limp with age. Your nose will also tell you whether fish is fresh. Truly fresh fish has no odour whatever; odour develops with age. Also, a fresh fish is never slimy, while an older one is.

You can reasonably expect to keep fresh fish refrigerated 2 or 3 days at the very most, because the flavour deteriorates very quickly.

Some frozen fish on the market today needs defrosting before cooking and some does not. Always read the label on the package. The best way to defrost fish is to transfer it from the freezer to the refrigerator. Defrost it only until it is pliable enough to handle easily; don't let it get too soft. A pound (500 gr) of frozen fillets usually takes from 8 to 10 hours to defrost in the refrigerator. Place the fish on a plate while it defrosts to keep it from leaking on to other foods.

Baking fish

You can bake any kind of fish — whole, stuffed or unstuffed, steaks or fillets. It's important to know the weight of the fish when it is ready to go into the oven so you can gauge the cooking time. This is another occasion when a kitchen scale is a handy thing to have.

Whenever possible, bake fish with its head on, except salmon. Keeping the head on prevents flavour loss and helps retain the marvelous juices. It also shortens the cooking time. If you find sight of the head unpleasant, cut it off before you serve the fish.

Wash the fish in very cold well-salted water. Use ¼ cup (60 ml) coarse salt for 2 to 3 quarts (2 to 3 L) water. Wash quickly; never let a fish soak in water. Dry thoroughly with paper towels.

Oil a shallow pan, line it with heavy-duty foil, then oil the foil. Place the fish on the foil. If the fish is to be stuffed, insert the stuffing and sew up the opening or fasten it with poultry pins laced with string. Shape the foil up around the sides of the fish, but do not cover it on top. The foil will hold the juices of the fish and make it easier to remove from the pan without breaking.

0➤ Never rub the pan or foil with either butter or margarine, because these will make the fish stick. Use salad oil, olive oil or bacon fat.

Whole fish steaks or fillets can be sprinkled with a variety of toppings before baking. Here are two favorites:

Bread-crumb topping

Rub the sides of the fish with a beaten egg, then sprinkle generously with fine bread crumbs flavoured with herbs or spices, or seasoned with salt and pepper. Use this topping on fish with edible skin, such as trout, whitefish and small haddock. It is not suitable for salmon. This topping helps to keep the fish juicy.

Flour topping

Sprinkle the top and sides of the fish lightly with flour and spread soft butter over it generously, or lay bacon strips over it.

The fish is now ready to bake. This work can be done a few hours ahead of time if the pan can be refrigerated. However, it cannot be kept waiting on the kitchen counter.

0➤ In taking any type of fish, stuffed or unstuffed, it is very important to put the fish in a pre-heated oven. The temperature should be at a constant 400°F (200°C) for any fish. It will take the oven 15 minutes to reach that temperature. When the fish is put in at precisely this temperature it will be baked properly. If you take the fish cold from the refrigerator and place it in a cold oven, or in an oven that hasn't yet reached 400°F (200°C) the fish will not bake but steam as the temperature of the oven and the fish slowly rise.

Basting fish

Fish will be tasty and moist if basted every 5 to 10 minutes while baking. Many types of hot or cold liquid can be used:

½ water and ½ butter, hot

½ water and ½ white wine, hot

½ water and juice of ½ fresh lemon, cold

Apple or tomato juice, hot

Dry white wine, cold

Sour cream or rich cream, cold

French dressing, cold

Obviously, each mixture imparts a different flavour as well as a different texture to the fish, but all can be relied on to give excellent results.

Baking times for fish

Professional chefs use the thickness and weight of a fish as a gauge for the cooking period, and it is the best way. A rule of thumb is to allow 10 to 12 minutes of baking for 1 inch (2.5 cm) of thickness. Measure the thickness before baking by holding 2 fingers (1 inch) across the thickest part of the fish. (This method was developed by Evelene Spencer when she was in charge of the Canadian government's experimental kitchen for fish). If you are in doubt, check with a ruler. The following table is a more professional guide and will give surer results. It can be used for whole fish, steak or fillets.

TIMETABLE FOR BAKING FISH

Type of fish	Thickness	Baking time in minutes
Flounder or sole	1 inch (2.5 cm)	2 per ounce (28 gr)
Haddock	3¼ inches (3.5 cm)	10 per pound (500 gr)
Mackerel	2½ inches (6.25 cm)	2 per pound (500 gr)
Pike	2¼ inches (5.5 cm)	1¼ per ounce (28 gr)
Salmon (head off)	2¼ inches (5.5 cm)	11 per pound (500 gr)
Sea bass	1½ inches (3.75 cm)	1½ per ounce (28 gr)
Striped bass	2½ inches (6.25 cm)	12 per pound (500 gr)
Whitefish	1½ inches (3.75 cm)	15 per pound (500 gr)

If you are baking a fish not listed on the chart, follow the rules for the type that is most similar.

○━➤ Never turn a baking fish, not even a small one; baked fish breaks too easily because of its delicate texture.

Cornell method for baking fish fillets

Brush fillets or steaks with butter, oil or soft bacon fat, then roll in very fine crumbs.

Place on a shallow baking pan such as a flat heat-proof glass or ceramic pan, or a jelly-roll pan. Preheat oven to 550°F (280°C); this will take 15 to 20 minutes.

Put the pan in the oven on the second rack from the bottom. Bake for exactly 8 minutes. The fish will have a nice brown colour and will be very well cooked. There is no effort involved.

Fish baked en papillote

The French method of cooking called *en papillote* might well be called "poaching in the oven" to distinguish it from poaching in liquid. In this method, in which the fish is wrapped in parchment or foil, no extra liquid is added but the fish's own liquid is retained. A fish cooked *en papillote* is delicious and the cooking method is most adaptable for the diet conscious, since fat can be cut down almost completely.

Use cooking parchment if possible. Cooking parchment can usually be found where kitchen or freezer paper are sold. Wet the parchment and then squeeze out the water; the paper will be soft and pliable. You can also use a piece of heavy-duty foil, large enough to wrap the fish completely. Brush one side of the foil or parchment generously with salad oil. Place the fish on the paper or foil and sprinkle with salt and pepper. A sprinkling of curry powder is also very good. Brush the fish with more oil. Sprinkle with lemon juice to taste. At this point, you can add an herb of your choice such as sage, dill, oregano or basil. Fold the parchment or foil and seal tightly by crimping the edges.

Place the wrapped fish in a shallow baking pan and bake in a preheated 400°F (200°C) oven for 12 minutes per pound (500 gr).

Unwrap the package carefully and slide the fish onto a hot platter. Pour all the juice accumulated on the paper over the fish. This is a perfect method for small fish, such as brook trout and smelts.

Broiling fish

This a favourite method of cooking fish steaks and fillets because it is quick, easy and always successful. You can also broil small whole fish without stuffing as well as split fish under 4 pounds (2 kg).

The heat used is 550°F (280°C). The distance from the source of the heat varies with the type of fish. Consult the timetable on page ... At this high temperature so close to the source of heat, fish cooks quickly, becomes golden brown, retains all its flavour, and has no fishy odour.

Fish steaks

Sprinkle lightly with flour and paprika. Dot the tops with soft butter, or drizzle salad oil over them. Preheat the broiler for 10 minutes. Place the fish on a generously oiled broiler pan, or on an oiled foil-lined pan. Broil 2 inches (5 cm) from the source of heat. Do not season before broiling. Baste once on each side with any of the combinations given for baked fish. Broil according to the following timetable.

TIMETABLE FOR BROILING FISH STEAKS

Type of fish	Thickness	First side, minutes	Second side minutes
Salmon	1 inch (2.5 cm)	3	5 (Baste only once when turned)
Halibut	1 inch (2.5 cm)	4	5
Bass	1 inch (2.5 cm)	4	5

Whole fish

Prepare exactly the same as fish steaks. Broil according to the following timetable, but baste three times during the cooking time.

TIMETABLE FOR BROILING WHOLE FISH

Type of fish	Distance from heat	First side minutes	Second side minutes
Carp (2½ to 3 lbs/1.25 to 1.5 kg)	6 inches (15 cm)	12	14
Flounder or sole	3 inches (8 cm)	10 in all;	do not turn
Pike	6 inches (15 cm)	5	8
Small bass	3 inches (8 cm)	4	5

Split fish

Any fish from 2 to 4 pounds (1 to 2 kg) can be split and broiled. If you leave the backbone in, the fish will be juicier and more flavourful. Do not turn splitfish. Place them skin side down in the bottom of a broiler pan, not on a rack. Proceed as for fish steaks.

TIMETABLE FOR BROILING SPLIT FISH

Type of fish	Distance from heat	Thickness	Broiling time, minutes
Bass	3 inches (8 cm)	¾ inch (1.9 cm)	8
Mackerel	2 inches (5 cm)	¾ to 1 inch (1.9 to 2.5 cm)	8 to 10
Pike	3 inches (8 cm)	¼ to 1¼ inches (6 mm to 3 cm)	8 to 10
Sea bass	3 inches (8 cm)	½ to 1 inch (1.25 to 2.5 cm)	6 to 8
Whitefish	3 inches (8 cm)	½ to 1½ inches (1.25 to 3.75 cm)	10 to 12

Fresh and frozen fillets

0→ Dry the fresh or properly thawed fillets by wrapping them in absorbent paper or cloth and leaving them wrapped for 20 minutes, to dry them as much as possible.

Roll each fillet lightly in fine bread or cracker crumbs, or in cornmeal. Then set on a broiler pan 2 to 3 inches (5 to 7.5 cm) from the heat source, just as for fish steaks. Do not turn fish fillets during the broiling period. The entire broiling time should take from 5 to 10 minutes for fillets from ¼ inch to 1 inch (6 mm to 2.5 cm) thick. When done, season and sprinkle with fresh lemon juice to taste.

Sautéing and panfrying fish

This is almost instant cooking and is probably the most used technique for cooking fish. Small dressed fish, steaks ½ to ¾ inch (1.25 to 1.9 cm) thick and fillets are used for sautéing. They can also be panfried.

To sauté fish, use an equal amount of butter and salad oil, bacon fat, shortening, margarine, or half margarine and half any other fat mentioned above. Use just enough to cover the bottom of the pan. For panfried fish, fill the pan about ¼ inch (6 mm) deep.

For either method use a large frying pan of heavy metal, cast iron, enameled cast iron or heavy stainless steel. Never attempt to sauté or to panfry in a small pan where fish would be crowded. Always use a heavy pan because the heat will be more evenly distributed for gentle cooking.

When preparing a fish for sautéing, simply roll the fillets or steaks lightly in seasoned flour. ⊶ Always use paprika as part of the seasoning, because it helps to brown the fish quickly.

For panfrying, roll the fish in seasoned flour or coat with egg and crumbs, or with cornmeal.

Whichever method you use, remember to turn the fish only once. Cook until the fish flakes. To test for flakiness, insert a fork in the thickest part of the piece of fish. Probe gently to see if the fish separates and falls easily into its own natural divisions, while at the same time showing a faint line of creamy, milky-white substance. The fish should be opaque but still moist. When the fish breaks, or shrinks, or looks dry, or has a fishy smell, it is overcooked.

There is, unfortunately, a tendency to overcook when sautéing or panfrying fish. Remember that the composition of fish is much like that of eggs — albumin and fat. Fish will therefore cook in almost the same time it takes to panfry eggs; most of the time, the only real danger is overcooking.

Deep-frying fish

Small fish such as smelts, moderately small fish such as lake perch, fish fillets of many kinds, croquettes and fish balls are all excellent deep-fried.

Clean fish when necessary in salted ice-cold water, or rub with cider vinegar. Dip into milk or into 1 egg beaten with 2 tablespoons (30 ml) cold water. Then roll in fine bread or cracker crumbs or in cornmeal.

It is best to use a frying basket, and be careful not to overcrowd the pieces. Heat shortening or salad oil 3 to 4 inches (8 to 10 cm) deep to 375°F (190°C). Use frying thermometer or thermostatically controlled electric fryer.

For fish to retain its moistness, yet turn to beautiful golden brown, 3 to 5 minutes of cooking time should be enough, depending on the size of the fish.

When the fish is done, take it from the pan, drain on paper towels and season with salt and pepper to taste while it is still hot.

For more about deep-frying and for a recipe for batter-fried fish, see Croquettes, Fritters and Doughnuts, Chapter 15.

Steaming fish

This method is as old as China and is one of the most appreciated ways of cooking fish because of the purity of flavour that it develops. It is also recommended for those on low-fat or reducing diets.

Any kind of fish can be steamed, and steamed fish is delicious whether served hot or cold, plain or with sauce.

Place 1½ to 2 inches (3.75 to 5 cm) of water in a deep large saucepan with a good cover that fits securely.

Place the cleaned fish, steaks or fillets on a small platter just as is, or with dots of butter and grated lemon or lime rind or fresh lemon or lime juice, with very little salt and pepper. (0—ᴙ Lime juice and a bit of grated fresh gingerroot on fresh salmon, by the way, is superb.) Place the platter on a rack, on an inverted low pan or in any other way so that it is above the level of the liquid. Cover tightly, place over medium-high heat, and steam.

Small fish, fillets or steaks less than 2 inches (5 cm) thick in their thickest part are steamed for 1 minute per ounce (28 gr). Fish fillets or steaks thicker than 2 inches (5 cm) are steamed for 10 minutes per pound (500 gr). The water should be at the boil all the time.

Steamed fish is best simply sprinkled with a little fresh lemon or lime juice. Do not add salt or pepper, but eat it just as is.

Poaching fish

0—ᴙ Whether fish is to be poached in a *court bouillon* or in plenty of salted water, and whether it is a whole fish or simply a piece, it should be tied in a cheesecloth, leaving long ends so that the fish can be lifted easily from the hot liquid without breaking.

0—ᴙ The liquid must never boil, but should always be kept at a simmer for perfect poaching.

Make a *court bouillon* with water, onion, carrot, herbs, wine or vinegar or lemon juice, and seasoning to taste. There must be enough liquid to cover the fish completely. Use wine or vinegar or lemon juice in proportions of 2 tablespoons to ½ cup water (30 ml to 125 ml water); (lemon juice is preferred with salmon).

Place all the flavouring ingredients in a saucepan, add the water, and boil uncovered, for 20 to 30 minutes before adding the fish.

If only salted water is used, then bring this to a full rolling boil.

When ready to put the fish in, remove the *court bouillon* or water from the source of heat. Once the fish is in, bring the liquid back to a very slow boil, then continue to simmer, covered, over low heat. Count 6 to 8 minutes per pound (500 gr) of fish, or allow 10 minutes per inch (2.5 cm) thickness of the fish.

As soon as a poached fish is cooked, take it out of the cooking liquid. To serve the fish cold, remove it from the liquid, then allow both the fish and the liquid to cool to tepid. Pour enough of the liquid over the unwrapped fish to cover it completely, then refrigerate until cold. Unwrap and serve.

Poaching can be done in the oven, too. Assemble the ingredients for the *court bouillon,* boil as above, then strain.

Pour the strained liquid over the cheesecloth-wrapped fish in a baking pan. Cover the pan and put it in a preheated 375°F (190°C) oven. Poach for about 10 minutes per pound (500 gr) or until the fish flakes easily when tested with a fork.

Canadian salmon

Spring and summer bring the enchantment of Canadian salmon to our tables from coast to coast. Some prefer the first salmon from the cold water of the Gaspé, while others say there's nothing like the British Columbia spring salmon from the deep sea. Some people, and these are an exclusive group indeed, eat only salmon they have caught themselves.

There are hundreds of interesting ways to cook and serve Canadian salmon. The secret of success is to cook it just right, and this does require a little practice and a few classic recipes.

Baked stuffed salmon

This is the king of all salmon dishes and should be prepared with a large salmon. Serve with new potatoes and fresh green peas in a cream sauce.

1 tbsp (15 ml) salt

3 tbsp (50 ml) lemon juice

1 8-12 lb (4-6 kg) whole fresh salmon

1 cup (250 ml) chopped celery

1 cup (250 ml) minced celery leaves

2 medium-sized onions, sliced thin

¼ cup (60 ml) butter or salad oil

4 cups (1 L) diced whole-wheat or rye bread

¼ tsp (1 ml) ground thyme or sage

Salt and pepper to taste

2 eggs, lightly beaten

Oil or bacon fat for coating

Mix the salt and the lemon juice together. Rub the cleaned fish inside and out with this mixture until all is used. It is best to use your fingers to do this.

For the stuffing: Sauté the celery, celery leaves and onions in the butter or salad oil over medium-low heat until the onions are soft, transparent and lightly browned here and there. Place the diced bread in a bowl and add the sautéed vegetables. Blend well, then add the herb, salt and pepper to taste, and the eggs. Stir until the whole is well mixed. Stuff the fish with the mixture, then sew the opening with coarse thread, or tie the fish securely. Weigh the stuffed fish.

Place the fish on a baking sheet well oiled or rubbed with a thick coating of bacon fat. Bake in a preheated 400°F (200°C) oven for 10 minutes per pound (500 gr) of weight after stuffing. Makes 10 to 16 servings.

This can be served hot with an egg sauce, or cold with a sour-cream cucumber sauce. Both are wonderful.

My best poached salmon

o—x

3 quarts (3.4 L) water

Juice of 1 lemon

2 carrots, sliced

2 onions, sliced

12 peppercorns

2 tbsp (30 ml) salt

6 to 10 parsley springs

1 bay leaf

1 5-10 lb (2.5 - 5 kg) whole salmon

Place the water and all the other ingredients except the salmon into a pot or saucepan large enough to hold the fish. A dripping pan covered with foil can be used for a large fish if you don't have a long fish poacher. Boil the mixture for 30 minutes.

Wrap the cleaned salmon in a piece of cheesecloth. Remove the pan from the heat, following the rule for poached fish, and place the fish in the liquid. Cover and cook over medium heat.

When ready, take the fish from the pan by inserting 2 large forks, one at each end of the fish, through the cheesecloth. Place the whole package on a hot platter, then carefully pull the cloth away from under the fish, or remove it by turning the fish over with the cloth. (The latter is more difficult to manage).

To serve the salmon hot, remove the skin, garnish with parsley, sprinkle the top with a little curry powder and spread a little egg sauce all along the back. Serve the rest of the sauce separately.

To serve the fish cold, place it on a platter. Soak a cheesecloth in the fish broth, then completely cover the fish with it. Pour a few spoonfuls of broth on top. This will keep the fish from drying out. Refrigerate until ready to serve. Remove the cloth carefully, then remove the skin. Spread the fish with mayonnaise and decorate with capers. Serve with a large bowl of Sour-Cream Cucumber Sauce (recipe follows). Makes 8 to 12 servings.

Sour-cream cucumber sauce

2 cups (500 ml) commercial sour cream

3 green onions, minced or ¼ cup (60 ml) minced chives

1 large cucumber

Salt and pepper to taste

2 tbsp (30 ml) lemon juice

To the sour cream add the minced green onions or minced chives. Peel and finely dice the cucumber. Add to the mixture with salt and pepper to taste and the lemon juice. Blend well.

Makes about 3 cups (750 ml) sauce.

English poached salmon

This is a most attractive way to serve salmon for a buffet supper or garden party.

1 4-6 lb (2-3 kg) whole salmon

2 cups (500 ml) milk

2 cups (500 ml) water

1 tbsp (15 ml) salt

2 bay leaves

¼ cup (60 ml) chopped parsley

½ tsp (2 ml) dried basil

¼ tsp (1 ml) dill seeds

1 cup (250 ml) mayonnaise

1 peeled lemon, cut into thin slices

2 hard-cooked eggs

2 carrots, cut into fine shreds

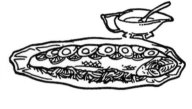

Wrap the salmon in cheesecloth. Bring the milk, water, salt, bay leaves, parsley, basil and dill seeds to a fast boil. Boil for 5 minutes. Add the salmon and simmer, covered, over medium-low heat for 20 to 35 minutes.

Let fish cool in the cooking liquid, then remove from the liquid but do not unwrap. Cover and refrigerate the salmon until ready to serve.

To serve, unwrap the salmon, remove the skin and place the fish on a platter. Spread the mayonnaise over the fish and place a long line of overlapping lemon slices on top. Grate the eggs and sprinkle over the whole fish. Place the shredded carrots all around to form a red crown. Makes 6 to 8 servings.

Poached salmon French style

The French use salmon steak for this colourful and tasty dish. When you use this recipe, it is as easy to make enough for 10 as it is for two. Serve the salmon cold with the classic sauce verte (recipe follows).

1 tbsp (15 ml) salad oil

4 to 6 salmon steaks

Juice of 1 lemon

Grated rind of ½ lemon

6 peppercorns, crushed

1 tbsp (15 ml) salt

1 small onion, quartered

Sauce Verte (below)

3 to 6 parsley sprigs

Spread the oil in a frying pan (preferably Teflon-coated) or in a flat baking dish. Place the salmon steaks next to one another, not overlapping. Add the lemon juice and rind, the peppercorns, salt, onion and enough hot water just to cover the fish. Cover. If you are using a frying pan, poach the fish on top of the stove over low heat for 10 to 20 minutes; if using a baking dish, poach in a 325°F (160°C) oven for the same length of time, or until the salmon flakes.

Allow the fish to cool in the liquid. Drain well and remove the skin. Arrange on a serving platter, then completely cover the fish with sauce verte and garnish with parsley sprigs. Serve with a cucumber salad. Makes 4 to 6 servings.

If you use a blender, this sauce will be ready in minutes. If not, the ingredients will have to be chopped very fine.

Sauce verte

½ cup (125 ml) green onion tops or chives

½ cup (125 ml) green-pepper pieces

¼ cup (60 ml) parsley leaves

½ cup (125 ml) uncooked spinach leaves

2 tbsp (30 ml) lemon juice

1 cup (250 ml) mayonnaise

Chop the vegetables into coarse pieces and place them in a blender with the lemon juice. Cover and blend until well mixed. Add the mayonnaise and blend again.

If you don't have a blender, chop the ingredients very fine and blend into the mayonnaise, crushing them in to give as much colour as possible to the sauce. Makes 1½ cups (375 ml) sauce.

This is an attractive way to use leftover pieces of poached or baked salmon. Or you can start with a thick slice of poached salmon.

Scottish molded salmon

2 to 3 cups (500 to 750 ml) cooked salmon

1 envelope unflavoured gelatin

¼ cup (60 ml) cold water

1 cup (250 ml) mayonnaise

2 tsp (10 ml) prepared mustard

1 tsp (5 ml) curry powder

Capers

Lemon wedges

Shredded lettuce

Remove the skin and bones from the salmon. Pack the pieces into an oiled mold of your choice. Cover and refrigerate for a few hours.

Sprinkle the gelatin over the cold water to soften; let stand for 5 minutes. Set over a pan of hot water to melt. Mix together the mayonnaise, prepared mustard and curry powder. Add the gelatin slowly while beating constantly. Refrigerate for 10 minutes or until it is partly set.

Unmold the fish on a platter. Spread generously with the jellied mayonnaise. If any is left, spread it around the unmolded fish. Decorate the top with capers. Place lemon wedges around, standing them up against the fish. Surround with a thick layer of shredded lettuce. Refrigerate until ready to serve. Makes 6 servings.

Swedish salmon and vegetable salad

This is another good way to use leftover salmon, but canned salmon substitutes very nicely.

1½ cups (375 ml) cooked salmon

2 peeled tomatoes, chopped

1 peeled cucumber, diced

1 cup (250 ml) cooked or canned peas

2 tbsp (30 ml) lemon juice

1 tsp (5 ml) sugar

1 tsp (5 ml) salt

½ tsp (2 ml) pepper

½ cup (125 ml) mayonnaise

Lots of chopped parsley

Flake the salmon and mix it lightly with the tomatoes, cucumber and peas. Beat together the lemon juice, sugar, salt, pepper and mayonnaise. Add to the fish mixture and blend lightly. Pile in a neat mound in a serving dish or bowl, and cover thickly with parsley. Cover and refrigerate until ready to serve. Makes 4 to 6 servings.

Marinated salmon

Scandinavians marinate all types of fish, providing themselves with fish that's always ready to serve. Marinated fish will keep in the refrigerator for 15 to 20 days. Cucumbers and green salads are good accompaniments, or you can serve this dish with hot boiled potatoes rolled in parsley.

½ cup (125 ml) cider vinegar

2 cups (500 ml) white wine

1 large onion, sliced thin

1 carrot, sliced thin

1 tbsp (15 ml) salt

3 whole cloves

¼ tsp (1 ml) dried thyme

6 peppercorns

½ tsp (2 ml) celery salt

10 to 12 small fish, any type, or 4 to 5 lbs (2 to 2.5 kg) fresh salmon

Place all the ingredients except the fish in a saucepan. Bring to a boil, then simmer, uncovered, for 20 minutes.

Clean the fish; if using salmon, slice it or leave it whole. Place fish in the hot liquid and simmer, uncovered, for 20 minutes for small fish and 40 minutes for a whole piece of salmon. Be sure not to boil. Then remove the fish to a dish and pour the cooking liquid over it. Cover and refrigerate until cold. Serve cold in the marinating liquid. Makes 6 to 8 servings.

Finnan haddie

I never knew what true finnan haddie was until I ate "cullen skink" at a friend's farm in Scotland, surrounded by great black fir trees through which the fierce winds off the North Sea shrieked. It was then I learned that finnan (or Findon) haddock was named after a small village near Aberdeen. It was there in the old days that haddock was smoked, dried over seaweed, and sprinkled with salt water during the smoking process.

Finnan haddie can be grilled, steamed, poached or made into a loaf. It has an affinity for butter, milk and potatoes. It is certainly economical and often appeals to those who, for the most part, care very little for fish.

Leftover finnan haddie is used for this savoury, which can be served as a creamy breakfast dish or on toast as an after-dinner treat. Use chutney or curry powder to flavour the breakfast dish, cayenne for the savoury served on squares of hot buttered toast.

Finnan savoury

1 tbsp (15 ml) butter

Cayenne, or ½ tsp (2 ml) curry powder

1 to 1½ cups (250 to 375 ml) cooked and flaked finnan haddie

2 tbsp (30 ml) heavy cream

1 tsp (15 ml) capers

Salt

Fresh parsley, chopped

Melt the butter and add cayenne to your taste, or the curry powder. Stir until the butter is light brown. Add the flaked fish, cream and capers. Simmer over low heat until the fish has absorbed most of the cream. Add salt to taste and sprinkle with parsley. Makes 4 servings.

Finnan farmhouse scramble

Serve this on a cold night with hot buttermilk biscuits. In Scotland it is a "crofter" specialty.

1 cup (250 ml) milk

1 lb (500 gr) finnan haddie

2 to 3 tbsp (30 to 50 ml) butter

Salt and cayenne to taste

¼ cup (60 ml) minced parsley

4 eggs

Juice of ½ lemon

Place the fish in a shallow pan and pour the milk over it. Simmer, covered, over low heat for 10 minutes, or until the fish is tender. Remove the fish from the milk and flake it. Reserve the milk. Melt the butter in a frying pan. Add the flaked fish, salt and cayenne to taste, and the parsley. Stir over low heat for 2 to 3 minutes.

Beat the eggs in a bowl and pour over the fish mixture. Cook slowly to make scrambled eggs. Do not overcook. When ready, remove from the heat, pour the lemon juice on top, and serve.

The remaining milk can be thickened with 1 tablespoon (15 ml) cornstarch mixed with 2 tablespoons (30 ml) cold water to make a parsley sauce to serve with the scramble. Add salt and pepper to taste and as much minced parsley as you like. The fish can be kept warm while you make the sauce. Makes 4 servings.

Finnan savoury pudding

A green salad is all that is needed to make an elegant and tasty meal of this light, soufflé-type pudding.

1 lb (500 gr) finnan haddie

2 slices bacon

4 tbsp (65 ml) butter

2 cups (500 ml) mashed potatoes

Salt and pepper to taste

Juice of ½ lemon

1 small onion, minced

½ tsp (2 ml) celery salt

3 tbsp (50 ml) minced parsley

¼ tsp (1 ml) dried savory

3 eggs

Place the fish in a shallow pan. Top with the bacon and add just enough water to cover the bottom of the pan. Cover and steam over medium heat for 10 minutes. Remove the fish to a plate. Rub the fish with 1 tablespoon (15 ml) of the butter. Cool. Flake the cooked fish and stir it into the mashed potatoes. Add salt and pepper to taste, the lemon juice, onion, celery salt, parsley and savory. Beat until the whole is thoroughly mixed. Melt the remaining 3 tablespoons (50 ml) of butter and stir into the fish and potatoes.

Separate the eggs. Beat the yolks until light and stir in. Beat the whites until stiff, then fold them gently into the mixture.

Butter a casserole or soufflé dish and pour in the mixture. Bake in a 350°F (180°C) oven for 30 to 40 minutes, or until golden and puffed up. Makes 6 servings.

For a party dish, set this cooled fish on a green platter or on a wooden tray, and surround with small wooden bowls filled with the garnishes.

Pink cod garnished

1 lb (500 gr) frozen cod fillets

1 tsp (5 ml) salt

¼ tsp (1 ml) pepper

3 tomatoes

1 tsp (5 ml) sugar

3 tbsp (50 ml) chopped fresh dill or parsley

2 tbsp (30 ml) margarine

½ cup (125 ml) light or heavy cream

3 hard-cooked eggs

½ cup (125 ml) chopped parsley

¼ cup (50 ml) prepared horseradish

Partially thaw the cod fillets, then cut the block into ½-inch (1.25 cm) slices with a sharp knife. Place the slices side by side in a buttered dish; you may overlap them slightly. Sprinkle with the salt and pepper.

Pour boiling water over the tomatoes and let them stand for 2 minutes. Peel and slice, then place them over the fish. Sprinkle with the sugar and dill or parsley. Dot with margarine and pour the cream over all. Cover the dish with a lid or foil and bake in a 375°F (190°C) oven for 25 to 30 minutes. Let the fish cool in the dish, still covered, then refrigerate until ready to serve.

Separate the eggs and chop or grate the whites, then the yolks. Place each in a little bowl. Place the chopped parsley in a third bowl, the horseradish in a fourth. Serve these as garnishes. No dressing or mayonnaise is needed with the fish. Makes 4 servings.

Pickled and marinated fish should be prepared with fresh fish. In this recipe, halibut steaks can replace the cod. This method of browning, cooking and marinating fish is most popular in Finland. The pickled cod needs to be refrigerated for at least 24 hours before it's served.

Pickled cod

3 lb (1.5 kg) cod

Pepper

Flour

1 cup (250 ml) salad or olive oil

2 medium-sized onions, sliced

10 peppercorns

3 bay leaves

1 cup (250 ml) green or ripe olives, pitted

½ cup (125 ml) cider or wine vinegar

1 tsp (5 ml) salt

Rub the fish on both sides with pepper, then dredge with flour. Heat the salad or olive oil in a large frying pan and quickly brown the fish pieces. When the fish is done, arrange it in a symmetrical pattern in a deep glass dish.

To the oil left in the pan, add the onions, peppercorns, bay leaves, olives, cider or vinegar and salt. Simmer for 3 minutes, then pour over the fish while still hot. Cover, cool a little, and refrigerate for at least 24 hours.

Garnish the fish with tomato wedges, lime or lemon quarters and parsley; serve with mayonnaise. Makes 6 servings.

Marinated fresh herring

In Scandinavia, they use 7 to 8-inch (17 to 20 cm) Baltic herring to make this colourful pickled fish dish. Any type of small fresh herring will do, or you can use fresh smelts.

The herring is very good with a bowl of unseasoned greens and a plate of cucumber sticks. Let each person use some of the fish liquid as a salad dressing.

1 ½ lb (750 gr) small fresh herring

2 tbsp (30 ml) cider vinegar

6 tbsp (100 ml) salad oil

1 tsp (5 ml) sugar

2 tbsp (30 ml) tomato paste

1 tsp (5 ml) salt

½ tsp (2 ml) pepper

Clean the herring, or ask your fish dealer to do it for you. Wash thoroughly in cold salted water and drain on absorbent paper. Place them side by side in a baking dish; do not use a metal pan. Stir together the rest of the ingredients and pour over the fish. Cover with a lid or foil, and simmer over low heat for 10 minutes. Cool and refrigerate for 24 hours before serving. Makes 4 servings.

Oven-poached trout with clam dressing

This is an excellent way to cook fresh trout, which will keep in the refrigerator for 3 to 5 days. Frozen sole fillets, sliced into ½-inch (1.25 cm) blocks, can replace the trout.

2 tbsp (30 ml) salad oil

1 to 2 lb (500 gr to 1 kg) fresh trout, whole or filleted

1 tsp (5 ml) salt

Chopped parsley or dill

Juice of 1 lemon

1 5-oz (140 gr) can baby clams

¼ tsp (1 ml) dried marjoram or thyme

12 to 15 stuffed olives, sliced

Spread the oil over the bottom of a baking dish and, without overlapping the pieces, place the whole or filleted trout on it. Sprinkle with the salt, parsley or dill, and lemon juice.

Drain and reserve the clams; pour their juice over the fish. Sprinkle with the marjoram or thyme. Cover the dish with a lid or foil. Poach the trout in a 375°F (190°C) oven for about 25 minutes.

Cool. Then carefully drain off the juice without disturbing he fish. Refrigerate the fish, broth and clams separately.

When ready to serve, mix together the reserved clams and the sliced olives. Add the broth, stir, and adjust seasoning. Pour the dressing over the fish. Serve with a bowl of radishes and tomato slices. Makes 4 to 5 servings.

Shellfish

Shellfish includes oysters, clams, mussels, scallops, shrimps, crabs and lobster. All provide excellent protein and are foods rich in vitamins and minerals that cooks can use as alternates to meat and poultry.

If it seems too expensive to serve shellfish, you may be surprised to find that in terms of weight, most shellfish costs no more than good-quality meat. If necessary, you can use a little less shellfish and serve a substantial first course; or add other ingredients to the shellfish to make a main dish. For example, a pint (500 ml) of shucked oysters contains no waste; nutritionally it is equivalent to 1¼ pounds (625 gr) of good-quality meat, and it costs about the same. If you find this is too much for your budget, buy only a half pint (250 ml) and combine the oysters with some other ingredients into a main dish, such as scalloped oysters or Louisiana Little Loaves.

Oysters

The oyster is a bivalve mollusk found in tidal waters along most coasts of the world. Different species live in different areas. Fresh oysters are available from September to April in the shell or shucked. Oysters in the shell are sold by the dozen or half dozen, and shucked oysters are sold by pint or half pint (0.5 or 0.25 L). They are graded according to size. Canned oysters, packed in water or oyster liquor, and frozen oysters are available in most markets.

Raw oysters on the half shell, the bottom half, are a popular and elegant appetizer. They are also served hot on the half shell, crowned with a spoon of seasoned vegetables or bread crumbs or bits of bacon and baked or broiled until sizzling.

Oysters are delicious cooked in many different ways — oyster stew, scalloped oysters, chicken and oyster pie, oyster omelet, and creamed mushrooms and oysters.

Thick batter should never be used for oysters. It makes them heavy and tasteless.

Fried oysters

½ pint (250 ml) shucked oysters

1 egg white

¼ cup (60 ml) cold water

½ cup (125 ml) flour

1 tsp (5 ml) salt

¼ tsp (1 ml) pepper

½ tsp (2 ml) paprika

1 cup (250 ml) dry bread crumbs

Peanut oil or lard

Rinse the oysters under cold running water. Drain and spread on absorbent towels to dry as much as possible.

Slightly beat the egg white with the water. Mix the flour, salt, pepper and paprika and place on a flat plate. Put the bread crumbs on another flat plate. Roll each oyster first in the seasoned flour, then in the egg-white mixture, then in the fine bread crumbs. Then place the coated oysters one next to the other on a large platter.

Put 2 inches (5 cm) of hot peanut oil or melted lard in a heavy pan. Heat to 375°F (190°C) on a frying thermometer, or until a 1-inch (2.5 cm) cube of bread browns in 40 seconds. Fry the oysters, a few at a time. As soon as each batch is browned, drain on absorbent paper. Serve with a dip or sauce of your choice. Makes 4 servings.

O—🗝 Since oysters are so full of liquid, they need to be drained for some dishes. The liquor can be used as part of the liquid in the recipe.

O—🗝 Another common preparatory step is to poach oysters gently in their own liquor until the edges curl. This is especially useful if the oysters are to be added to sauce mixtures; otherwise, they would dilute the sauce.

Louisiana little loaves

Serve for lunch, with a salad of endive or mixed greens, or as an after theatre supper.

8 crusty French rolls

5 tbsp (80 ml) butter

½ pint (250 ml) shucked oysters

Grated rind of ½ lemon

Pinch of grated nutmeg

¼ tsp (1 ml) salt

⅛ tsp (0.5 ml) pepper

1 tbsp (15 ml) flour

½ cup (125 ml) milk

¼ tsp (1 ml) MSG

2 tsp (10 ml) mayonnaise

1 tsp (5 ml) fresh lemon juice

Minced parsley or chives

Slice the tops from the rolls and hollow out the interiors, saving the crumbs. Melt 2 tablespoons (30 ml) of the butter and brush insides and outsides of the hollow rolls. Place the rolls in a 350°F (180°C) oven to brown. Melt 2 more tablespoons (30 ml) butter in a frying pan. Add the crumbs removed from the rolls and sauté over low heat until golden brown. Toss the crumbs and butter with a fork to brown evenly. Place the oysters in another saucepan with the lemon rind, nutmeg, ¼ teaspoon (1 ml) salt and ⅛ teaspoon (0.5 ml) pepper. Simmer over low heat until the edges ruffle.

Make a cream sauce with the remaining 1 tablespoon (15 ml) butter, the flour and milk. When creamy, add the MSG., salt and pepper to taste, then the mayonnaise and fresh lemon juice. Stir until blended and add to the oysters. Stir gently until the whole is well mixed; then stir in half of the sautéed crumbs. Spoon the mixture into the hot rolls. Sprinkle the tops with the remaining sautéed crumbs and minced parsley or chives. Makes 8 small servings.

Clams

The clam is another mollusk. Soft-shell clams live in the area between high- and low-tide limits and burrow into the sand. They are dug out with clam rakes. Hard-shell clams are found beyond the low-tide limit, where they are dug out with rakes or dredges. The shells are creamy white, and ridged. Soft-shells are thinner and flatter and the shell itself is thinner and can be broken by finger pressure. Hard-shells are often referred to as "quahogs", especially around Cape Cod; their shells are rock hard and they are rounder and fatter in shape than soft-shells. Cherrystone and Littleneck clams, which are small quahogs, are usually served raw on the half shell, like oysters. Larger clams are chopped and used for chowder. Clams can be bought in the shell, like oysters, and they are available canned whole, large or baby type, as well as minced. Bottled clam juice is also available.

Steamed clams

Soft-shell clams are usually served steamed. Scrub them carefully. Put them in a deep heavy pot and add about ½ cup (125 ml) water. Do not add salt, as clams are very salty. Cover the pot and steam the clams for 10 to 12 minutes, until the shells are opened. Turn them over after 3 or 4 minutes to ensure even steaming. Lift them out with a slotted spoon and serve in bowls.

Serve them with a dipping sauce. The best is 1 cup (250 ml) of the strained broth heated with ¼ cup (60 ml) butter, the juice of 1 lemon and 1 teaspoon (5 ml) Worcestershire sauce. Allow about 4 dozen clams for 4 servings.

Whole or chopped clams make delicious sauces for spaghetti or linguini, and they are delicious fried in the same fashion as oysters. Clams are often added to other seafood to make such dishes as *cioppino* and *paella*.

Mussels

Mussels are bivalve mollusks resembling clams, with rather thin, bluish-black shells. There are saltwater and freshwater varieties. They are a most delicious shellfish. Mussels are sold in the shell by weight. You will need to open them yourself by steaming. Buy 1 pound (500 gr) of mussels for 2 or 3 main-course servings.

Mussels require thorough cleaning, which is a little tedious. First, scrub each shell with a rough brush under running water. Then remove the beard, which the mussel uses to hold onto rocks, poles and wharves. It resembles old dried grass and is usually tightly caught between the shell. Cut off the part that shows with scissors. Then cover the cleaned mussels with very cold water and let them soak for 2 hours. During this soaking they will throw off any sand that remains inside the shells. Lift them out of the water to drain; the sand will remain in the water. Discard any that are open or broken. The rest are now ready to be steamed.

The liquid used to steam them can be plain salted water or half white wine, half water. Put only 1 inch (2.5 cm) of liquid in the bottom of a large heavy pan. Add the cleaned mussels. Cover the pan and steam the mussels for 5 minutes, or until the shells open. If you are cooking a large quantity of mussels, turn them with a large spoon or skimmer after 2 minutes to allow them to steam evenly. Lift them out of the pan and discard any that have not opened; these may be filled with mud. Serve the mussels, still in their shells, on large plates. To eat, pick them out of their shells, one by one, and dip them into plain or lemon butter or their own broth. To use the broth, strain it through a fine sieve lined with a double layer of moistened cheesecloth.

Moules marinière

This is a famous French preparation and is one of the best ways to serve mussels.

½ cup (125 ml) dry white wine

1 green onion, chopped

¼ cup (60 ml) butter

2 to 3 lb (1 to 1.5 kg) mussels

1 tbsp (15 ml) butter

1 tbsp (15 ml) flour

1 tbsp (15 ml) minced parsley

Clean the mussels. Then combine in a saucepan wine, chopped green onion and butter. Heat until the butter is melted. Add the mussels. Cover and simmer over medium heat until the mussels open, about 5 minutes. Lift out the mussels and divide them among large deep plates. Remember to discard any that have not opened. Strain the broth through a fine sieve lined with a double layer of moistened cheesecloth into a hot bowl. Make a beurre manié with the butter and flour and use it to thicken the broth. Add the minced parsley. Or if you prefer, stir in ¼ cup (60 ml) heavy cream, or a mixture of the cream and 1 egg yolk. Spoon some of the thickened sauce into a small bowl for each person. Makes about 6 appetizer servings.

Scallops

This is another mollusk, but only a part of the creature is used — the muscle that opens and closes the shell. In Europe the whole scallop comes to market and the roe or coral, looking like a small orange tongue, can be used as well. We never see this on our side of the Atlantic, but European recipes that call for the coral can be made without it. As there is no waste at all in scallops, they can be an economical buy when in season, from November to May for deep-sea scallops.

Bay scallops are available in the East during the early fall. They are usually more expensive, but they are very delicate in flavour and very tender.

Place the scallops in a sieve and spray with cold water. They should never soak in water. Then turn the scallops on to an absorbent towel or a clean cloth and pat as dry as you can. Roll up in the cloth and refrigerate until ready to cook.

When using frozen scallops, always defrost them before cooking and roll in a cloth just as for fresh scallops.

Sautéed scallops

Roll scallops in seasoned flour. Melt some butter or margarine, or heat some olive oil, in a heavy frying pan. When very hot, add as many scallops as the pan will accommodate. Sauté quickly over medium heat, turning only once, for 2 minutes. Do not cook scallops or they will lose flavour and tenderness. Scallops are all white and they look better when garnished with parsley or chives or sautéed cherry tomatoes. For 4 to 6 servings, allow 1 pound (500 gr) scallops. If they are very large, they can be cut into smaller pieces.

Shrimps

Shrimps are crustaceans with 10 legs, but usually the legs have been removed along with the heads before they are brought to market.

Uncooked shrimps are often referred to as green shrimps, though they are not truly green in colour. However, the familiar shrimp-pink colour appears only after the shrimps have been cooked, and it is the shells that have the most colour.

There are many different kinds of shrimps, from large to small, and there is considerable variety in the colour of the uncooked shells. Related species are langoustines, prawns and scampi, all of which are larger, although there is much disagreement about which name belongs to which. All of them can be cooked by the methods used for shrimps.

Poached shrimp

1 lb (500 gr) uncooked fresh shrimp

3 slices unpeeled lemon

¼ tsp (1 ml) dried thyme

1 bay leaf

1 tbsp (15 ml) chopped celery leaves

2 tsp (10 ml) salt

Place fresh shrimps in a saucepan. Add lemon slices, dried thyme, bay leaf, chopped celery leaves, salt and enough cold water to cover the shrimps. Then bring to a boil, uncovered, over medium heat. As soon as the water boils, lower the heat and simmer gently for 3 to 5 minutes, or just until shrimps turn pink. Drain immediately and cool. Peel off the shells and remove the black veins down the backs with the point of a knife. The shrimps are now ready to use just as they are, or they can be added to other preparations. If you are not ready to use them, refrigerate, covered, until needed.

Frozen shrimps

Shrimps frozen in their shells should be thawed and washed under running cold water. Place in a pan with just the water that clings to them, cover tightly, and cook them in their own steam over medium heat for about 5 minutes, or until the shells turn pink. Some water will accumulate during the cooking period; drain it off. Peel the shrimps and they are ready to use.

When the shrimps are frozen without their shells, thaw, devein, and drop them into enough boiling water to cover. Add 1 teaspoon salt per pound (5 ml salt per 500 gr) of shrimps and 2 slices of unpeeled lemon. Bring the water to a rolling boil, cover, and simmer over low heat for 3 minutes.

When adding frozen shrimps to a sauce, peel if needed, devein, and add them directly to the sauce without thawing.

Whether fresh or frozen, 1 pound (500 gr) of shrimp can be the basis of a main dish or salad to serve 3 or 4 persons.

Fried shrimps

This recipe can also be used for clams or mussels. The batter is light and crispy, so it does not disguise the delicate flavour of the shellfish.

24 fresh shrimp, uncooked or cooked

½ cup (125 ml) flour

¼ tsp (1 ml) salt

½ tsp (2 ml) paprika

¼ tsp (1 ml) curry powder

1 egg

1½ tsp (7 ml) lemon juice

⅓ cup (80 ml) milk

Peanut oil or lard for deep frying

Clean the shrimp. Then mix together the flour, salt, paprika and curry powder.

Beat the egg, add the lemon juice and milk, and beat the liquids into the flour until the mixture is smooth. If the batter is too heavy, add a little milk, 1 teaspoon (5 ml) at a time.

If you do not have a deep fryer, use a deep pan and put oil or lard in the pan to a depth of 2 inches (5 cm). Heat the fat to 350°F (180°C) on a frying thermometer. Dip the shrimps one by one into the batter and then slide them carefully into the hot fat. Fry for about 3 minutes, until brown on both sides, turning once. Drain on absorbent paper and serve. Makes 4 servings.

Crabs

Like the shrimp, a crab is a decapod crustacean. There are many different species of crabs and they are found all over the world.

Fresh crabs in the shell are expensive; also, one has to learn how to open the shells and extract the meat, and it is a lot of work to collect enough for a meal.

It is more economical and much less work to buy fresh or frozen crab meat. Also, no basic cooking is needed because the crab is already cooked. Canned crab is also available.

Soft-shell crabs are hard-shell crabs that have sloughed off their tight old shells and whose new, larger shells have not yet had time to harden. It takes about 48 hours for the new shell to harden, so there is only this short time to capture the defenceless soft-shell. This is what makes this delicate seafood hard to get and usually expensive.

Fried soft-shell crabs

Clean the soft-shell crabs by removing the spongy substance under the pointed flap and the feathery gills on either side. Then cut across the front to remove the eyes and sandbag; or ask your fishmonger to do this for you.

Sprinkle cleaned crabs all over with a mixture of equal amounts of salt and MSG. Dip them into flour. Heat enough butter in a heavy cast-iron frying pan to fill it ½ inch (1.25 cm) deep. Fry the crab on both sides over medium heat for about 3 minutes on each side, turning only once, until golden in colour. Serve with melted butter mixed with lime juice, or with tartar sauce.

A ramekin is a round or oval individual ovenware dish. This quick and easy recipe will give you light seafood mixture with a crunchy topping. It is delicious made with any type of cooked seafood, but it is best with crab and lobster.

Seafood ramekins

6 tbsp (100 ml) butter

¼ cup (60 ml) dry sherry

1 to 1½ cups (250 to 375 ml) flaked crab or lobster meat

2 tbsp (30 ml) flour

¾ cup (200 ml) light cream

2 egg yolks

Salt and pepper to taste

¼ cup (50 ml) cracker meal

¼ tsp (1 ml) paprika

Grated rind of ½ lemon

1 tbsp (15 ml) crushed potato chips

2 tsp (10 ml) grated Parmesan cheese

Melt 2 tablespoons (30 ml) of the butter and add the sherry. Heat together, then simmer for 1 minute. Add the crab or lobster meat. Stir to blend, cover, and let stand away from heat.

Melt another 2 tablespoons (30 ml) of the butter, stir in the flour, and stir together for 1 minute. Remove from the heat and stir in the cream. Drain the hot liquid from the sherried crab or lobster meat and add it to the mixture. Return the sauce to the heat and cook, stirring constantly, until smooth and creamy.

Beat the egg yolks and stir them into the hot sauce while beating. Add the shellfish. Taste for seasoning and add salt or pepper if desired. Divide into 4 to 6 buttered ramekins (or use large custard cups or other individual baking dishes).

Combine the cracker meal, paprika, lemon rind, crushed potato chips and grated cheese. Melt the remaining 2 tablespoons (30 ml) butter and stir into the crumb mixture. Sprinkle evenly on top of the ramekins. Bake in 300°F (150°C) oven for 10 minutes, or until the tops are delicately browned. Makes 4 to 6 servings.

Lobster

Fresh lobster tops the list of seafood for elegant eating, but it also is the most expensive because there is a great deal of waste. Nevertheless, you have been deprived of the full romance of the sea if you have never cooked live lobster. When cooked with care, lobster can be spectacular in taste and appearance. I suspect that many avoid lobster, not because of its price but because it seems so difficult to cook and shell.

The shells of live lobsters are dark green, almost black, to blend in with their natural surroundings of rock and kelp. They become buff red and fragrant when cooked. Both the male and female lobster contain tomalley, the green liver considered by many the most delicate part of the meal, but the coral or red-coloured roe, which is also delicious, is found only in the female.

Lobster is often referred to as the "treasure from the bottom of the sea." You may think it is indeed a treasure if you plan to serve it whole in the shell, for you will need a lobster for each person. Each should weigh about 1½ pounds (750 gr). The same lobster can serve 2 people if the meat is removed from the shell and prepared in a sauce.

Another kind of lobster — the rock lobster or spiny lobster or crawfish —

is a related species but has no large front claws. The tail meat of the rock lobster is the chief edible part; these tails are frozen and shipped all over the world, chiefly from South Africa. While the flavour is similar, these are not as tender as our northern lobster. There is less waste in lobster tails and they can be used in any recipe calling for lobster meat.

Boiled live lobster

Many cookbooks tell you to "plunge live lobsters head first into boiling water". A better way is to put the lobster to sleep, gently and humanely.

First, choose a large saucepan or soup kettle. Place the lobster on a large piece of clean cotton or cheesecloth and tie the corners together at each end. (This is not absolutely necessary, but it makes it easy to remove the lobster from the cooking liquid later — simply lift the cloth bag with long forks slipped into the knotted ends.)

Cover the lobster completely with cold water and add 1 tablespoon (15 ml) coarse salt. If you're lucky enough to be near the sea, use sea water and omit the salt. Bring the water to a boil over high heat and let it boil for 3 to 4 minutes. Then lower the heat to simmer and cook for another 12 to 18 minutes, depending on the size of the lobster. An over-cooked lobster will have stringy or mushy meat.

As soon as the lobster is cooked, re-move it from the water and dip it brief-ly into a bowl of cold water. This will stop the cooking without cooling the meat.

Steamed lobster

Only baby lobsters, Eighths (1⅛ pounds / 560 gr), Quarters (1¼ pounds / 625 gr), and Selects (1½ pounds / 750 gr) should be steamed.

Place lobsters on a rack in a large sau-cepan containing 2 to 4 cups (500 ml to 2 L) of boiling water under the rack. Cover tightly. This is very important. If the cover does not adjust properly, place a sheet of foil or a large cloth between saucepan and cover and fasten tightly to the pot. Steam for 6 to 8 minutes, at most, after the water has come to a boil. Keep on high heat during the whole cooking period.

If the lobster is to be served cold, let it cool completely before removing the meat.

Broiled lobster

Do not attempt to broil or bake a cooked lobster. It will be hard, dry and stringy. Ask your fish dealer to split a live lob-ster and remove the stomach sac and sand vein for you.

Rub each half with melted butter and add a sprinkle of grated lemon rind or a pinch of tarragon to taste. Place on a rack 4 inches (10 cm) from the source of heat and broil, with the door of the oven partly open, for 10 to 15 minutes. Serve direclty from the oven when ready.

Baked lobster

Split and clean as for a broiled lobster. Place shell-side down in a shallow drip-ping pan. Brush with this herb butter: 2 tablespoons (30 ml) melted butter, pinch of dried tarragon or rosemary, ¼ teaspoon (1 ml) dry mustard, ¼ teaspoon (1 ml) salt and some fresh-ly ground pepper. Bake in a preheated 450°F (230°C) oven for 15 to 18 minutes. Transfer to a warm platter and pour remaining herb butter on top.

This makes a delicious summer meal to serve with a basketful of hot buttered crackers, and followed by strawberries, thick cream and maple sugar. The stew needs to be made at least 12 hours before serving to develop its full flavour.

Creamy lobster stew

2 Select lobsters 1½ lb/750 gr each)

or 3 Quarter lobsters (1¼ lb/625 gr each)

3 tbsp (50 ml) butter

4 cups (1 L) milk

1 cup (250 ml) heavy cream

Salt and pepper to taste

Steam the live lobsters. Remove the meat from the shells. Cover and cool.

Melt the butter in an enameled cast-iron or steel saucepan. Add the lobster meat and simmer over low heat for a few minutes. Add the milk and stir most of the time until hot, then add the cream and keep on stirring. When hot, simmer for a few minutes, but do not boil. Cool. Cover and refrigerate for 12 to 24 hours before serving, to develop the full flavour of the lobster. Reheat, without boiling. Just before serving, season with salt and pepper to taste. Makes 4 to 6 servings.

HOW TO EAT A COOKED LOBSTER

1. Twist off the claws.

2. Crack each claw with a nutcracker, hammer or rock.

3. Separate the tail from the body by arching the back until it cracks.

4. Bend back and break off the flippers from the tail-piece.

5. Insert a narrow fork where the flippers broke off and push out meat.

6. Unhinge the body (which contains the green tomalley or liver) from the back.

7. Crack the remaining part of the body apart sideways to find some more good meat.

8. The succulent meat in the small claws can be sucked out.

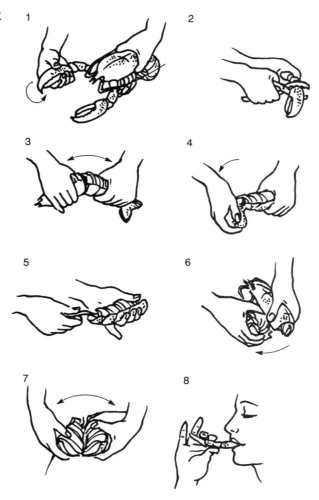

Lobster Newburg

A true Newburg is more than canned lobster stirred into a white sauce coloured with paprika. It is said that the recipe originated at Delmonico's, a New York restaurant famous in the 19th century. The sauce was made with Madeira in those days, and spiced with cayenne.

4 egg yolks, lightly beaten

1 ½ cups (375 ml) heavy cream

⅓ cup (80 ml) milk

2 tbsp (30 ml) flour

⅓ cup (80 ml) soft butter

Pinch of grated mace

2 to 2 ½ cups (500 ml to 625 ml) cooked fresh lobster meat

Salt to taste

2 tbsp (30 ml) dry sherry

Place egg yoks, cream and milk in the top part of a double boiler and heat to scalding, stirring often.

Mix the flour, butter and mace into a paste. Add this to the egg-yolk mixture and cook until creamy and smooth, stirring often. Thin sauce to consistency you prefer with a little milk. Add lobster meat and salt to taste. Let simmer for 10 to 12 minutes. Add sherry. Serve on buttered toast points. Serves 4 to 6.

Spring sauce for lobster

This a classic French sauce to serve with broiled or baked lobster.

2 shallots or spring onions, minced

½ cup (125 ml) dry white wine

4 tbsp (65 ml) butter

3 tbsp (50 ml) flour

1 ¼ cups (310 ml) milk or light cream

Salt and pepper to taste

1 tbsp (15 ml) lemon juice

Slowly simmer the shallots in the white wine until reduced to 2 tablespoons (30 ml); this will take about 30 minutes, with no stirring or attention.

Make a cream sauce with 3 tablespoons (50 ml) of the butter, the flour, and the milk or light cream. Season with salt and pepper to taste. Add the reduced wine and shallots; blend well. Add the remaining 1 tablespoon (15 ml) butter and the lemon juice. Stir just enough to melt the butter, and serve. Makes about 1 ½ cups (375 ml) sauce.

For a recipe for barbecued lobster, see Seafood Sakana, in Barbecuing, chapter 12.

CHAPTER 12

Barbecuing

BROILING OR GRILLING OUTDOORS over an open fire has become a favourite national pastime. All the knowledge you have about indoor broiling will be useful here, but remember that the source of the heat is below the food and juices will fall down into the fire unless you take special precautions. Also, the heat is less easy to regulate than in your indoor broiler.

All kinds of barbecuing equipment is available, from small Japanese hibachis to Mexican black-iron braseros. Whatever you buy, it will come with instructions. Familiarize yourself with these directions.

Equipment

Covered barbecues which offer highly efficient control over heat, wind and even rain are by far the best type for covered cooking and smoking, with their excellent dampers and deep firebeds. They do not, like other types, flare up when melting grease oozes out of the meat, or excess oxygen gets in at the charcoal level. When the cover is on, oxygen enters through the bottom dampers and is consumed by the charcoal, allowing only the heat to rise, hit the cover, rotate, and cook the food. Natural juices and flavours are sealed in by heat reflected from the cover into the food from all sides. And, most interesting, cooking time is greatly reduced because the cover keeps the heat in the barbecue.

In a covered barbecue, roasts can be done directly on the grill — and they do not even have to be turned. You can grill by direct or indirect heat in a covered barbecue and you can give your roast or chicken a beautiful smoked flavour if you wish.

In the direct method, the meat is placed on the grill over the charcoal; this is perfect for steaks and chops, hambergers and split broilers. With the indirect method, the fire is placed on the sides of the grill, with a foil drip pan in the centre. The meat is placed on the grill, directly over the foil pan, and the cooking is done by reflected heat; this is the way to cook whole roasts, chickens and hams.

How to build and control the fire

Whatever type of equipment you use, the firebed is the most important part. The right kind of heat in a barbecue can cook your food to perfection; the wrong heat will burn it to a crisp.

If your barbecue requires you to build a fire, remember that a little wind and a lot of patience are what you need most. Once the fire is started, it has to be kept going, but neither too fast nor too slow, until coals start to form. The coals should be allowed to burn until they are an ash-gray colour, shot through here and there with a red glow. This is your guarantee of a constant heat.

I prefer to use maple hardwood, but I am lucky enough to have a lot around me, so I am not concerned with cost. Its drawback is that it takes a long time to reduce to glowing coals. Whatever you do, make sure you stay away from pine, a soft wood that gives a resinous smoke and never develops adequate coals.

Charcoal and briquettes are easy and quick. Although both are more expensive than wood, they have the advantage of being uniform in size and therefore easy to arrange under the grill. If you are using briquettes, remember that different brands are made from different materials, so be sure you use the same brand each time. Each type burns differently. Briquettes are also devilishly hard to light. Allow 45 to 55 minutes between the time you light them and the time you plan to start cooking over them.

0—➤ Never cook over coals that are not completely covered with a white ash. It is not the flame that cooks barbecued foods, but direct, red-hot radiation. This comes only from completely heated coals. If you must add coals or briquettes during cooking, place them at the edge of the fire, well away from the food. They will take about 15 minutes to get red.

Briquettes and charcoal absorb moisture rapidly and once damp are next to impossible to start. **0—➤** So transfer them to a plastic bag for storage.

Don't use more charcoal than is necessary. For instance, if you are barbecuing only a small amount, build a small bed in the middle, making the charcoal layer only slightly larger than the area covered by the food to be cooked.

The importance of a good draft

Charcoal and briquettes burn from the bottom to the top, so they require a draft from below to burn perfectly. If your barbecue has a solid metal box, the bottom must be covered with sand or gravel. Lining the fire box with heavy foil makes it easier to clean and increases the radiant heat. When cold, the foil containing all the mess can be lifted out and thrown away.

Fire control

When low heat is required for long slow cooking, use tongs to spread the red coals so they aren't touching each other. If you need more heat, just flick the white ashes off the tops; you will get 6 to 10 more minutes of heat. When more fuel is required, place it around the edge of the fire, never on top.

To eliminate flare-ups caused by fat falling on the fire, douse the flames with a small amount of water sprayed out of a basting tube or a child's water pistol. **0—➤** It's best to have a water-filled bottle with a spray attachment handy at all times.

The distance from the top of the coals to the food determines the rate of cooking. The greater the distance, the less heat and the slower the barbecuing.

A hood on the back of a grill intensifies the heat, shortening the cooking time slightly.

Timing

Timing is a matter of judgment. The cooking period varies with the type of grill used, the size of the firebox, the degree of heat, and the amount and direction of the wind. **0—➤** Keep a diary of the cooking times you have the most success with for different foods.

Barbecuing uses the same heat principle as oven grilling, so the timetable for grilling meat in an oven broiler will help you estimate how long to barbecue most meats. As in all types of meat cooking, differences depend on the meat used, its texture and quality.

About 3 inches (8 cm) above the coals is a good average distance to place the grill. 0—🔑 Here's a trick for judging the intensity of the heat: Hold your hand 3 inches (8 cm) from the coals and count the seconds until you have to pull it away — 1 second means high heat; 3 seconds indicates medium heat; 5 seconds means low heat.

What can be barbecued

All foods that can be panfried or broiled can be barbecued — meat, poultry, fish and vegetables.

The best beef cuts to barbecue are all loin cuts — sirloin, pinbone, porterhouse, T-bone and club steaks. The rib is also a good barbecue cut.

For a large party, buy a 10-inch (25 cm) rib roast. It will give you 7 good steaks, and 1 to 2 pounds (500 gr to 1 kg) short ribs, a few pounds of soup bone, and 2 small pot roasts. You can see from this that buying a large rib cut can prove more economical than merely buying a few steaks.

Have steaks cut 1½ to 2 inches (3.75 to 5 cm) thick. Steaks should be well marbled with fat; look for tiny lines of fat running throughout the meat.

Veal is too dry for successful barbecuing, but calf's liver is very quickly and successfully cooked this way.

Every cut of lamb is delicious cooked on the barbecue, but a butterfly leg of lamb, lamb steaks cut from the leg and lamb kebabs made from cubed or ground lamb are especially good.

Among pork cuts for barbecuing, none is more popular than spareribs. However, pork chops are also good, as is a whole pork loin or a part of a loin. Cured pork is also good. Ham steaks are successful if not too thin. If you have a covered barbecue, you can do a whole ham.

As for chicken, whole, split or cut into pieces, it is the easiest meat to barbecue. However, chicken tends to be dry and it should be basted frequently.

Barbecuing brings out the finest flavour in all seafood. Whole fish, steaks, fillets or any boneless cuts can be barbecued. Just remember that fish, like chicken, needs frequent basting to keep it from getting too dry. Fish is fragile, and can break apart when turned. Also, it sticks easily to the grill. It is best to place fish on a toasting rack, or in a hinged box grill that can be turned with the fish inside.

Potatoes, corn on the cob and other vegetables can be cooked on the barbecue wrapped in foil. Small pieces of meat, fish or shellfish, mixed with vegetables or fruits, whole or in pieces, make wonderful barbecued kebabs. 0—🔑 Remember to salt the foods only at the end of the cooking period. Salt tends to release juices, and you want to keep all of them in the food you are cooking.

Also do not turn meats with a fork. This punctures the sealed outer layer and lets rich juices escape and sizzle into the fire. Use tongs. If you must use a fork, jab it into the fat only.

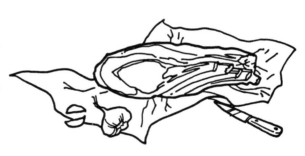

MARINADES AND BASTING SAUCES

In barbecuing, the scope for a really distinctive touch lies in the endless variety of special marinades and sauces that can be used.

Marinating does more than add seasoning to barbecued food. It is used to sharpen the flavour of meat, fish or fowl; to supply fat to meats that lack natural oils (by oil penetration); and to tenderize meats (by acid penetration) such as spareribs, shoulder pork, lamb chops and short ribs.

Marinades can be made with olive or salad oil. You can use any type of vinegar, or a mixture. Hundreds of different herbs and spices, fresh or dried, can be used to season a marinade to your taste.

Place the meat in a glass, enamelware or ceramic container and pour on the marinade. Turn the meat frequently. Most foods require only 2 to 6 hours at room temperature, but large or tough cuts of meat should be kept in the refrigerator for a few days; cover them tightly to prevent their strong seasoning odors from reaching other foods.

0—🔧 One trick is to place the meat and a relatively small amount of marinade in a tough plastic freezer bag, tightly tied.

You will find more about marinades and their uses in other cooking process in chapter 6, vol. I.

Basic marinades

Use 2 parts oil, 1 part vinegar, 1 minced onion or 1 crushed garlic clove, and salt, pepper, herbs and spices to taste.

For a very special steak, use ½ cup (125 ml) olive oil, 3 tablespoons (50 ml) red-wine vinegar, 1 teaspoon (5 ml) garlic salt, 1 tablespoon (15 ml) paprika and 1 teaspoon (5 ml) MSG.

For chicken use olive oil, wine vinegar, tarragon, thyme and parsley.

For duck use melted butter and red wine in place of oil and vinegar; add rosemary, chopped celery leaves, sage and grated lemon rind.

For lamb use olive oil or salad oil, red-wine vinegar, fresh mint, shallots and garlic.

For fish use equal parts of soy sauce and water and crushed garlic to taste. Marinate for at least 5 hours. Baste with fresh lemon or lime juice while broiling (see also Seafood Sakana, p. 292)

Honey mint marinade for lamb

½ cup (125 ml) water

1 tbsp (15 ml) cider vinegar

1 cup (250 ml) honey

¼ to ½ cup (60 to 125 ml) minced fresh mint

Bring to a boil the water and cider vinegar. Add the honey and stir until dissolved. Remove from heat and add the mint.

Marinate lamb in this for 4 to 6 hours. Use the marinade for basting while the lamb is cooking.

1 garlic clove, sliced

½ cup (125 ml) salad oil or melted butter

Soak the sliced garlic in the oil or melted butter. Cover and let stand overnight. Remove the garlic with a fork and use the oil as a marinade for chicken, or for relatively dry cuts of meat such as chuck steak. It can also be used as a basting sauce.

If you use melted butter instead of salad oil, brush this onto the meat for the marinade. Some can be scraped off when you are ready to barbecue, but what is left will help to form a delicious crust on the meat.

Garlic marinade

Italian marinade

Mix together 1 part sweet (Italian) vermouth and 1 part olive oil. Season with rosemary and basil to taste. This is delicious with both chicken and fish.

This has a subtle flavour with the wonderful tang of lemon. It is perfect with chicken, fish, pork or hamburger.

¾ cup (190 ml) butter

2 tsp (10 ml) paprika

1 tsp (5 ml) sugar

1 tsp (5 ml) salt

½ tsp (2 ml) pepper

¼ tsp (1 ml) dry mustard

Pinch of cayenne

½ cup (125 ml) lemon juice

½ cup (125 ml) hot water

Melt the butter, being careful not to brown it. Add the paprika, sugar, salt, pepper, mustard and cayenne. Stir until thoroughly blended. Then add the lemon juice and hot water. Beat until well mixed.

Use as a basting sauce. It keeps refrigerated for 2 to 3 weeks. Warm to use. Makes 1½ cups (375 ml) sauce.

Lemon basting sauce

Lemon butter sauce

Any type of grilled or barbecued seafood is absolutely delicious dipped into this. It is so simple, yet so right.

1 cup (250 ml) butter

2 tbsp (30 ml) lemon juice

¼ tsp (1 ml) salt

¼ tsp (1 ml) paprika

⅛ tsp (0.5 ml) pepper

¼ cup (60 ml) chopped parsley

2 tbsp (30 ml) chopped chives (optional)

Heat together in a small saucepan the butter, lemon juice, salt, paprika and pepper. Do not let the butter brown. Add the parsley and chives and serve.

To use as a plain basting sauce, omit the parsley and chives. Makes 1 cup (250 ml) sauce.

B.C. basting sauce

This is the favorite basting sauce of a friend in Vancouver. It is delicious with both barbecued chicken and lamb.

¼ cup (60 ml) liquid honey

¼ cup (60 ml) prepared mustard

1 tsp (5 ml) curry powder

Simply mix the honey, prepared mustard and curry powder.

You will find other ideas for marinades and basting sauces with the recipes that follow.

Barbecued steak

Marinate steak for 1 to 12 hours, depending on how sharp a flavour you want. Sprinkle the steak generously with brandy 15 minutes before you start to barbecue. Rub the steak with a piece of suet or brush it with oil to prevent it from sticking to the grill. Place the steak on the grill about 3 inches (8 cm) above the glowing charcoal. Cooking time will depend on the thickness of the meat, temperature of the fire, and how you like your steak done. A basic timing, however, is 6 minutes for one side and 6 minutes for the other. Baste the steak with soy sauce or H.P. Sauce while cooking. Turn the steak only once during broiling. Never use a fork, because this punctures the meat and allows the juices to escape.

Just before removing the steak from the grill, throw a few bay leaves on the charcoal and smoke each side of the steak over this for a few seconds. At the moment of serving, top each sizzling steak with Seasoned Butter (below).

Barbecue a steak 1½ inches (3.75 cm) thick — porterhouse, sirloin, T-bone or rib steak (about 4 pounds/2kg) — 3 inches (8 cm) from the glowing coals for 6 to 10 minutes per side for rare, medium, well-done.

Barbecue a steak 1 inch (2.5 cm) thick, also 3 inches (8 cm) from the coals, for about 4 minutes per side.

Barbecue a cube steak cut from the round or flank 3 inches (8 cm) from the coals for 7 to 8 minutes per side.

4 tbsp (60 ml) butter

1 tsp (5 ml) seasoned salt

½ tsp (2 ml) paprika

1 tsp (5 ml) Worchestershire sauce

Blend together all the ingredients. Form into balls and refrigerate until ready to serve.

Steak can also be served with just salt and pepper and a dab of butter.

Seasoned butter

Steak can be basted with a special sauce while barbecuing.

1 garlic clove

½ tsp (2 ml) dried thyme

1 cup (250 ml) salad or olive oil

Mix together the ingredients. Let the mixture blend for 12 hours then dip the steak into it before cooking. More can be brushed on during cooking to keep the steak from getting too dry.

Steak sauce

This recipe comes from a friend in British Columbia and makes a memorable barbecue.

¼ cup (60 ml) peanut oil

¼ cup (60 ml) Canadian rye whisky

2 tbsp (30 ml) soy sauce

1 tbsp (15 ml) chutney

½ tsp (2 ml) garlic powder

Coarse pepper to taste

Blend together the peanut oil, Canadian rye, soy sauce, chutney and

½ teaspoon garlic powder. Add a generous amount of freshly ground coarse pepper. Soak the steaks in this for 2 hours. Then brush it off the steaks and barbecue them. While the steaks are cooking, brush them 3 or 4 times with the remaining sauce.

Serve with big baked potatoes, with either sour cream or butter on them, and thick slices of tomatoes. These should be generously sprinkled with minced chives but no dressing.

Barbecued club steak

Calf's liver brochettes

Brochettes *is the French name for skewers. Cook these over direct heat on your covered barbecue.*

1 lb (500 gr) calf's liver

¼ cup (60 ml) hot melted butter

¼ lb (125 gr) sliced bacon

Fine dry bread crumbs

Grated rind of ½ lemon

¼ tsp (1 ml) ground thyme

Have the liver cut into ½-inch (1.25 cm) slices. Cut each slice into 1-inch (2.5 cm) squares. Heat the butter until it is light brown. Dip the liver pieces into the hot butter just enough to stiffen the meat. Then cut the bacon into squares.

Alternate liver squares and bacon squares on the skewers, leaving a small space between each 2 squares. Blend the fine bread crumbs with the lemon rind and thyme. Foll each brochette in this mixture. Barbecue for 4 to 5 minutes. Makes 3 to 5 servings.

Herb butter

4 tbsp (60 ml) butter

Juice of 1 lemon or lime

½ tsp (2 ml) crumbled dried basil

1 tsp (5 ml) MSG

1 tsp (5 ml) instant coffee powder

Melt the butter; add the remaining ingredients and mix.

Barbecued wieners
This recipe comes from a German friend.

Split the wieners (big frankfurters or knockwurst) and spread with a good coarse liverwurst, but not too generously. Top with prepared mustard and minced dill pickle. Then roll each wiener in slice of boiled ham. Secure with metal skewers. Broil over hot coals until the meat browns.

Serve with a choice of toasted buns or black bread, and very cold beer.

Hamburgers or lambburgers
Make 6 large patties with 2 pounds (1 kg) of ground meat. Grill 5 inches (13 cm) from the coals for 4 to 6 minutes on each side.

Butterfly leg of lamb
Ask the butcher to bone a 5- to 6-pound (2.3 to 2.7 kg) leg of lamb. Spread the boned meat out flat so that it forms a shape resembling a butterfly. Insert 2 long metal or wooden skewers through the meat in the form of a cross. The skewers keep the meat flat while cooking and also help in turning it.

Place the meat fat side down on the grill, 3 inches (8 cm) above a medium fire. Grill for 30 minutes on the first side, then turn and grill on the second side for 30 minutes. This will give you medium-rare lamb. While cooking, brush the meat frequently with Herb Butter (below).

To carve the butterfly lamb, start at one end and cut the meat across the grain into ¼-inch (0.625 cm) slices. Makes 6 to 8 servings.

Lamb steak
Have your butcher cut ¾-inch (2 cm) steaks from a leg of lamb. Place the steaks on the grill. Brush them while they cook with Herb Butter (above). Cook for about 8 minutes a side, turning only once.

Lamb chops
Have lamb chops cut 1 to 1½ inches (2.5 to 3.75 cm) thick, from the loin, rib, or arm. Barbecue them 4 inches (10 cm) from the coals for about 8 minutes per side.

Marinate lamb chops overnight in a basting sauce made with fresh mint and dry rosemary. Or use Honey Mint Marinade to baste the lamb chops while broiling.

Persian kebab

There are hundreds of ways to make kebabs. This simple method uses ground lamb. Cheaper cuts of meat can be used.

2 lb (1 kg) ground lamb

Chopped onion to taste

1 egg

Salt and pepper to taste

2 tbsp (30 ml) flour

1 tsp (5 ml) curry powder

1 tbsp (15 ml) chopped fresh mint

2 tbsp (30 ml) crushed dried mint

Tomatoes cut into thick slices

Mix the ground lamb with all the other ingredients, except the tomatoes, until smooth. Shape into oblong patties about 5 inches (13 cm) long, 1½ inches (3.75 cm) wide and 1 inch (2.5 cm) thick. Refrigerate, covered, for a few hours.

Push a skewer through each patty and add a thick slice of tomato. Barbecue for 10 minutes on each side. Serve on a bed of hot rice sprinkled with fresh mint. Makes 6 servings.

Crisp-crusted rolled pork roast

Try this on your covered barbecue to practise indirect cooking. The result is a moist, tender roast of pork with a crisp, crunchy crust on top.

4 to 4½ lb (1.8 to 2 kg) boned and rolled loin of pork

2 tbsp (30 ml) soy sauce

1 tsp (5 ml) ground ginger

1 tsp (5 ml) dry mustard

Grated rind of ½ an orange

½ tsp (2 ml) curry powder

⅛ tsp (5 ml) cayenne

½ tsp (2 ml) salt

2 tbsp (30 ml) honey

2 tbsp (30 ml) ketchup

1 tbsp (15 ml) cider vinegar

Make sure the meat is at room temperature before starting to cook, which will take 1½ to 2 hours.

Rub the roast all over with soy sauce. Combine the ginger, mustard, orange rind, curry powder, cayenne and salt. Rub this all over the roast; use as much of it as you can.

Open all dampers in the cover and bottom of your barbecue. If you are using briquettes place 25 on each side of the fire pan, with a foil dripping pan in the centre. When the fire is ready, place the top grill directly over the foil pan. Put the meat on the grill over the foil pan. Cover and cook for 1 hour.

Then add 8 briquettes to each side. Mix together the honey, ketchup and vinegar. Brush this mixture on the meat every 10 minutes for the next 40 minutes. Keep covered. If you have a thermometer in the meat, cook until the thermometer registers 185°F (67°C). Serve sliced thin. Makes 8 servings.

Barbecued pork chops

4 pork chops, loin or rib, 1 ¼ to 1 ½ inches (3 to 3.75 cm) thick

Sage, fresh or dried

Salt and pepper

Cut the edges of the pork chops to prevent curling. Rub the surface of the chops with sage. Place the chops over low heat so that they will cook slowly and brown without burning. Turn once. Cook just until pinkness has disappeared when a cut is made near the bone. Season with salt and pepper and serve hot with baked apples. Makes 4 servings.

Barbecued spareribs

4 lb (1.8 kg) pork spareribs

1 cup (250 ml) ketchup

½ cup (125 ml) water

½ cup (125 ml) wine vinegar

1 tsp (5 ml) garlic salt

3 tbsp (50 ml) brown sugar

2 tbsp (30 ml) Worchestershire sauce

1 tsp (5 ml) salt

2 tsp (10 ml) dry mustard

Cut the ribs into serving portions. Place them in a large kettle, cover with boiling water, and simmer for about 45 minutes. Remove and drain.

To make the barbecue sauce, combine the remaining ingredients. Dip the ribs into the sauce and place them on the grill over a prepared fire. Cook about 6 inches (15 cm) from the hot coals for 20 minutes, or until the lean shows no pink when cut and the surface is nicely browned. Baste frequently with sauce during cooking. Serve hot. Makes 5 or 6 servings.

NOTE: Simmering the spareribs before placing them on the grill cuts down on the barbecue cooking time and usually eliminates the need for a drip tray in the grill. But uncooked spareribs can be placed over a low barbecue fire. Baste with barbecue sauce and cook slowly, turning occasionally. The ribs are ready to serve as soon as the meat loses its pink colour and the surfaces are well browned, which takes 40 to 60 minutes.

A glazed ham that retains its moisture can be cooked by indirect heat in a covered barbecue.

7 lb (3.1 kg) ready-to-eat rolled or half ham

Whole cloves

1 cup (250 ml) maple or brown sugar

2 cups (500 ml) ginger ale or cola drink

½ tsp (2 ml) ground cinnamon

Pineapple cubes

Remove any rind on the ham. Score the fat diagonally, giving it a diamond effect. Insert a clove in the centre of every diamond.

Open all dampers in the cover and bottom of your barbecue. If preparing a fire, place 25 briquettes on each side of the pan, with a foil dripping pan in the middle. When the fire is ready, place the top grill directly over the foil pan. Place the ham directly on the grill over the foil pan. Cover and start to cook, counting 10 minutes per pound (500 gr). Every hour, add 8 briquettes to each side.

Mix together the maple or brown sugar, ginger ale or cola, and cinnamon. Baste the top of the ham with the mixture, every 20 minutes. When the ham is ready, set it on a hot platter and garnish with the pineapple cubes. Makes 8 to 12 servings.

Glazed barbecued ham

Use only moist tenderized ham. Have the ham cut 1½ to 3 inches (3.75 to 8 cm) thick; a thin slice simply dries up. Remove any thick rind. Place the ham on the grill over medium-hot heat and cook for 20 to 30 minutes, turning 3 or 4 times. Baste frequently with the following paste:

2 tsp (10 ml) dry mustard

1 cup (250 ml) brown sugar, firmly packed

½ cup (125 ml) orange juice, sherry or pineapple juice

A thinner slice of cooked ham can be barbecued 3 inches (8 cm) from the coals for 10 to 12 minutes. Baste the meat often with a mixture of ½ cup (125 ml) commercial sour cream and 1½ to 2 tablespoons (22 to 30 ml) horseradish mustard. It keeps the ham moist and gives it a perfect flavour.

Barbecued ham steak

Golden glazed broilers

The attractive golden glaze on these barbecued birds comes from undiluted frozen orange juice. Cook them on your covered barbecue.

2-2½ lb (1.25 kg) broilers

½ tsp (2 ml) crumbled dried rosemary or basil

Salad oil

6 oz (200 ml) condensed frozen orange juice, undiluted

1 tbsp (15 ml) soy sauce

½ tsp (2 ml) ground ginger

½ tsp (2 ml) salt

2 or more oranges, cut into thin slices

Sprigs of fresh mint

Truss each chicken firmly. Place ¼ teaspoon (1 ml) of the rosemary or basil in each of the chicken cavities. Rub the outsides with salad oil. Combine the orange juice, soy sauce, ginger and salt.

Prepare the barbecue for indirect cooking. Place the chicken on the grill and cover the barbecue. Cook for 1 hour. Then cook for another 20 to 30 minutes, basting the birds with the orange mixture every 5 minutes.

Place the cooked chickens on a hot platter over a thick layer of thin orange slices. Pour any drippings left in the foil pan over the chickens. Push a bouquet of fresh mint into the opening of each cavity and serve. Makes 4 to 6 servings.

Barbecued split broilers

Split the chickens and cut the leg and wing tendons so the halves will lie flat. Cook slowly about 4 inches (10 cm) above the coals, turning every 10 minutes, or use a basket on a motorized spit. A split 2-pound (1 kg) broiler takes from 45 to 60 minutes.

If you put the bird closer to the coals — 3 inches (8 cm) away — it will cook in a shorter time — 20 to 30 minutes. It should be turned every 5 minutes and should be basted as it turns. Lemon Basting Sauce is very good with this. Another good sauce for chicken is the one that follows:

½ cup (125 ml) salad oil
½ cup (125 ml) butter
½ cup (125 ml) sherry, white wine, lemon juice or chicken bouillon
1 tsp (5 ml) salt
¼ tsp (1 ml) pepper
1 tsp (5 ml) crumbled dried tarragon or rosemary
1 garlic clove, crushed (optional)

Mix all the ingredients together and bring to a boil. Keep the sauce hot while using it. Put it on with a brush. Makes 1½ cups (375 ml) sauce.

Charcoal-baked whole fish

Use a 5- to 7-pound (2.2 to 3.1 kg) salmon, striped bass, lake trout or other fish. Clean, but leave the head and tail on. (Remove them after the fish has been grilled if you wish).

Rub the fish all over with a lemon half. Slice a whole lemon and place it in the fish cavity with a few sprigs of parsley or a few green onions. Wrap in heavy foil, rolling the edges tightly upward to prevent the juices from leaking out. Barbecue for 1¾ to 2 hours.

Another method is to roll the prepared fish in chicken wire, tie securely, and place on the grill for 1 to 1½ hours.

Oil and lemon juice give a special flavour to halibut and help to keep it juicy. Try this for a delicious change from the usual steak and chicken.

Grilled halibut steaks

½ cup (125 ml) salad oil

¼ cup (60 ml) fresh lemon juice

6 halibut steaks, ¾ inch (1.9 cm) thick

2 tsp (10 ml) salt

1 tsp (5 ml) MSG

½ tsp (2 ml) pepper

Combine in a shallow dish the salad oil and lemon juice. Roll the halibut steaks in the mixture. Cover and let stand for 30 minutes to 1 hour, turning once or twice. Drain just before cooking and save the remaining oil and lemon juice.

To barbecue, use indirect cooking on a covered barbecue, the same as for the rolled Pork Roast or the golden Glazed Broilers.

Place the drained fish steaks on the grill. Grill for 3 minutes, brush with the oil-lemon mixture. Turn the fish, brush again, and grill for another 3 minutes. Mix the salt, MSG and pepper. Sprinkle half on the fish. Turn, and sprinkle on the other half of the seasonings. Grill the fish steaks until they flake when tested with a fork. Serve very hot. Makes 6 servings.

Use a whole salmon or a large piece of boned salmon. If you have a whole fish, leave the two sides attached at the back; the skin will hold them.

Indian barbecued salmon

5 to 12-lb (2.2 to 5.4 kg) salmon

2 lemons, sliced thinly

3 tbsp (50 ml) brown sugar

2 tbsp (30 ml) butter

1 tbsp (15 ml) salt

1 to 3 tsp (5 to 15 ml) cider vinegar or lemon juice

On a double layer of heavy-duty foil, arrange the lemons slices to make a bed. Place the salmon on this.

Make a paste of the brown sugar, butter and salt. Moisten the paste slightly with cider vinegar or lemon juice. Make more or less of this, depending on the size of the fish.

Spread the paste over the salmon. Turn the foil up at the edges of the salmon to form a pan and to prevent dripping. Place on the rack. Cook by indirect heat in a covered barbecue. Salmon is done when it flakes easily. The time will vary with the size of the fish. The approximate time is 35 to 45 minutes for a 4-pound (1.8 kg) fish; 90 minutes for a 10 to 12-pound (4.5 to 5.4 kg) salmon. Remember to avoid overcooking.

Barbecued fresh trout

Here are two ways to cook trout.

Take fresh trout, 8 to 10 inches (20 to 25 cm) long, and wrap in bacon slices. Secure with skewers or wet bamboo sticks. Or omit the bacon and baste with lemon butter during the grilling. Grill them 3 inches (8 cm) from the coals for 7 to 8 minutes.

For any small fresh fish, or for thawed frozen fish, cut 6 squares of aluminum foil measuring about 12 inches (30 cm) each. Use 1 layer of heavy-weight foil, or 2 layers of light-weight foil. Place it shiny side up and grease it. Put one fish in the centre of a piece of foil. Season. Arrange slices of vegetable around it if you wish. Add a lump of butter or margarine to each. Fold the foil in drugstore wrap, Vol. I, Freezing, and seal the edges well.

Packages can be put directly on glowing coals. The fish will cook in approximately 15 minutes without being turned. Handle gently so that the foil is not punctured by the coals. Or, if desired, cook on the top grill of the barbecue for approximately 25 minutes, turning once.

You can use this method for larger fish, too. Just cut them into serving pieces and put a piece in each foil packet.

Seafood sakana

This soy-ginger marinade is delicious for barbecuing any seafood.

1 cup (250 ml) soy sauce

¼ cup (50 ml) brown sugar

1 tsp (5 ml) grated, unpeeled green gingerroot

You can find green gingerroot at Oriental food stores.

Mix the marinade and pour it over 2 pounds (1 kg) of thick fish fillets, small whole fish, split lobster or large shrimps. Let stand for 1 hour.

Turn once; then shake off excess marinade from the fish. Broil. Allow 5 to 8 minutes a side for thick fillets. Small whole fish should be grilled for about 10 minutes on one side, 4 minutes on the other.

Grill the marinated lobster, shell side down, about 5 inches (13 cm) from the coals. Grill for about 20 minutes. Grill shrimps for about 3 minutes on each side.

Live lobsters of about 1½ pounds (750 gr) — not marinated — can be split (ask your fish man to do this for you) and grilled; they are delicious basted frequently with Lemon Butter Sauce. These, too, will take about 20 minutes.

Hot buttery roast corn

Barbecued corn on the cob is the best corn you have ever tasted. It is a perfect accompaniment to any barbecued meat, poultry or fish.

Loosen husks of freshly gathered corn only enough to remove the silks. Dip the ears into a deep pail of water; shake well. Rewrap husks around the ears. Plunge into the water again and let them stand until the husks are thoroughly soaked.

Place them on the grill of a covered barbecue. Cook, covered, for 45 minutes to 1 hour, depending on the size of the corn.

To make buttered roasted corn on an open barbecue, remove both husks and silks. Cream ¼ cup (60 ml) butter with ½ teaspoon (2 ml) sugar and ¼ teaspoon (1 ml) each of salt and paprika. Spread on the ears. This is enough butter for 6 to 10 ears.

Wrap each ear loosely in heavy-duty aluminum foil, sealing carefully. Place 3 inches (8 cm) from glowing coals. Roast for 20 to 25 minutes, turning frequently. Serve in the foil wrappings.

CHAPTER 13

Be kind to vegetables

THE POWERFUL virtues of vegetables were recognized long ago by the Greeks and the Romans, to whom the pungency of a vegetable was a guarantee of its effectiveness. They ate leeks to improve their voices (the Welsh still do), and they gave soldiers a daily ration of garlic to excite their courage. They also fed garlic to fighting cocks to make them fight well. Cabbage was regarded as a panacea for just about everything from drunkenness to baldness, and at one point it practically put Roman physicians out of business.

It was Tiberius who introduced what probably was the first forced growth of vegetables. He liked cucumbers so much he wanted to be able to eat them out of their normal season.

Potatoes, tomatoes and eggplant were not eaten until very recently; as members of the same plant family as the deadly nightshade, they were thought to lead to death or insanity.

Today we take vegetables much for granted, although we often wish that we could always pick them dewy fresh from the garden and cook and eat them immediately afterward. Most cooks must rely on their skill in selecting the best and freshest vegetables from the vegetable stalls of supermarkets and specialty shops. You can develop this skill by learning as much as possible about the qualities of vegetables and their seasons.

Here is a golden rule: ⚷ Always buy the best you can afford. It is far better to have a higher-priced firm cabbage, for instance, all of which can be used, than a cheaper one of the same size that is damp, soggy and only three-quarters usable. This is a case of the cheaper being the more expensive.

It is fairly easy to judge the freshness of a vegetable by its texture, colour and appearance. Look for crisp, plump, well-coloured produce. Do not settle for dry, soft, bruised or faded vegetables.

PRESERVING NUTRITIVE VALUE AND FLAVOUR

Of all foods, vegetables — fresh, frozen, or canned — are the most abused by poor cooking.

Many cooks think "boil and drain" is the only way to cook vegetables. Under those conditions, the only thing left is a little starch and cellulose, and vegetables become flavourless, mere shadows of their former selves. It's small wonder that so many people are disinclined to eat vegetables. Follow these keys and your vegetables will be cooked properly:

⚷ Never let vegetables stand in cold water before cooking. The one exception is members of the cabbage family which should be soaked in cold salted water to dislodge any insects, but even this soaking should last for no more than 30 minutes.

0—🗝 Prepare vegetables just before cooking; this includes the peeling, slicing, or dicing. When exposed to air or soaked in water, vegetables lose much of their vitamin content and flavour.

0—🗝 Never add baking soda when cooking green vegetables. It keeps them green but destroys their vitamin content.

0—🗝 Do not add salt to vegetables while cooking, except for potatoes. Use ½ teaspoon (2 ml) salt for 6 potatoes.

0—🗝 Add ½ teaspoon (2 ml) of sugar to all vegetables while cooking. This will improve the flavour and in some cases even improve the colour. It will not make vegetables taste sweet; simply restores their natural sweetness. Add salt only when ready to serve the vegetable.

0—🗝 Cook vegetables whole or in large pieces whenever you can. For example, nutritive elements are present next to the skin of potatoes. When they are peeled and cut into pieces, their surfaces become exposed to air — the greatest enemy of vitamins.

0—🗝 Use herbs frequently with vegetables, while cooking and after cooking; they can spark a vegetable without destroying its natural flavour — for example, savory with green beans, mint and peas, sage with lima beans and thyme with carrots.

0—🗝 Covering vegetables while cooking is a subject about which experts disagree. Some think all vegetables should be covered. Others say never to cover green vegetables. Obviously, baked or braised vegetables are covered, and spinach steamed in the water that clings to its leaves must be covered. In the descriptions of cooking methods that follow, you will see that each method has its own rules.

0—🗝 Cook vegetables only until barely fork tender; they must retain a bit of their original crispness.

0—🗝 To give your vegetables a meaty flavour when they are served with a roast or chops, add ½ a chicken or beef bouillon cube to the cooking water. It usually salts the vegetables sufficiently.

Why not serve hot vegetables as a separate course, instead of serving a salad? This is especially good during the cold season. The unexpected is often most welcome.

KINDS OF VEGETABLES

We use the word "vegetables" for all sorts of plants, and we eat different parts of the plants. Here are some of them:

tubers are swelling off the roots, such as Jerusalem artichokes and potatoes

roots, such as carrots and turnips

bulbs, such as onions

stalks are whole plants with leafy tops, such as celery and cardoons

leaves, such as spinach and other greens

flowers, such as cauliflower

fruits, such as eggplant and tomatoes

pods, such as green beans and wax beans

seeds, such as green peas and dried beans

For our purpose these classifications fall into two main categories — root vegetables and green vegetables.

Root vegetables include the tubers and roots. They contain a large percentage of water and store nourishment in the form of starch. They are also, in most cases, high in mineral salts. Practically no protein or fat is present. Their fibres are formed by a woody substance known as cellulose, which in some cases must be softened before the digestible content can be extracted. The older the vegetables are, the coarser the cellulose. This explains why winter turnips, beets and carrots take longer to cook than younger, spring ones. Of course, some roots can be eaten raw — carrots and radishes, for example.

Bulbs, such as dried onions, are sometimes grouped with root vegetables. Like roots and tubers, they can be kept stored for winter use. On the other hand, fresh onions, such as scallions and leeks, are perishable like other green vegetables.

Potatoes are an exception to the rule of longer cooking for older vegetables, although there is a difference between new and old potatoes. The cell walls in new potatoes are ripe, but they still have a very hard, close texture. ⊶ Rapid boiling is needed because the heat has to penetrate to the inside starch. The cell walls of old potatoes have stretched the accomodate the increasing size of the grains of starch. ⊶ If old potatoes are boiled too rapidly, the cellulose breaks down, the starch bursts and the potato falls to pieces. Knowing this may help you serve potatoes with a neat appearance as well as good taste.

Green vegetables include the other groups. Even white, red or purple vegetables, such as califlower, tomatoes and eggplant, have green leaves. As with root vegetables, the cellulose toughens with age. Young, fresh green vegetables naturally have a much sweeter flavour than older ones. Young or old, they contain practically no starch, no fat and no protein. They do have a lot of mineral salts, which are the chief value of greens in the diet. Green vegetables are quite perishable and should be eaten within 3 or 4 days of purchase.

The general rule for all vegetables is "the fresher the better." Use them as soon as possible after purchase, but in the meantime some need to be protected from moisture evaporation, while others should be kept in a cool storage bin outside the refrigerator. Still others need room temperature and as much air circulation as possible. Learn which is which.

KEEPING QUALITIES

Perishables: Asparagus, corn, cucumbers, green onions, green and red peppers, radishes, tomatoes and all salad greens. Keep them in plastic bags in your refrigerator crisper.

Semi-perishables: Green and wax beans, broccoli, Brussels sprouts, cabbage, cauliflower, celery, and peas in the pod. Remove excess dirt, put in plastic bags or covered containers, and store on a shelf in the refrigerator. It is important to store peas in their pods; otherwise they dry.

Staples: Eggplant, pumpkin, squash; beets, carrots, onions, parsnips, potatoes, and turnips. These keep their quality the longest during storage.

Onions do well at room temperature, providing air can circulate around them. Keep them in a net bag or wire basket, and keep them away from humidity.

Squash, pumpkins, turnips and winter beets can be kept where it is cool and dry. The others need a cool and moist atmosphere. Store them, unwrapped, in the refrigerator.

Basic cooking methods for vegetables

Some vegetables need special attention, but these are in the minority. Most are cooked according to a few basic methods. It is important to learn about basic cooking methods for all foods, but perhaps even more so when it comes to cooking vegetables. As to the flavouring and the seasoning, let your own taste buds be your guide.

Blanching and refreshing, professional method

To serve a deep-green vegetable, even greener than when fresh, follow the chef's trick — blanch the vegetable before cooking it further. This does not require a second saucepan and it has the advantage of enabling you to cook vegetables hours ahead of time. When ready to serve, dip them into hot water for a few minutes to reheat, or sauté briefly in butter or oil, or heat in an appropriate sauce. They will lose none of their flavour, quality or colour. If convenient, you can serve them immediately after blanching and draining.

To blanch, fill a large saucepan with water and bring it to a rolling boil. Gradually add the cleaned vegetable. **0➤** If you have lots of water, it will quickly return to the boil; this is important because the quicker the water returns to the boiling point, the greener the vegetable will be.

The cooking period varies with different vegetables, their degree of freshness and the way they are cut. As an average, a vegetable that has been left whole will require 8 to 12 minutes. One that is sliced or diced will take only 3 to 4 minutes. To test, take a piece out of the water and taste it. You will be surprised how quickly most vegetables cook.

If the vegetables are to be served without delay, then drain, butter and serve. If they are to be served cold, or later in the day, they must be refreshed. This is another trick used by the professional chef. **0➤** To refresh blanched vegetables, drain the water or lift the vegetables out with a wire skimmer or a perforated spoon and toss them into a bowl of ice-cold water. This cold bath stops the cooking immediately, sets the colour and preserves both the texture and the flavour. Place an absorbent cloth in a dish. Skim the vegetables out of the cold water and place them in the cloth-lined dish. Refrigerate until ready to serve. To reheat, place the vegetables in a saucepan and pour over them enough boiling water to cover. Boil for ½ minute, drain, and they are hot and ready to serve.

Steaming

Vegetables — whole, or pared and cut into serving pieces, or sliced or diced — can be cooked by this method. However, green vegetables cooked this way do not retain the beautiful green colour they keep if blanched.

First, use a thick stainless-steel or enameled cast-iron saucepan. Add just enough liquid to cover the bottom of the pan. The liquid can be water, bouillon, consommé, milk or vegetable water. Do not salt and pepper before cooking, but you can add herbs and spices to the water. Bring the liquid to a rolling boil. Add the prepared vegetables and return to a rolling boil. Cover the saucepan and cook over medium-low heat until tender. The degree of heat is important because the steam developed by the water should cook the vegetables. If the water boils too fast, it will not cook by steam; also, it may boil away. The average time needed to cook vegetables ranges from 5 to 25 minutes. Uncover the pan as infrequently as possible. Experience will soon teach you the correct timing.

As soon as the vegetables are cooked to the desired tenderness, pour them into a sieve to drain. Place in a hot vegetable dish, add salt, pepper and butter, or any other seasoning you like, and serve. **0→** Do not put the vegetables back into the hot saucepan to wait; they will continue to cook from the heat retained by the pan, wilting and losing both flavour and colour.

Vegetables can be steamed ahead of time and refreshed, as described for blanching, then reheated in water or in a sauce at serving time.

Pan-cooking

This method was created in the 1930s by Ida Bailey Allen, who may have been inspired by the ancient Chinese method of stir-frying vegetables.

Melt 2 tablespoons (30 ml) fat — any fat you prefer — in a heavy, wide frying pan. Add 1 inch (2.5 cm) of boiling water and bring again to a fast rolling boil. Add the vegetables and cover the pan. Reduce the heat and simmer slowly until the vegetables are tender. Holding the cover, shake the pan from time to time to distribute the vegetables and ensure even cooking.

At first this may seem to be the same as steaming vegetables, but there is more liquid in pan-cooking and the fat makes a difference. This is an excellent method for sliced or diced winter root vegetables, shredded cabbage, sliced onions and slivered carrots.

Chinese stir-frying

The Chinese prepare vegetables with as much care as fish or meat. A cooked vegetable should be crisp, excellent in flavour and bright in colour. For these reasons, vegetables cooked by Chinese methods are never soft, with the colour and flavour boiled out of them, but neither are they raw. To true vegetable lovers, the Oriental way of cooking, serving and eating vegetables is the height of perfection.

Once you have learned this technique, you can apply it to any vegetable. The time is almost the same for all; if there is a difference, it is only a matter of a minute or two. The wok is the perfect pan to use.

Cut the vegetable into slivers on the bias. For each pound (500 gr) or approximately 3½ to 4 cups (875 ml to 1 L) prepared vegetable, measure ½ cup (125 ml) water or bouillon and add ½ teaspoon (2 ml) sugar. As a variation, add 1 tablespoon (15 ml) soy sauce, or fresh lemon juice, or cider vinegar. Set this aside.

For each pound (500 gr) of vegetable, heat 2 tablespoons (30 ml) salad oil in a large frying pan. Add ½ teaspoon (2 ml) salt; stir for a few seconds. As a variation, you can add 3 thin slices of fresh gingerroot. Add the prepared vegetable to the hot salted oil and stir over high heat until the vegetable is well coated with the oil, just a few seconds. This seals the pores so the vegetable retains colour and flavour.

Add the prepared liquid. Stir quickly for a few seconds over high heat. Cover, lower the heat, and simmer until the vegetable is tender, from 3 to 5 minutes.

To cook whole vegetables or vegetables cut into large pieces, they must be blanched first for 3 to 5 minutes and refreshed, as explained previously. Drain them, pat dry, then stir them into the hot oil and cook just as the slivers are cooked.

When a stir-fry vegetable cannot be served immediately, do not cover. The heat retained by covering the vegetables will created a moist steam that will soften the crisp texture and fade the colour, making the pieces limp and grey.

When several vegetables are cooked together, those needing a longer cooking period, such as onions, celery, green peppers and carrots, go into the pan with the hot oil first; they are stirred for a few seconds longer than usual. Then the more tender vegetables, such as tomatoes, spinach and green onions, are added.

The more you use the stir-fry method for your vegetables, the more variations you will discover and the more you will enjoy them. You can vary the liquid and flavouring in so many ways. It is the easiest and the most creative and exciting way to cook vegetables.

Steam-baking

We seldom consider that any vegetable besides the potato can be baked, yet many vegetables, especially the winter roots, gain by being baked. Some are steam-baked, while others are baked with dry heat.

To steam-bake, scrub the vegetable — carrots, beets, parsnips — and remove any imperfections. Then rub all over with salad oil or bacon fat or soft margarine. An easy way to do this is to place a small piece of fat in your hand, or pour a little oil into your palm, then roll the vegetable around in it. Then place the oiled vegetables into a casserole they fit comfortably. Add just enough boiling water to cover the bottom of the casserole. Cover tightly. Steam-bake in a preheated oven, 350°F to 375°F (180°C to 190°C) for 40 to 50 minutes, or until the vegetable is tender. Time varies according to the size of the vegetable and the oven heat. This flexibility enables you to steam-bake your vegetable while the oven is used for other baking.

When the vegetable is half done, turn the pieces over in the casserole, then finish. Uncover if you prefer to have the liquid completely evaporated and the vegetable slightly browned on top.

Baking with dry heat

Beets, onions, potatoes, pumpkin and squash can all be baked. If you have never tasted a baked onion, you are in for a pleasant surprise. There is a world of difference between onions that have been boiled and those that have been baked.

Baking potatoes

To bake potatoes or any other vegetables, scrub but do not peel. Remove the imperfections, just as for steam-baked vegetables. Rub with oil or fat, and roll in coarse salt until a few grains stick to the vegetable.

Set on a sheet of foil placed on the oven rack to protect the stove from drippings. Preheat oven at 375° to 400°F (190°C to 200°C) and bake the vegetable until tender. The average time is about 1 hour.

Cut pumpkin and squash into halves. Scoop out the seeds and strings. Dot the inside with butter. Add a few spoonfuls of honey or maple to relieve the bland flavour without making it too sweet.

French frying or deep-frying

French frying can be used for preparing vegetables besides potatoes — cauliflowerets; finger-length sticks of eggplant; blanched and refreshed carrots and parsnips; pieces of pumpkin or winter squash; rings of onions or green peppers.

Wash and prepare the vegetables. Do not let them soak in cold water, except in the case of potatoes. Put enough vegetable oil, shortening or lard in a deep heavy saucepan or French fryer to fill it to one-third of the depth. Heat to 350°F (180°C) on a frying thermometer, or until the oil will brown a 1-inch (2.5 cm) cube of bread in 1 minute. Carefully slide in the vegetable, a bit at a time, and fry until golden brown. Remove with a perforated spoon. Drain on crumbled paper towels. Dust with salt.

For *French-fried potatoes,* cut 12 to 16 finger-length pieces from a good sized potato. Soak in ice-cold water for 1 hour, drain and dry.

For *French-fried eggplant* cut it into finger-length strips. Dust with flour, salt and little MSG. Dip into 1 egg slightly beaten with ¼ cup (60 ml) water. Coat at once with fine dry crumbs.

For *French-fried carrots, parsnips, pumpkin or winter squash,* half-cook them, then cut into finger-length strips and dip into egg and crumbs as for eggplant.

For *French-fried cauliflower,* wash and separate into its natural flowerets; do not pre-cook. Dip into egg and crumbs as for eggplant.

For *French-fried onion rings,* use large Spanish onions. Peel and cut into ½-inch (1.25 cm) thick crosswise slices and separate into rings. For these and green-pepper rings, dip into egg and crumbs as for eggplant.

Of course, vegetables can be cooked in pressure cookers and waterless cookers. Follow the directions that come with the utensil. They can also be broiled or sautéed, which is different from pan-cooking or Chinese stir-frying because no extra liquid is added.

If you can't think of how to cook a vegetable, you can't go wrong if you follow this golden rule: Place the prepared vegetable in a saucepan, add ½ teaspoon (2 ml) sugar, and pour over the least amount of boiling water — just enough to keep the pieces from sticking to the pan in cooking. Cover and cook for the shortest possible time necessary to your taste. "It's foolproof." When you know more about the vegetable, you can try other methods until you find the one that is best suited to it and to your taste.

The way you cut a vegetable makes a significant difference in the final flavour and texture of the dish. Of course, many vegetables can be cooked whole; small onions, small new potatoes, tender young snap beans, baby carrots and tiny zucchini can be blanched, steamed or stir-fried just as they are. And whole, larger vegetables can be baked. We often cut up larger vegetables or those that are not young and tender to reduce cooking time and to ensure they are cooked evenly.

You will find directions for cutting vegetables in the chapter entitled Science and Seasoning, Vol. I.

Vegetables can be sliced, diced or minced; they can be cut into julienne, chiffonade, shreds or diagonal slivers, or they can be scraped into curls. Remember, when cut into small or thin pieces they need the least amount of cooking. For instance, julienne or chiffonade vegetables should be cooked by steaming or pan-cooking or stir-frying for just a few minutes.

ROOT VEGETABLES

Potatoes

The name potato is derived from bata-ta, a word from a language used by the Arawaks. Indeed, the potato is a native of the Americas.

It took 200 years for the potato to reach its present popularity, and today nobody could imagine that it would ever lose its place. It is a sensible and valuable food.

TO PREPARE: Valuable nutrients lie close to the skin of the potato, so it is wasteful to peel them when not absolutely necessary, or to peel them and let them stand in cold water for hours. The quantity of the vegetable remains, but part of the essential quality is destroyed.

When possible, keep the skin on old potatoes but scrub it with a stiff brush. This retains the flavour and mineral salts and much waste in material and time is avoided. On the other hand, new potatoes lose much of their skin when scrubbed because it is thin and delicate. Simply wash and cook in their skins.

Boiling potatoes

TO COOK: There are hundred of ways to cook potatoes, but the most used is plain boiling. **0➤** Old or winter potatoes should be started in cold water and allowed to come to the boiling point, then simmered until tender. **0➤** New potatoes should be added to rapidly boiling water. **0➤** Try to choose potatoes for boiling, or cut the larger ones to match the size of the smaller ones, so that all will be cooked at the same time and none overcooked. To test boiled potatoes for doneness, use a skewer or a cake tester. Do not use a fork. Too many holes will make the potatoes watery.

When the potatoes are cooked, drain the water and put the saucepan uncovered, back over medium heat. Shake the pan gently for a minute or two to dry them out quickly; wet and soggy boiled potatoes are unappetizing.

0➤ When boiled potatoes cannot be served immediately, remove the pan from the heat. Place a folded cloth or double thickness of absorbent paper towelling on top of the potatoes. Set the cover loosely on the cloth. Keep on the back of the stove. The hot steam will be absorbed by the cloth; the potatoes will stay dry instead of becoming soft and mushy. Potatoes can stand like this for 15 to 20 minutes.

Scalloped potatoes

Peel 6 large potatoes. Slice thin and place in layers in a buttered 2-quart (2.5 L) baking dish. Cover each layer with a sprinkle of flour. Dot with butter and season with salt and pepper. Fill the dish up to the top layer of potatoes with hot milk.

Bake slowly in a 350°F (180°C) oven for about 1¼ hours, or until tender. Cover for the first 20 minutes, then keep uncovered for the remaining period. Makes 6 servings.

Fried mashed-potato puffs

4 bacon slices

4 cups (1 L) mashed potatoes, leftover or fresh

2 eggs, beaten

1 cup (250 ml) flour

2 tsp (10 ml) baking powder

1 tsp (5 ml) salt

Fat for frying

Fry bacon until crisp. Crumble into small pieces. Combine with mashed potatoes and beaten eggs. Sift flour, baking powder and salt into the potato mixture. Blend well.

Heat fat in a deep pan to 385°F (195°C) on a frying thermometer; you need about 2 inches (5 cm) of fat. Drop the potato mixture by tablespoons into the hot fat. Fry for 3 to 5 minutes, or until brown. Excellent with roast beef. Makes about 8 servings.

NOTE: You can substitute 4 cups (1 L) instant mashed potatoes, prepared as directed on the package, for the fresh or leftover potatoes.

Duchess potatoes

This is a very useful recipe when you want to prepare potatoes 6 to 8 hours before dinner. Keep refrigerated, and just warm in the oven when needed.

2 cups (500 ml) mashed potatoes

2 tbsp (30 ml) melted butter

2 eggs

½ cup (125 ml) milk

Salt and pepper to taste

Combine mashed potatoes and melted butter and beat until creamy. Add well-beaten eggs, milk, and salt and pepper to taste. Place in a greased 1½-quart (2 L) baking dish or casserole, and bake at 375°F (190°C) for about 20 minutes, or until browned on the top. Makes 4 servings.

Fisherman's potato cakes

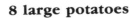

These are as Canadian as can be and are simply wonderful when served with poached fish.

8 large potatoes

1 lb (500 gr) saltpork fatback

2½ cups (625 ml) sifted flour

3 tsp (15 ml) baking powder

Boil and mash potatoes. Cut saltpork fatback into large pieces and fry until the fat is rendered and pork is golden. Add the scrunchions to the mashed potatoes. Mix in the sifted flour and baking powder. Form into cakes. Bake at 350°F (180°C) for 30 minutes. Serve with fish. Makes 8 or more servings.

My favourite mashed potatoes

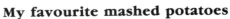The secret of creamy, white mashed potatoes is simple: Use commercial sour cream and lemon juice.

A perfect mashed potato is prepared with winter potatoes. Peel the potatoes and cut into equal-size pieces. Boil, drain and dry over low heat. Mash with a potato masher, pass through a potato ricer or place in the bowl of an electric mixer and use slow speed to mash. Do this very quickly so the potatoes remain hot. Add salt, pepper, parsley, and chives or savory to taste; then add ½ to 1 cup (125 to 250 ml) commercial sour cream and 1 tablespoon (15 ml) lemon juice for 6 to 10 potatoes. Beat until creamy.

Sweet potatoes

The sweet potato is a plant of a different family from the white; it is a relative of the morning glory and has no poisonous associations. It, too, is an American native.

Baked sweet potatoes

Scrub sweet potatoes. Trim away any blackened bits. Bake in the oven just as for white potatoes. At 400°F (200°C), they should be fork tender in 40 to 45 minutes. Serve with whipped butter and a shaker of cinnamon sugar.

Sweet potatoes California

6 large sweet potatoes

3 oranges

¼ lb 125 gr) butter

1 cup (250 ml) light brown sugar

⅛ tsp (0.5 ml) ground cinnamon

½ tsp (2 ml) salt

1 cup (250 ml) unsweetened pineapple or apple juice

¼ cup (60 ml) brandy (optional)

Peel potatoes and slice thin. Grate the rind of one of the oranges and set it aside. Pare the oranges and cut them into slices. Arrange potato and orange slices in layers in a buttered 1½-quart (2 L) baking dish, dotting each layer with butter and sprinkling with a mixture of sugar, cinnamon, salt and the grated orange rind. Pour pineapple or apple juice over the potatoes. Cover and bake in a 375°F (190°C) oven for 1 hour. Thick syrup should have formed by this time. Pour brandy on top and serve. Makes 6 to 8 servings.

6 to 8 sweet potatoes

Butter to taste

Pinch each of ground cinnamon, ground cloves and crushed cardamom

2 tbsp (30 ml) heavy cream, orange juice or brandy

Peel the sweet potatoes. Cut into quarters. Boil in salted water for about 15 minutes, or until fork tender. Drain.

Add a big lump of butter, the ground cinnamon, ground cloves and crushed cardamom, and the heavy cream, orange juice or brandy. Beat to a fluff. Serve. Makes 6 to 8 servings.

Whipped sweet potatoes

Carrots

The carrot seems almost indispensable all year round, but is by no means beneath the notice of an epicure when it is cooked with care.

TO PREPARE: Here are two important points ⚬━➤ Most of the vitamins in carrots are near the skin, it is advisable to take off as little of the skin as possible. Use a potato peeler to peel off only a very thin layer. When carrots are very young and small, scrub them instead of peeling them. Trim the root and stalk ends.

⚬━➤ The second important point is to remove the stalk ends before storing them. If they are left on, the stems and leaves absorb too much of the natural moisture in the roots and the carrots simply do not keep fresh as long.

TO COOK: All the methods used to cook vegetables can be applied to carrots, depending on their age, size or the way they are cut. The carrot is another vegetable that loses flavour when overcooked. Always keep carrots on the crunchy side.

Carrots Véronique

Véronique, in the classic French repertoire of food terms, means a food garnished with seedless green grapes, cooked to an opaque texture. This recipe is a variation on this classic, and it is an epicure's delight.

2 to 3 cups (500 to 750 ml) diced carrots

⅔ cup (160 ml) seedless green grapes

3 tbsp (50 ml) heavy cream

Pinch of grated nutmeg

¼ tsp (1 ml) ground basil

Salt and pepper

Blanch the diced carrots for 3 minutes. Freshen. This can be done ahead of time. Drain and refrigerate.

Place all the ingredients in a saucepan. Simmer, uncovered, until the sauce is slightly thickened or reduced. This takes 15 to 20 minutes. Serve. Makes about 6 servings.

Carrot vegetarian casserole

A luncheon or light dinner meal can be made of this tasty casserole. I have often used it cold for a picnic, served with thin slices of ham and a good mustard. I first learned to make it while visiting a friend in Avon, England, who used her own garden-fresh carrots and served the casserole with her own homemade bread.

3 cups (750 ml) thin carrot rounds

2 eggs, beaten

4 to 6 tbsp (60 to 100 ml) melted butter

¼ cup (60 ml) light cream or milk

1 cup (250) grated sharp cheese

½ tsp (2 ml) minced fresh sage or ¼ tsp (1 ml) dried thyme

1½ cups (375 ml) tiny bread croutons

Salt and pepper to taste

Paprika

Blanch the carrots for 3 minutes, freshen, and drain. Beat together the eggs, butter, cream or milk, cheese and fresh sage or dried thyme.

The croutons can be left as is, or dry-browned in the oven, or browned in butter. They are at their best when oven dried to a crisp brown. Add the croutons and carrots to the cheese mixture. Salt and pepper to taste. Grease a baking dish, pour in the mixture, and sprinkle the top with paprika. Bake in a preheated 400°F (200°C) oven for 20 minutes, or until browned on top. Makes 4 servings.

I call this dish a colcannon because I was inspired by the traditional Irish cabbage and potato mixture to create a dish that combines carrots and potatoes. You can substitute turnips for the carrots, and add about ½ cup (125 ml) of grated cheese. The casserole goes well with roast turkey or chicken.

Elegant Irish colcannon

4 to 6 carrots, peeled and cubed

3 medium-size potatoes, peeled and cubed

1 medium-sized onion, sliced

⅛ tsp (0.5 ml) dried thyme or ½ tsp (2 ml) dried basil

3 tbsp (50 ml) butter

⅔ cup (160 ml) milk or water, approximately

1 egg

¼ cup (60 ml) commercial sour cream

Salt and pepper to taste

¼ cup (50 ml) chopped parsley

Place in a saucepan the carrots, potatoes, onion, thyme or basil, and 1 tablespoon (15 ml) of the butter. Add enough water or milk to cover 1 inch (2.5 cm) of the bottom. Cover and simmer until the vegetables are tender, 10 to 15 minutes.

If you have a blender, pour in the drained vegetables and add just enough of the cooking liquid to make a thick purée; or make a purée by pressing the vegetables through a food mill or sieve.

To the hot purée, add the egg, sour cream and remaining butter. Add salt and pepper to taste. Whip over low heat until creamy and fluffy. Serve sprinkled with parsley. Makes 4 to 6 servings.

This is how the professionals glaze carrots to perfection.

Chef's glazed carrots

1 bunch carrots

1 tbsp (15 ml) salad oil

2 tbsp (30 ml) butter

⅓ cup (80 ml) boiling water

½ tsp (2 ml) salt

½ tsp (2 ml) sugar

Cut the carrots on the diagonal into long ovals. Heat the oil and butter in a heavy frying pan with a good cover. Add the carrots and stir-fry over high heat for 2 minutes, until the carrots are shiny and have a deep rich colour. Stir constantly.

Add the boiling water, salt and sugar. Stir, then cover tightly. Keep over low heat for 7 to 10 minutes. By that time most of the water will have evaporated and the carrots be beautifully glazed. If too much liquid is left when the carrots are ready, simply uncover and cook, stirring gently, over high heat. In a minute or so you will have only buttery carrots left. Serve. Makes 6 to 8 servings.

Variation: I use 4 to 6 carrots, cut the same as above, and 4 celery ribs, also cut on the diagonal, along with 2 to 4 sliced green onions. Proceed in the same manner with the 3 vegetables. Flavour with a pinch of thyme. Makes 4 to 6 servings.

Parsnip

The parsnip does not deserve to be ignored. It has good nutritive value and is delicious when properly cooked.

In choosing parsnips, look for smooth, firm, well shaped roots. Never buy those that are soft, shriveled or too large. Parsnips do not have to be refrigerated.

Parsnips can be sautéed, stir-fried, deep-fried, steambaked, added to soups and stews, or served in a sauce. They are also delicious mashed, either by themselves or with an equal quantity of potatoes, mixed with butter, cream, parsley, salt and pepper. Fat is needed to bring out the best flavour in this vegetable, and butter is the best to use.

Do not peel parsnips ahead of time; this will not only discolour them but cause a loss of vitamins. As you peel and cut them, drop them into acidulated cold water to prevent discolouration — 1 tablespoon (15 ml) vinegar or lemon juice for each 3 to 4 cups (750 ml to 1 L) of water. Do this just before cooking. Cut into dice or sticks, or leave whole. Always remove tough or woody cores.

All recipes for carrots can be applied to parsnips.

Oyster plant or salsify

This is a root vegetable, shaped like a carrot. The root is dark ivory in colour and half as fat as a large carrot. The flavour is like that of oysters, which explains the unusual name, but it is also called salsify.

Handle quickly to keep the vegetable from discolouring. Wash and scrape, then plunge into cold water acidulated with a little lemon juice or vinegar. Slice or dice, and cook in a small amount of boiling salted water, covered, for 15 to 20 minutes. Drain and add cream or white sauce and season with salt and pepper to taste. One pound (500 gr) of oyster plant roots will make 3 servings.

Turnips

This name is used for two root vegetables. One is actually the *rutabaga,* a vegetable of Swedish or Lap origin that is none other than our own large yellow turnip. It contains 92 per cent water, no starch or sugar but has a pungent essential oil. It is crisp, solid and nutritious and does not have an odour if it is properly cooked. There is also a white *rutabaga,* as large as the yellow but more delicate in flavour. The *true turnip* is the small white tuber, topped with a crown of purple. Turnip and rutabaga can be cooked by the same methods.

To PREPARE: The turnip has a thicker peel than most other vegetables. There is a thin well-marked coloured line between the peel and the inside of the turnip. This marks the point to which the peel must be removed, because this is where the bitterness is. Peel the vegetable only when you are ready to cook it.

To COOK: Slice or cut into pieces, add just enough boiling water to cover, and add a pinch of sugar and a pinch of pepper. Cook, uncovered, for 20 to 35 minutes. Do not overcook, for prolonged cooking changes the colour of the turnip and makes it hard to digest. When peeled and grated, a turnip cooks in 5 minutes.

Turnips are very good sliced thin and stir-fried, served with lots of minced fresh parsley.

1 turnip

½ tsp (2 ml) sugar

¼ tsp (1 ml) MSG

1 tbsp (15 ml) commercial sour cream

2 tbsp (30 ml) butter

⅛ tsp (0.5 ml) pepper

Parsley, minced

Peel the turnip and cut into thin strips. Cover with boiling water and add the sugar and MSG. Boil for 8 to 9 minutes over high heat. Drain in a sieve and return the turnip to the saucepan. Add the sour cream, butter and pepper; mash. Stir well and serve, garnished with minced parsley. Makes 4 to 6 servings.

My special mashed turnip

2 cups (500 ml) mashed turnips

1 egg

5 tbsp (80 ml) butter

Pinch of ground savory

Salt and pepper

3 tbsp (50 ml) flour

1 cup (250 ml) milk

½ cup (125 ml) grated cheese

Blend together the mashed turnips, egg, 2 tablespoons (30 ml) of the butter, the savory, and salt and pepper to taste. Stir well. Place in a buttered baking dish.

Make a thick white sauce with the remaining 3 tablespoons (50 ml) of butter, the flour and the milk. Spoon the sauce over the turnips and sprinkle with the grated cheese. Bake in a 400°F (200°C) oven for 25 minutes, or until the cheese has melted. Makes 4 servings.

Turnips have leafy green tops that can be used as a green vegetable. For directions for cooking turnip greens, see the section on Greens.

Turnips gratiné

Beets

Did you know that beets are first cousins to spinach? And did you know that beet tops are a good source of vitamins A and C, iron and riboflavin?

Since you get them free, look for young beets with fresh green tops when you buy them. For information on beet greens, see the section on Greens.

TO PREPARE: Cut off the leafy tops, but leave 2 to 3 inches of the stems on the beets, otherwise the beets will lose their deep red colour while cooking. Scrub the beets, but do not peel or remove the root end.

TO COOK: Bring some water to a boil, enough to half cover the beets. Add the juice of 1 lemon or 2 tablespoons (30 ml) vinegar. Add the beets. Cover and boil over medium-low heat from 30 minutes to 1½ hours, depending on the age, size and type of beets you are cooking. You can tell they are cooked when the skin slips off easily.

After cooking, drain them and plunge them into cold water. Slip off the skins by rolling the beets, one at a time, between your fingers.

TO SERVE: Slice, dice, or leave whole. Season with butter and salt and pepper to taste, or with a few tablespoons (15 to 50 ml) of fat gravy when they are being served with a roast.

Boiled new beets are delicious simply stirred with commercial sour cream and chopped green onion to taste.

Make cooked beets into a salad by shredding them into matchsticks and mixing with diced apples, lemon juice, and sour cream to taste. Then season with salt and pepper to taste and a bit of brown sugar.

Mashed beets

I learned one of my favourite recipes for beets many years ago from the owner of a little inn, which unfortunately no longer exists, in Strasbourg. She wore a large black taffeta headdress and a long black skirt, summer and winter. A fabulous cook, she made this recipe to perfection. She served the beets with a smoked loin of pork sitting on a bed of thick unsweetened applesauce, which was topped with a large piece of unsalted butter.

8 to 10 medium-sized beets

Juice of 1 lime

Pinch of ground cloves

1 tsp (5 ml) sugar

Salt and pepper to taste

1 tbsp (15 ml) cornstarch

⅓ cup (80 ml) dry red wine

1 tsp (5 ml) butter

Chives or parsley to taste

Boil or steam-bake the beets until tender. Skin them and mash in a blender or pass them through a food mill. Return to the saucepan and add the lime juice, cloves, sugar, and salt and pepper to taste. Mix the cornstarch with the red wine. Add this to the beets. Cook over medium heat, stirring most of the time, until hot and creamy.

Remove from the heat and stir in a teaspoon of butter and chives or parsley to taste. Serve. Makes about 6 servings.

Beet raita

Serve this side dish with an Indian curry.

2 cups (500 ml) cooked beets

1 cup (250 ml) yogurt

1 small onion, grated

Hot pepper sauce

Salt to taste

½ tsp (2 ml) sugar

Juice of 1 lime

Grate the cooked beets. Mix them with the other ingredients, adding the hot pepper sauce and salt to taste. Refrigerate for a few hours before serving.

This salad is most attractive served over spinach; it is a nice accompaniment to a plate of cold cuts. You can replace the garlic with grated orange or lemon rind.

New beet salad

6 to 8 beets, cooked or canned

2 garlic cloves, crushed

6 tbsp (100 ml) salad oil

3 tbsp (50 ml) cider or red wine vinegar

Salt and pepper to taste

1 lb (500 gr) fresh spinach, chopped

Juice of ½ a lemon

Chives or parsley, minced

Drain the beets well and cut into slices. Blend them with the crushed garlic, 4 tablespoons (70 ml) of the salad oil, the vinegar, and salt and pepper to taste.

Marinate in the refrigerator until ready to serve.

Heat the remaining 2 tablespoons (30 ml) salad oil in a large frying pan. Add the chopped spinach and stir over medium heat for 2 to 3 minutes until the spinach is limp. Pour it into a bowl and add the lemon juice and salt and pepper to taste. Chop with 2 knives until it is well mixed and chopped very fine. Then place it in a mound in the middle of a round plate.

To serve, make a ring of the marinated beets around the spinach and place a few beets on top. Sprinkle the beets with minced chives or parsley to taste. Makes 6 servings.

Celeriac or celery root or celery knob

This is an excellent root vegetable. Though related to celery, its leaves and stalks are not significant and only the root is used. In England it is often referred to as turnip-rooted celery; it's true the shape and size of celeriac resemble the shape and size of the turnip, but the taste is entirely different.

TO PREPARE: Peel just as you would a turnip, then quarter, slice or dice. As soon as the root is cut, place the pieces in water acidulated with a few spoonfuls of vinegar to prevent discolouration.

TO COOK: Use the professional method, steam-bake, steam or stir-fry, as described at the beginning of this chapter.

TO SERVE: Just toss with butter and chopped parsley or grated lemon rind. It's perfect with roasted chicken.

Dice and add to a white sauce, to which you can add grated cheese to taste.

For a salad, cut into thin slices, blanch for 10 minutes, freshen, and cool. Serve tossed with a dressing of your choice, or simply marinate in vinegar with a little sugar, just as with beets.

Peel, dice and boil with an equal amount of potatoes. When done, drain, mash as for mashed potatoes, and serve with roast beef or veal.

To serve uncooked as a salad or hors d'oeuvre, a French specialty, peel the celeriac and grate on a fine grater. Toss with lemon juice, rubbing it in well with your hands to prevent discolouration. Toss with a little French dressing, then with a few spoonfuls of mayonnaise. Place in a mound on a dish. Sprinkle with minced parsley. Refrigerate for a few hours before serving.

Jerusalem artichokes

This vegetable is a tuber that resembles a badly shaped potato. It has nothing in common with the globe artichoke, despite its name. This plant belongs to the Helianthus family and has a large blossom like a sunflower. The tuber is very easy to digest and has a mild, pleasant flavour. Jerusalem is a corruption of the Italian name for sunflower, girasole. North American Indians were cultivating this plant and apparently greatly appreciating its flavour as far back as 1600.

The basic cooking methods can be applied to Jerusalem artichokes. Peel the tubers, wash and wipe them. Or cook them in their skins like new potatoes. The skin comes off easily after cooking. Blanch for 5 minutes; freshen. Place around a roasting chicken or a roast of veal for the last 40 minutes of cooking. They will brown and cook. Serve them instead of potatoes.

They can also be eaten raw, in the same way as radishes. They have a crunchy texture and slightly earthy taste.

Radishes

These are seldom served any way but raw — as a garnish, appetizer or salad ingredient. They are perishable. Wash and trim them as soon as they arrive from the market. Then put them in a glass jar and cover with cold water; this keeps them crisp. They will keep for 4 to 5 days if you change the water daily. Cooked, their flavour is similar to that of turnips.

ONIONS AND THEIR RELATIVES

Onions, members of the lily family, rank among the oldest vegetables in the world. Down through the ages, magical healing properties have been attributed to them. They actually were sacred in ancient Egypt.

While the most-used domestic onions are available year long, some of the others, such as Bermuda and Spanish onions, appear only seasonally. Most onions are sold dried or "cured", but green onions, leeks and chives are sold fresh.

Yellow onions: Globe shaped, sometimes called cooking onions. They vary in size from small to large and are pungent. Good for chopping, boiling and soup.

Bermuda onions: Flatter in shape and quite large. They are pale yellow or white, and milder than the yellow onion.

Spanish onions: These have brown or yellow skins; they are mild. Excellent for slicing; good for deep-frying and stir-frying.

White onions: Small sized, sometimes called silver-skins. Fairly mild. Use whole to boil, or in stews and casseroles.

Red onion: The large ones are mild, even sweet, and are used for salads. Medium-sized, they are strong and are used for frying as well as in stews and hash.

Green onions, or scallions: Very young onions, pulled before the bulbous base has been formed. Both the green and white parts can be used. Trim and wash, then wrap in absorbent cloth and refrigerate; these are perishable. Used chiefly for flavouring, garnish or salad, but they can be served as a vegetable as well. Cook them as you would cook asparagus. They are delicious served on toast with a butter sauce.

TO PREPARE: Peel under running cold water or follow the chef's way, especially if you are cooking a lot of onions: ⚷⟶ Drop unpeeled onions into a saucepan of rapidly boiling water and leave them there for 1 minute. Drain, throw into a bowl of ice water, and simply slip off the skins.

TO COOK: Overcooked onions lose their true flavour and give off a strong smell. Onions can be cooked by any of the various basic methods, depending on how they are cut and how you plan to serve them.

Shallots

Shallots are the aristocrat of the onion family. A favorite of French cuisine, the shallot combines the best flavour characteristics of onions, garlic and scallions. The flavour is unique — pungent yet delicate, savoury yet freshly sweet. The shallot is small and shaped like a head of garlic. It has a brown outer skin and an onion like interior, shading from light green to violet. Several shallots grow together in a cluster, each one as a clove of the larger bulb; each little clove has its own purple-brown skin. They are sold cured, like dry onions.

Select shallots that are firm, with glistening brown skin. Stored in a cool dry place, they will keep for up to 4 months.

TO PREPARE: Peel off the outer brown skin, then slice or chop or mince according to recipe directions. When a recipe calls for 1 shallot, this means 1 clove of a shallot.

TO COOK: Shallots can be used in a variety of ways. Whip together softened butter and minced shallots and serve as a topper for broiled steaks. Add chopped fresh shallots to scrambled eggs and omelets. Substitute shallots for onions in creamy sauces for meats and vegetables. Add chopped shallots to salad dressings; slice thin and add to the salads. Use them minced in a marinade for meats and seafood. Stir a small amount of chopped shallots into your favorite rice, macaroni or noodle casserole. Use them to replace onion or garlic whenever you wish a mild, intriguing flavour.

Leeks

Leeks also belong to the lily family, and can be considered a kind of onion. They are delicate in flavour. In France, where they are readily available, leeks are known as "the poor man's asparagus". In Wales, they are the national emblem.

Leeks have long, flat green leaves, closely folded together. The white bottom, or bulb, is only a little fatter than the leaves, unlike the more familiar onion, which develops a much larger-sized bulb.

TO PREPARE: Cut off the root ends and about 2 inches of the green tops. Then peel off the first leaves, from top to bottom. Soak the trimmed leeks in cold water to loosen the soil. Leeks are very gritty, so they must be carefully and thoroughly cleaned. After a brief soaking, run water into the tops, down through the leaves, opening them as you do to let the water go down as deep as possible. If they are to be sliced, make 2 lengthwise cuts in the green part so you can open the tightly folded leaves and wash them.

TO COOK: Leeks can be cooked and served in much the same way as celery and asparagus. They can be blanched whole for 20 minutes, then freshened, cooled, and served with a French dressing for a salad. They are the base of the well-known soup vichyssoise, which is served hot or cold.

Garlic

Some are afraid of this small but powerful member of the onion family, but it can work wonders in flavouring certain foods. When used well it is a friend, not an enemy. You will find more about garlic in the chapter on herbs and spices, Vol. I.

Chives

Chives, another member of the onion family, are used as a flavouring herb. They look like miniature green onions. You will find out more about them in the chapter on herbs and spices, Vol. I.

Welsh leek pie

This a superb recipe that makes a pleasant change for the often served quiche. It is a good buffet dish. Serve it hot with sliced cold chicken or turkey.

6 leeks

½ cup (125 ml) chicken stock

Juice and grated rind of ½ a lemon

2 tbsp (30 ml) butter

4 eggs

¼ cup (60 ml) heavy cream

2 cups (500 ml) fine cottage cheese or 8 oz (225 gr) cream cheese

Salt and pepper to taste

3 tbsp (50 ml) fine dry bread crumbs

Pie pastry for a 1-crust, 8-inch (20 cm) pie

Clean the leeks and cut both the white and the green parts into 1-inch (2.5 cm) pieces. Bring the chicken stock to a boil along with the lemon juice, rind and butter. Add the leeks and cook, uncovered, over medium heat for 12 to 15 minutes.

Beat together the eggs, cream and cheese until well blended and creamy. Add ½ cup (125 ml) of the cooking stock while stirring. Then add the whole mixture to the cooked leeks and remaining stock. Simmer for a few moments, stirring, until the mixture thickens to the consistency of a light cream sauce. Add salt and pepper to taste.

Grease a pie plate and dust it with fine bread crumbs Line with the pastry and flute the edge. Pour in the leek mixture. Bake in a preheated 375°F (190°C) oven for about 40 minutes, or until the top is golden brown and the custard is set. Makes 4 to 6 servings.

THE CABBAGE FAMILY

The cabbage family includes red and green cabbages with large, heavy heads somewhat flattened on the top; Savoy cabbage with a smaller, looser head and very crinkly leaves; Chinese or celery cabbage with a long head or stalk like an overgrown stalk of celery; broccoli; Brussels sprouts; cauliflower; kale; and kohlrabi. The cabbage itself is a native British plant. The others have been developed through long cultivation that started in the 16th and 17th centuries.

The mortal sin commited against cabbage — apart from reducing it to cole-slaw — is to overcook it. People complain about its obnoxious smell, but this is present only if it is overcooked. The moment a member of the cabbage family loses its original colour, you can be sure it has been overcooked. It is at this point that it develops a strong smell. What's more, the Vitamin C that is plentiful in cabbage is lost through overcooking.

Cabbage

All true cabbages may be cooked following the same methods.

TO PREPARE: Remove coarse or discoloured outside leaves. Halve the head. Cut out the thick white stem; either discard it, or shred it and cook it with the cabbage.

The leaves can be cut into fine or coarse shreds with a sharp knife, or cut into pieces of about 2 inches (5 cm) square, or cut into quarters.

Cover any kind of cabbage in cold water and soak for 30 minutes. Add a teaspoon (5 ml) of coarse salt to dislodge any slugs or other unwelcome guests. If you plan to shred the cabbage, cut it into halves or quarters and soak it before shredding it.

TO COOK: The best way to cook cabbage that has been quartered is the professional method — blanching and refreshing.

Shredded cabbage is best cooked by pan-cooking or stir-frying.

If cabbage is cut into big squares, steam it or steam-bake it.

The average cooking time will be from 7 to 15 minutes for shredded and cut squares and 20 minutes for larger pieces, quarters or halves. Add a few more minutes for Savoy cabbage.

Broccoli

TO PREPARE: Soak the broccoli in cold salted water for 10 minutes; drain. Cut off the ends of the stems and the large leaves around the flower head. Peel the stems.

TO COOK: Broccoli can be cooked whole, chopped, or cut into small serving pieces; or the stems can be slivered and the heads cut into flowerets.

To cook the whole broccoli, use the professional method — blanching in lots of water for 20 minutes. Freshen quickly.

To cook in small pieces, use the pan-cooking method.

The stir-fry method is the best for the slivered stems and flowerets.

Red cabbage bruxellois

Belgians excel in the cooking of red cabbage, and this is one of the classic ways they prepare it. In autumn, when small wild birds or small ducks are available, they brown them in butter, stuff them with chestnuts, and bury them in cabbage and simmer slowly. This can be quite a treat on a cold day.

1 medium-sized red cabbage

3 apples

4 tbsp (60 ml) butter

1 bay leaf

3 tbsp (50 ml) brown sugar

4 juniper berries (optional)

3 whole cloves

¼ cup (60 ml) red wine or apple juice or orange juice

1 tsp (5 ml) salt

¼ tsp (1 ml) pepper

1 tsp (5 ml) butter

Clean and shred the cabbage. Cut the unpeeled apples into thin slices. Melt 4 tablespoons (60 ml) of the butter in a large saucepan, add the apples, and stir for a few minutes. Add the cabbage and stir to mix. Add the rest of the ingredients. Mix well and simmer, covered, for 1 hour. Most of the liquid should evaporate. If too much is left, uncover the pan and boil fast for a few minutes. Stir in a teaspoon (5 ml) of butter just before serving. Adjust seasoning. Makes 4 to 6 servings.

Brussels sprouts

TO PREPARE: Trim away any jutting stalks and discoloured outer leaves, and be very particular about soaking in salted cold water to dislodge any insects.

TO COOK: In the cabbage family, Brussels sprouts represent quality versus quantity. They are dainty and delicious, but easily ruined when badly cooked. The smaller ones are best. When possible, select all the same size.

To cook Brussels sprouts successfully every time, use the professional method of blanching for 5 to 8 minutes, then quickly freshening them in cold water. Cook the sprouts early in the day and refrigerate until ready to serve, when only a tossing in melted butter over low heat will warm them up in 5 minutes.

TO SERVE: Browned butter, toasted sesame seeds or toasted almonds are perfect companions to Brussels sprouts. The very best accompaniment is chestnuts.

Brussels sprouts and chestnuts

Use canned, unsweetened, water-packed chestnuts, imported from France, or buy fresh chestnuts.

Use 1 pound (500 gr) fresh chestnuts or one 8-ounce (225 gr) can of water-packed chestnuts for each 2-quart (2.5 L) basket of Brussels sprouts. To prepare the fresh nuts, make a crisscross on the flat top of each chestnut with a sharp-pointed knife. Cover with cold water, bring to a boil, and boil for 20 minutes. Then remove the hard shell and the brown skin covering the chestnut. Cook the chestnuts in salted water, or in chicken or beef bouillon if you prefer, for 10 to 20 minutes, or until tender; then drain.

If using canned chestnuts, just drain them.

Cook the Brussels sprouts. Melt 2 to 4 tablespoons (30 to 60 ml) butter in a saucepan. Fry a couple of green onions, chopped fine, in this melted butter. Add the drained, cooked Brussels sprouts and the chestnuts and toss together until hot. Add salt and pepper to taste, and serve. Makes about 8 servings.

Algerian stuffed cabbage leaves

Stuffed cabbage leaves are made in almost every country in the world. The Algerian method is unbeatable for lightness and flavour. The original hot spices have been replaced with allspice.

3 or 4 lamb bones, any type

4 cups (1 L) water

1 cinnamon stick

1 cup (250 ml) rice

1 head white or Savoy cabbage

½ to 1 lb (250 to 500 gr) ground lamb

¼ cup (60 ml) melted or soft drippings or oil

½ tsp (2 ml) ground allspice

Salt and pepper to taste

Juice and grated rind of 1 lemon

2 tbsp (30 ml) salad oil (optional)

Cover either long- or short-grain rice with cold water and let it soak for 1 hour. Drain.

Pour the water over the lamb bones, add the cinnamon stick, and simmer, covered, for 2 hours.

Remove the core from the cabbage with a pointed knife. Separate the leaves. Blanch for 5 minutes and freshen in the professional way. When cool, wrap in an absorbent towel to remove excess moisture. Cut the large leaves into halves.

Prepare the filling by mixing together the ground lamb, the well-drained soaked rice, the drippings or oil, the allspice, and salt and pepper to taste. Put a tablespoon (15 ml) or so on each cabbage leaf. Close like an envelope, tucking down the ends.

Remove the lamb bones from the broth and place them in a wide-bottomed saucepan. Set the stuffed, rolled leaves across the bones, making successive layers if needed. Add enough of the broth to cover the rolls. Sprinkle the whole with a little salt. Set a plate or a cover on top of the rolls to hold them in place. Cover the pan tightly and simmer over low heat for 1 hour.

Place the rolls on a hot platter. Measure 1 cup (250 ml) of the broth and add to it the lemon juice and rind. Add salad oil to the broth if you wish, pour the mixture over the rolls. Serve hot. Makes 8 or more servings, depending on the size of the cabbage and the amount of lamb you use.

Cauliflower

TO PREPARE: Cut off the hard stem and any big leaves. The small leaves close to the flowerets may remain. Soak in salted water, head down, for 10 minutes.

TO COOK: When cooking cauliflower whole, it is important to cut crisscross slashes into the thick stalks to ensure even cooking.

Use the professional method: Blanch, head up, for 15 to 18 minutes, or until tender to taste. Avoid overcooking.

0—⚷ If the head is rubbed with half a cut lemon before cooking, it will keep its beautiful creamy-white colour.

Broken into flowerets, cauliflower can be stir-fried or pan-cooked.

TO SERVE: Grated cheese, butter and lemon, hollandaise sauce and buttered browned croutons are the best garnishes to use with cauliflower. It is also very nice served in a cream sauce, topped with grated cheese, and browned under the broiler or in the oven.

Kale

This is a member of the cabbage family that forms loose heads, like a coarse spinach plant. It has smooth or crinkled leaves, depending on the variety; the crinkled leaves must be washed carefully. Usually the tough stems and ribs should be discarded. Kale is cooked like other leafy greens. See the section on Greens for more about this. Kale is usually plentiful in winter, when other greens are scarce and expensive.

Kohlrabi

TO PREPARE: Kohlrabi is sometimes called kale-turnip. This relative of the cabbage has a stem that swells out into a small turnip-shape or knob just above the soil. It is this knob that is eaten. Remove the leaves as near as possible to the knob. Pare off the outside skin, but try not to cut off any of the knob itself.

TO COOK: Kohlrabies can be cooked whole or diced. Cook by the pan-cooking method when diced. Steam-bake them when whole. They can also be steamed. Any recipe for turnip can be used for kohlrabies; they can be used instead of turnips.

TO SERVE: Dress with butter and lemon juice.

Cook them diced with a peeled, diced apple, and mash together. Add butter and either chopped fresh mint or parsley.

They are also very nice served with a well-seasoned white sauce.

Broccoli divan à la moderne

A true broccoli divan is a wine-poached chicken breast that is set on a bed of cooked broccoli heads, topped with hollandaise sauce and a layer of grated Swiss cheese, and baked. This version can be made quickly when you are in a hurry.

**1 bunch of broccoli
or 2 10-oz (280 gr) packages
frozen broccoli**

2 7-oz (198 gr) cans albacore tuna

3 green onions, chopped fine

**1 10½-oz (294 gr) can cream of
mushroom soup, undiluted**

1 tsp (5 ml) curry powder

**½ cup (125 ml) commercial sour
cream**

⅓ cup (80 ml) grated cheese

2 tbsp (30 ml) butter

Paprika

Prepare the fresh broccoli and cut into slivers or leave whole, according to your taste. Butter a baking dish. Cook the slivered broccoli by the stir-fry method or the whole heads by the professional method. Drain, and place in the bottom of the baking dish. If you are using frozen broccoli, cook as directed on the package and leave whole.

Break the tuna into large pieces and make a layer over the broccoli. Sprinkle the green onions on the tuna. Blend together the undiluted soup, curry powder and sour cream. Pour over the tuna. Top with the grated cheese, dot with the butter, and sprinkle paprika on top. Bake at 375°F (190°C) for 20 to 25 minutes, or until browned on top. Makes 6 to 8 servings.

NOTE: Leftover sliced fish, turkey or chicken can replace the tuna in this recipe.

Golden cauliflower

Ruth Conrad Bateman is an American food expert who has written many books on the subject and has a wonderful flair with food. This golden cauliflower is her idea.

1 cauliflower

**½ cup (125 ml) grated Swiss
cheese**

¼ cup (50 ml) mayonnaise

1 egg white

1 tsp (5 ml) lemon juice

**2 tbsp (30 ml) grated Parmesan
cheese**

Separate the cauliflower into flowerets. Cook by the professional method, blanching for 10 minutes.

Drain the flowerets and place them in a shallow baking dish that can go under the broiler. Otherwise, protect the edges of the dish with a collar of foil.

Combine the Swiss cheese and the mayonnaise. Beat the egg white and fold into the cheese and mayonnaise mixture. Add the lemon juice and spread this mixture over the cauliflower. Sprinkle with Parmesan. Broil 6 inches (15 cm) from the source of heat until the sauce puffs up and is golden. This takes about 5 minutes. Makes about 6 servings.

FRESH LEGUMES

These plants have seeds that grow within pods, which open along the sides when the seeds are ripe. Some, like green or yellow snap beans and snow peas, we eat pod and all, before the seeds are developed. Others we eat after the seeds are developed but still green, peas and lima beans, for example. Chick-peas and lentils are also legumes and, surprisingly, so is the peanut.

Fresh snap beans

Green beans, yellow or wax beans and the hard-to-find mottled green and purple beans are the best-known and most-used beans of those eaten in the pods. Of course, there are many other kinds. Every country has its own tasty and different way of cooking and serving them.

TO PREPARE: Wash beans in cold water. Snip off the top and bottom ends. Some have threads or strings that should be pulled away when the ends are snipped off. If you trim the beans ahead of time, place them in a plastic bag and refrigerate until you are ready to cook them.

TO COOK: The beans can be left whole, or cut into 1-inch (2.5 cm) pieces or into halves, or cut on the diagonal into 3 pieces, or cut into long thin shreds with a sharp knife or a special cutter. Beans cut into shreds are referred to as "French-style".

The usual method of cooking them is to blanch them, but they can be stir-fried. Wax beans can also be steam-baked.

All fresh beans will cook in 5 to 12 minutes, depending on the way they are cut and the season. Avoid overcooking them, as they are more tasty and far more digestible when a bit on the crunchy side.

TO SERVE: The classic way to serve green beans is with butter and lemon juice or lemon rind.

The Germans add a pinch of dried savory to the water while cooking the beans; then only butter is used to dress them.

The Greeks fry an onion in salad oil, then add chopped parsley and mint and a tablespoon (15 ml) of tomato paste. When these ingredients are well mixed, a little water is added and whole green beans are added to the boiling liquid. They are cooked quickly and served in their own juice with a bowl of rice.

Amandine garnish

This is a delicious garnish for French-style beans.

1 lb (500 gr) green beans

¼ cup (60 ml) blanched almonds

2 tbsp (30 ml) butter

1 tbsp (15 ml) fresh lemon juice

Cook the beans. Sliver the blanched almonds into thin shreds. Brown the butter, add the almonds, and cook until the almonds and butter have a deep brown colour. Add the lemon juice. Pour over the beans as soon as they are cooked. Serve.

When delicious new potatoes are available, serve these beans with a dish of steamed new potatoes.

Mennonite green beans

2 tbsp (30 ml) butter

⅓ cup (80 ml) water

¼ to ½ tsp (1 to 2 ml) dried savory

Salt and pepper to taste

1 lb (500 gr) green beans, cut into halves

1 tbsp (15 ml) cornstarch

1 tbsp (15 ml) tomato paste

½ cup (125 ml) light cream

⅓ cup (80 ml) grated strong Cheddar cheese

Melt the butter in a saucepan; add the water, savory, and salt and pepper to taste. Bring to a boil. Add the beans, cover tightly, and steam for 15 minutes. Drain the beans into a hot serving dish, reserving the cooking liquid.

Put the reserved liquid back in the pan. Mix the cornstarch with the tomato paste and the cream. Add to the bean liquid. Cook, while stirring, until the mixture turns into a slightly thickened sauce. Add the cheese and stir until it melts, then pour over the beans. Makes 4 servings.

This is another masterpiece of the ever-surprising and always-interesting Scandinavian cuisine. This dish is delicious served very hot, with paper-thin slices of cold smoked salmon.

Scandinavian wax beans

1 lb (500 gr) wax beans

2 tbsp (30 ml) unsalted butter

1 small onion, diced

1 tomato, diced

¼ tsp (1 ml) sugar

¼ cup (60 ml) water

Salt and pepper to taste

Juice of ½ a lemon

1 tsp (5 ml) dried dillweed or 1 to 2 tbsp (15 to 30 ml) minced fresh dill

Clean the beans and cut into diagonal shreds. Melt the butter in a heavy metal saucepan. Add the onion and stir until soft, then add the tomato, sugar, water and beans. Bring to a boil, then cover tightly and simmer over low heat for about 20 minutes.

Uncover after 10 minutes; if you find there is too much liquid, boil fast over high heat until only about one third of the liquid is left. Add salt and pepper to taste. Then add the lemon juice and dill and serve. Makes 4 servings.

Snap-bean salad

This is an excellent salad to serve with barbecued steak. If you soak the onion rings in ice water, you will take the bite out of them and make them very crisp.

1 lb (500 gr) green or yellow snap beans

1 tsp (5 ml) sugar

1 white onion

2 tbsp (30 ml) salad oil

Juice of ½ a lemon

1 or 2 pinches of dried oregano

Salt and pepper

Trim and wash the beans and place them in a saucepan with the sugar. Cover with boiling water and boil for 6 to 8 minutes.

Drain and rinse in cold water. Drain again on absorbent paper, cool, and refrigerate.

Slice the onion as thinly as possible. Break the slices into rings and place in a bowl. Cover with ice cubes and let stand until ice has melted.

When ready to serve, mix the beans with the salad oil, lemon juice, oregano, and salt and pepper to taste. Toss until all the beans are well coated, and place in a salad bowl. Drain the onion rings and sprinkle over the salad. Makes 4 to 6 servings.

Lima beans

Unlike the other fresh beans just described, the pods of lima beans are not eaten, for they are too tough. Instead, they are allowed to ripen until the beans inside reach an edible size.

TO PREPARE: If possible, do not shell the beans until you are ready to cook them. Limas are difficult to shell. Use a sharp knife to cut a lengthwise slice down the pod, then pry apart the sides of the pod. The pods are so tight that the beans do not need to be washed before cooking.

TO COOK: Lima beans can be blanched and refreshed, or steamed. These take longer to cook than other fresh beans, 15 to 25 minutes. Taste a bean to avoid overcooking.

TO SERVE: Add salt, pepper and a bit of butter. Try lemon juice for an interesting change.

If you have a blender, place the cooked lima beans with ½ cup (125 ml) of their cooking water in the blender container. Cover and blend into a purée. Add butter and salt and pepper to taste.

Cook lima beans in chicken bouillon instead of water, and thicken the liquid to a cream sauce. Serve with the addition of a few slices of diced fried bacon and chopped fresh parsley.

To make the famous American succotash, add a package of cooked frozen lima beans to a package of buttered corn kernels. Add butter and salt to taste.

Peas

Green peas are a favourite vegetable all around the world. They have been cultivated for a long time — they have been found in the remains of Bronze Age dwellings — and they have been known in China for more than 5,000 years. They are available fresh, frozen or canned. Peas are perfectly delicious when picked young from the garden and cooked immediately.

A variety of peas with edible pods is a popular ingredient in Oriental cooking. Called snow or sugar peas, they are eaten pod and all. The pod is flat and of a much paler green than the regular green peas; the peas inside the pod are tiny. Although expensive, there is no loss since the whole vegetable is eaten.

TO PREPARE: Shell green peas when ready to cook; if you do it sooner the peas will dry out. One pound (500 gr) in the pods equals about 1 cup (250 ml) of shelled peas.

Snow peas are not shelled. Trim the ends and pull off any strings; wash.

TO COOK: Peas and snow peas are usually cooked by the professional method — blanch them ofr 10 to 15 minutes. Stir-fry, pan-cook or steam.

TO SERVE: Butter, fresh mint, minced shallots, cooked small white onions and parsley are all good additions to cooked green peas.

DRIED LEGUMES AND CEREAL GRAINS

Dried legumes are excellent winter fare, because they are both nourishing and warming, as well as being extremely economical. They double in bulk when cooked; 1 cup (250 ml) of a dried legume can make 4 servings.

They can be served as a main dish, a soup, or a vegetable. You can cook more than is needed for a single meal because they can be stored in the refrigerator for as long as 8 to 10 days without spoiling. They also freeze very well. They take a fairly long time to cook, but they require no supervision and can be reheated without problems.

⚷ If you are searching for a way to economize, substitute a dried legume dish for meat. There are many, such as dried lima and kidney beans and chickpeas. The most interesting for casseroles and soup are lentils and split peas.

Lentils

Lentils are like miniature peas except they are flat. They have an outer membrane with the seed inside. The seeds of lentils are split like the seeds of peas. Whole lentils are sold as brown lentils and have a greenish-brown colour; the inside is a golden orange. The split or so-called Egyptian lentils are easier to find than the whole brown lentils. The split ones will cook in 20 to 30 minutes; the whole ones take 1 to 1½ hours. Neither requires a soaking period. Brown lentils have more flavour than split lentils.

Creamed lentils

Serve as a vegetable, or as a main dish by adding diced leftover meat at the same time as the sour cream.

1 lb (500 gr) brown lentils

10 cups (2.5 L) cold water

Salt and pepper to taste

1 tsp (5 ml) celery salt

1 cup (250 ml) commercial sour cream

2 tbsp (30 ml) butter

Place the lentils in a colander and rinse under running cold water. Place in a saucepan and add the cold water. Set over low heat, cover, and *slowly* bring to a boil. **0—➤** This is important, because the slow cooking will give a preliminary softening to the lentils. This usually takes 40 to 45 minutes. When the water is boiling, cook a little faster, as the water must be evaporated when the lentils are cooked. This should take another 45 minutes.

Toward the end of the cooking, add the salt and pepper to taste and the celery salt. When the lentils are soft and the water is all absorbed, add the sour cream and the butter. Adjust seasoning. Stir gently until the cream and butter are well blended in. Serve.

As a variation, sprinkle with minced parsley or fried onions.

Makes about 6 servings.

Lentil soup

This delicious soup makes a perfect winter lunch accompanied by a thick wedge of warm apple pie with cheese and a big cup of hot tea.

2 cups (500 ml) brown lentils

4 cups (1 L) cold water

2 tbsp (30 ml) salt

¼ tsp (1 ml) pepper

½ cup (125 ml) butter

1 large can tomatoes

1 large onion, diced

2 tbsp (30 ml) fresh dill or 1 tbsp (15 ml) dill seeds

2 garlic cloves, crushed

2 bay leaves

Place the ingredients in a saucepan. Slowly bring to a boil. Cover and simmer over low heat for 2 to 2½ hours. Makes about 6 servings.

Split peas

Green split peas are usually hulled from peas called Small Blues or Imperial. The process used for hulling gives a larger, more tasty split pea, and also accounts for the difference in size between these and other split peas. The peas are washed lightly, soaked, and dried; this loosens the skin, which is then easily removed, and the peas fall apart. They cook quickly.

Barley

Barley is a hardy cereal, not a vegetable at all, but it can be used in the same way as dried legumes. Rich in phosphorous, it is perhaps the most ancient of the cultivated seed foods. Hulled barley, referred to as "pot" or Scotch barley, has the best flavour and is lowest in calories. Pearl barley is grain that has been steamed and rounded and polished in a mill; some of the nutritive value is lost in the process, but pearl barley cooks quickly.

This old-fashioned dish is similar in texture to "Scotch brose", a pudding made with oatmeal. Boiled bacon or lamb, homemade rhubarb chutney and pease pudding is a true Scottish country meal, wonderful after a day of hunting or just roaming in the woods.

Scottish pease pudding

3 cups (750 ml) green split peas

4 tbsp (60 ml) butter

1 tsp (5 ml) salt

¼ tsp (1 ml) pepper

1 tsp (5 ml) brown sugar

1 egg, lightly beaten

Soak the peas in cold water overnight. Drain, then tie them loosely in cheesecloth, leaving room for them to swell. Place in a large saucepan. Add enough boiling water to cover by about 2 inches (5 cm). Cover and simmer over low heat for 3 hours, until they have become soft. Remove from the water and drain thoroughly.

Place the peas in a bowl and add the butter, salt, pepper, brown sugar and egg. Beat together with a wire whisk or a rotary beater. The mixture will be soft but quite thick. Lightly flour the cheesecloth and return the mixture to the cloth. Tie up the cheesecloth tightly to shape a pudding. Put it in a pan of boiling water and boil for 30 to 40 minutes. Unwrap and place on a hot dish. Pour melted butter to taste on top. Slice and serve. Makes about 8 servings.

If you happen to have any leftover pudding, slice it cold, then brown the slices slowly in butter or bacon fat.

Barley pilaf

Barley pilaf is a wonderful accompaniment to game birds, Cornish hens and venison.

4 tbsp (60 ml) butter

2 onions, minced

½ lb (250 gr) mushrooms, chopped

1½ cups (375 ml) pot barley

3½ cups (875 ml) consommé

½ tsp (2 ml) salt

Melt 2 tablespoons (30 ml) of the butter in a large frying pan. Add the onions and mushrooms. Cook over high heat until lightly browned, stirring most of the time. Remove the vegetables from the pan with a slotted spoon, draining out as much of the browned butter as possible.

Melt the remaining butter in the frying pan. Add the barley to this and stir over medium heat until the grains have a nutty brown colour. Add the onions and mushrooms and mix. Pour the mixture into a casserole and add the consommé and the salt. Cover and bake in a 350°F (180°C) oven for 45 to 55 minutes. If necessary, add a little hot water during the cooking period. Makes about 8 servings.

Varation: For a main dish, brown chicken wings or legs or pieces of breast in butter and bury them in the barley. Add an extra cup of consommé or water. Bake in the same manner.

Rice

The bland flavour of rice allows it to be combined with almost every type of food. Rice can be served with a main course, as a salad, and as a dessert, and it's also most useful as a hot or cold cereal. When properly cooked, rice is delightful.

Rice comes in three basic forms — brown, white and converted. All forms can be cooked by the same general method, only the time differs. However, there is quite a difference in the vitamin value.

Brown rice is the natural grain, not polished; the vitamins and minerals are still there. This rice is harder than white rice and somewhat chewy.

Converted rice is a specially processed rice; although it is white in colour, most of the vitamin content has been restored.

White rice, which can have long or short grains, has lost a great deal of its vitamin and mineral content in milling, so be sure to include with it or in the meal some other food high in thiamin, riboflavin and iron to make up for the deficiency.

TO COOK: Follow the directions given on the package you buy, or use one of the following methods:

Instant rice, somewhat pre-cooked white rice, cooks very quickly. There is a long list of rice convenience foods, such as canned rice pudding, ready-seasoned rice, a mixture of brown and wild rice (by the way, wild rice is not a rice at all) frozen rice, canned and frozen fried rice. Whether to use them is a matter of choice. But remember: Regular short- or long-grain rice is the best buy, since 1 cup (250 ml) of raw rice will yield 3 full cups (750 ml) cooked, which is not the case with all types of processed rice.

Actually, rice is a true convenience product all by itself, since it keeps very well after cooking. Cover it tightly and refrigerate, and it will keep for as long as 8 days. To reheat, put a few tablespoons (15 to 50 ml) of water in a saucepan, add the rice, cover and heat over low heat for 5 to 6 minutes, stirring once with a fork. Or put the water and rice in a baking dish, cover and heat in a 350°F (180°C) oven for 10 minutes.

With 1 cup (250 ml) of uncooked rice — 3 cups (750 ml) cooked — you can usually make 4 generous servings as an accompaniment to a main dish.

Slow-cooking brown rice

Follow the same method as for white rice. Use 2 cups (500 ml) brown rice, 1½ teaspoons (7 ml) salt, and 4 cups (1 L) cold water. Cook the rice for 35 minutes, and let the cooked rice dry for 10 minutes.

Slow-cooking converted rice

Follow the same method as for white rice. Use 2 cups (500 ml) converted rice, 1½ teaspoons (7 ml) salt, and 3½ cups (875 ml) cold water. Cook for 22 minutes, and let the cooked rice dry for 5 minutes.

Baked rice

This is a very useful method, especially when the oven is already in use.

Place 1 cup (250 ml) long- or short-grain white rice in a baking dish with a cover. Bring to a boil 2 cups (500 ml) water with 1 teaspoon (5 ml) salt. Pour it over the rice and stir; cover the pan. Bake in a 350°F (180°C) oven for 25 minutes.

For brown and converted rice, bake for 45 to 50 minutes.

Steamed rice

Place in a saucepan 2 cups (500 ml) white rice, 2 cups (500 ml) water, hot or cold, and 1 teaspoon (5 ml) salt. Set over high heat, uncovered. When the water boils vigorously, stir several times with a fork, then cover the pan with a tight-fitting lid. Cook over heat as low as possible for 14 minutes. Take off the heat and lift the grains gently with a fork to let the steam out. Water will all be absorbed.

For brown rice, increase the liquid to 1½ cups (625 ml). Cook for 45 minutes.

For converted rice, cook for only 20 minutes.

2 cups (500 ml) rice

4 cups (1 L) cold water

1½ tsp (7 ml) salt

1 tsp (5 ml) salad oil

Pour long- or short-grain rice into a 2-quart (2 L) saucepan. Add the cold water, salt and salad oil. Cover with a tight-fitting lid. Bring to a brisk boil; it should take 3 to 5 minutes. Then reduce the heat to the lowest possible, and cook for 18 to 22 minutes, or until all the water is absorbed. This makes a rice with firm grains. If you like softer rice, use an extra ⅓ cup (80 ml) water and cook for 5 minutes more than the 18 to 22 minutes. Then, in either case, remove the cover when the time is up and let the rice steam dry away from the source of heat. This will give you flaky, separate grains.

Slow-cooking flaky white rice

Italian buttered rice

1 to 3 tbsp (15 to 50 ml) butter

1 cup (250 ml) rice

2¼ cups (560 ml) hot chicken stock or beef stock or consommé

2 chicken or beef bouillon cubs

2¼ cups (560 ml) boiling water

Salt to taste

Grated Parmesan cheese

Melt the butter in a heavy metal saucepan. Add long- or short-grain rice. Stir constantly over medium heat until the rice is golden in colour. Then add hot chicken or beef stock or consommé. Or add chicken or beef bouillon cubes to the boiling water. Stir well, add salt if necessary, and pour into a 2-quart (2.5 L) casserole. Cover and bake in a 350°F (180°C) oven 35 to 40 minutes. Serve with a bowl of grated Parmesan cheese.

Chinese fried rice

4 tbsp (60 ml) peanut oil or sesame-seed oil

½ tsp (2 ml) salt

¼ tsp (1 ml) MSG

2 eggs, beaten

2 scallions

4 cups (1 L) cold cooked rice

½ tsp (2 ml) sugar

2 tbsp (30 ml) soy sauce

In a 9- or 10-inch heavy metal frying pan, heat the peanut or sesame-seed oil with the salt and MSG. Beat eggs until well mixed but not frothy. Pour the eggs into the hot oil and fry over low heat like a pancake, but do not brown. Remove from the pan with a wide spatula; cool. Roll the pancake into a sausage shape and cut it into fine shreds.

Chop scallions on the bias and add to the fat remaining in the frying pan. Stir for a few seconds and add cold cooked rice, any type, sugar and soy sauce. Stir constantly with a fork over a moderate heat until the rice is hot. Then stir in the shredded egg, mix with the rice for a second or two, and serve.

Double-boiler rice

This method is frequently used for dessert rice, for instance rice pudding where the rice is cooked in milk. It can also be used as cereal.

Place 1 cup (250 ml) short- or long-grain rice in the top part of a double boiler with 3½ cups (875 ml) milk and 12 teaspoon (5 ml) salt. Heat to boiling over direct heat, then place over boiling water and cook, covered, for 40 to 45 minutes, or until the milk is all absorbed.

Freezing rice

Cook any rice you prefer, by one of the above methods. Cool it, chill it, then place it in freezer containers in portions to suit your needs. Seal and label. It will keep up to 8 months.

To reheat, thaw the frozen rice; takes about 2 hours in the refrigerator or 1 hour at room temperature. Proceed as you would for refrigerated rice.

Savoury rice ring

Prepare rice by any of the methods described. For each 3 cups (750 ml) of cooked rice, beat 1 egg well and add a pinch of grated nutmeg and a pinch of powdered garlic. Stir into the hot cooked rice and blend thoroughly. Salt and pepper to taste. Pack into a generously buttered ring mold. Bake in a 350°F (180°C) oven for 10 minutes. Let the mold stand on a wooden board for 5 minutes. Then turn out on a hot platter, in a swift turn. Fill to taste.

GREENS

Under this general heading we usually include all the plants we cultivate chiefly for their leaves. First, the whole family of salad greens — chicory, dandelion greens, endive, escarole, watercress, and Boston, Bibb, iceberg, romaine and garden leaf lettuces. There also is kale, a member of the cabbage family, and turnip tops, beet greens and the leaves of other plants we usually grow for the roots. The most famous green is spinach. Another green is fiddleheads, a specialty in the Maritime provinces, and Maine.

TO PREPARE: All salad greens except iceberg lettuce should be washed under cold running water. Shake the water out well, then place absorbent cloth in the bottom of a plastic bag. Fill the bag loosely with the cleaned greens and refrigerate in the vegetable crisper. The cloth will absorb any moisture left in the greens and prevent rusting as well as keeping them crisp and fresh.

If you trim salad greens before storing them, do not use a knife, but break off the parts you wish to discard. Using a knife on greens causes rust spots on the leaves.

Greens to be cooked should be cleaned carefully; they are likely to have grit and soil attached to them. Wash repeatedly by immersing them in a large bowl of tepid water. Change the water and repeat. Separate the leaves — especially important for kale — and run under cold water.

TO COOK: Do not drain the greens after the final cleaning; the water clinging to the leaves is usually sufficient liquid in which to cook them. All recipes for celery and spinach can be used for cooking greens.

Dandelions

There is a certain ironic humor in the pleasure we can derive in the springtime from consuming the lowly dandelion, this enemy of our lawns. Dandelions were thought to have medicinal properties and are supposed to purify the blood. The young green leaves can be used raw or cooked. Gather dandelions early in the morning.

TO PREPARE: There is only one thing to remember: Use lots of water and exercise lots of patience. Cut off the roots, then wash in several waters, always lifting the leaves up from the water. When thoroughly cleaned, wrap them in absorbent cloth and refrigerate for a few hours to crisp them.

TO COOK: Any recipe for spinach can be used to cook dandelions. They can be mixed with an equal amount of spinach, as a matter of fact, and cooked together. They can also be chopped and stir-fried with a chopped onion for 5 or 6 minutes.

To remove all bitterness, cook in the professional way — blanch for 10 minutes and then freshen. Uncooked and crisp, use them as one of the greens for a salad, or make them into a salad alone, garnished with sliced hard-cooked eggs or cooked beets.

Braised endives

The endive is one of the most interesting cooked greens. When well done, endives are an epicure's delight. They are fairly expensive, but a treat for a special occasion.

Allow 2 heads per person. Trim off roots without cutting leaves and remove any discoloured leaves.

Rub the bottom of a casserole generously with butter and add the endives, the juice of ½ lemon, and enough chicken stock (your own or canned) to half-cover the endives. Bring to a boil on top of the stove. Place a round of buttered waxed paper directly on top of the en-

dives. Cover the casserole and place it in a preheated 325°F (160°C) oven. Cook for 1 hour, or until the endives are tender when pierced with the point of a small sharp knife; they should be lightly browned.

To serve, lift the endives onto a hot serving dish. Boil down the liquids in the pan over high heat, uncovered, until you have about 1 tablespoon (15 ml) per person. Pour this over the endives. Sprinkle with minced fresh parsley.

Fiddleheads

These are actually young fern leaves that, before unfolding, resemble fiddle, or violin, heads. Fiddleheads, like dandelions, appear in May. They are found in dark moist places, usually along or near brooks or streams. If they are picked very young, the stalks are as tender as the heads. If picked late, when the green colour has started to yellow, then only the heads are tender and should be eaten.

TO PREPARE: Shake out each stalk and head carefully so as not to break off the head. To remove the brownish scale, wash well in several waters. Use warm water. Lift the greens up and out of the water. Then let them stand in salted cold water for 30 minutes or longer before cooking.

TO COOK: Cook in a small amount of boiling water for only a few minutes, until the stalks are tender; drain. Season with salt and pepper, butter, and a few drops of vinegar or lemon juice.

Fiddleheads can be enjoyed frozen or canned during the rest of the year.

Spinach

Spinach is supposed to have come originally from Asia through Spain, which is a curious odyssey for so simple a vegetable. It is available fresh all year long. The whole of a small plant is pulled up and the root end and stems are often very sandy. Thorough washing is necessary.

This chore makes frozen spinach increasingly popular, but the fresh vegetable is far more delicious. The glossy green leaves are the basis of many an epicurean dish, such as sole florentine and spinach soufflé.

TO PREPARE: Use a large pan filled with cold water, which you change a few times. Lift the spinach from the water, or use the direction given to clean greens. Even packaged, cleaned spinach should be washed to freshen it. Cut off stems and remove wilted leaves.

TO COOK: Do not use too much water, which not only washes away the mineral salts in spinach but deprives it of its fine flavour. It should be cooked quickly in its own juices, which will develop in cooking, and in the moisture adhering to its leaves after washing.

Pack tightly in a stainless-steel saucepan. Cover and set over high heat. After 2 minutes, lift the cover and turn the spinach over from top to bottom. The bottom will then be almost cooked. Cover again and cook for another 2 or 3 minutes. Throw the spinach into a colander and press out the water. The water will be dark green; reserve this for soup or gravy. Chop the spinach as fine or as coarse as you wish; use a sharp knife and a fork and chop directly in the colander. The spinach is then ready to be used as you wish.

A good quick way is to cream it. When cut and drained, return to the saucepan. Sprinkle the top with 2 teaspoons (10 ml) flour. Add a piece of butter and 1 tablespoon (15 ml) of light cream or milk. Add salt and pepper to taste and a dash of grated nutmeg. Stir together over medium heat until creamy and well blended. It takes about 1 minute. Serve.

To serve cooked spinach as a base for a soufflé, cook it by the professional method — blanch for 1 minute, freshen, and drain thoroughly in a sieve.

With slight variations this recipe is used in Greek, Turkish and Armenian cuisines. It is especially good served with roast lamb and chutney.

Spinach and cucumber salad

1 lb (500 gr) fresh spinach

2 cucumbers

1 cup (250 ml) slivered celery

½ cup (125 ml) minced fresh parsley

½ cup (125 ml) green olives, chopped

½ cup (125 ml) black olives, chopped

¼ cup (60 ml) pine nuts or almonds

¼ cup (60 ml) salad oil

⅛ cup (30 ml) red wine or cider vinegar

½ tsp (2 ml) salt

¼ tsp (1 ml) freshly ground pepper

Pinch of dried oregano or marjoram

Wash the spinach and dry thoroughly. Cut the stems and chop into coarse pieces. There should be about 4 cups (1 L) of the pieces. Peel and dice the cucumbers; discard seeds if they are large. Place the dice in a large bowl and add the celery, parsley, green and black olives, pine nuts or almonds, and the chopped spinach.

Mix together the salad oil, vinegar, salt, pepper, and oregano or marjoram; pour over the vegetable mixture. Toss together until well blended. Makes 4 servings.

EDIBLE THISTLES

Artichokes
The French or globe artichoke is one of the oldest cultivated vegetables in the world. It takes its name from the Arabic word *alkhurshuf*. It is a kind of huge thistle, of which only the fleshy base of each leaf and the heart can be eaten.

TO PREPARE: Dip each vegetable, tips down, into a bowl of cold water. Do it many times, shaking out the water each time, until the artichoke is free of all dust and any foreign particles. Cut off the stems, leaving no more than about 1 inch (2.5 cm) of stem. Pull off any dried or discoloured leaves on the outside. With scissors, cut off the sharp spiny leaf tips. To avoid discolouration, rub a cut piece of lemon on all parts that have been cut.

TO COOK: Blanch and freshen by the professional method; blanch for about 30 minutes, or until a leaf can be pulled away easily. The age and size of the artichoke can vary the cooking time by 10 to 12 minutes. Drain thoroughly.

TO SERVE: Serve with a bowl of melted butter, or butter melted with fresh lemon juice, or with hollandaise sauce.

Cardoons
These delicious vegetables are grown extensively on the Continent but are little known in North America, although you will find some early in the autumn in markets in the Italian districts of any city.

Cardoons are unlike any other vegetable. Members of the same family (Cynara) as the French artichoke, they are tall and upright, and the ribs of the leaves have a fleshy consistency. With artichokes, it is the flower heads that are eaten, but the cardoon rib is like the fleshy rib of celery, and it is this part that is edible.

The cardoon is a very large vegetable, pale green in colour, and reveals its family by having prickly edges on the ribs. In Italy they clean cardoons, cut the hearts and stalks into long pieces, soak overnight in cold water, refrigerate, and then eat them raw, dipped into a sauce. However, it is better to cook them as described below.

TO PREPARE: Cut into lengths of 4 to 5 inches (8 to 10 cm), removing any prickly parts. Place in boiling water and cook until the outer skin, which is woolly, will rub off. Drain and place in ice-cold water until cool. When cool enough to handle, scrape them and remove the strings. They are then ready to be cooked. Yes, they do get cooked twice.

TO COOK: The professional method is the best to use with cardoons. Blanch them for 30 to 40 minutes, or less, until they are tender. Freshen. They are very nice when cooked slowly in consommé.

TO SERVE: Toss with diced fried bacon, or butter and lemon juice, or serve in a white sauce.

This recipe comes from a friend who was a true gourmet and a genius with gardens à l'anglaise. His vegetable garden was as beautiful a sight as his rose garden. When he served artichokes, sometimes cold as a luncheon dish, sometimes hot with dinner, he used this superb dressing.

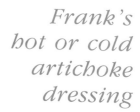

Frank's hot or cold artichoke dressing

2 hard-cooked eggs

2 tbsp (30 ml) tarragon or cider vinegar

2 green onions, chopped fine

1 very small piece of garlic, minced

Juice of ½ a lemon

¼ tsp (1 ml) sugar

¼ tsp (1 ml) dry mustard

¼ tsp (1 ml) curry powder

4 tbsp (60 ml) chopped fresh parsley

1 cup (250 ml) olive or salad oil

Separate the whites of the eggs from the yolks. Mash the yolks and add the other ingredients one by one, stirring and washing as you go.

If you have a blender, simply place all except the egg whites in it and blend for 1 second.

To serve, place the mixture in small individual bowls, or in a large bowl. Mince the egg whites and sprinkle on top of the dressing.

CRUNCHY STALKS

Celery

Celery is as well known and as widely used as carrots. A wild maritime plant, it has a watery, crunchy texture, strong aromatic odour and a freshness that gives it an attractive, appetizing flavour. It is a good food for dieters because it has few calories.

TO PREPARE: Purchase heads of celery with as many fresh leaves as possible. Hold the whole head, leafy end up, under running water to rinse. Shake out as much water as possible. Cut off the leaves with as much of the ribs as you wish. Place the leaves in a plasting bag and keep them to chop and add to salads, soups, sauces, stews, meat loaves, poultry and fish. The leaves can also be dried to use for flavouring when fresh celery is not available.

Trim the root end and then rub with a cut lemon or a little vinegar to prevent discolouration. The ribs may be left together on the root, or separated, washed, or brushed under running water. When separated, keep them in a plastic bag in the vegetable crisper of your refrigerator. When celery is cut into matchsticks for hors d'oeuvre or salad, keep them in a glass jar of water in the refrigerator.

TO COOK: Although celery is mostly eaten raw, it can be cooked whole, halved, diced, sliced or chopped. The most successful methods to follow when cooking are blanching, stir-frying, pan-cooking, steaming and steam-baking. Whatever the method, however, remember that celery, being mostly water, should be cooked in a very small amount of water or consommé, usually ¼ cup (60 ml) to each 2 cups (500 ml) of vegetable. The cooking time varies from 7 to 10 minutes.

Celery amandine in casserole

This is an attractive and tasty luncheon casserole. It is very nice served with curry-flavoured rice.

1 head of celery

2 eggs, well beaten

1 cup (250 ml) chicken stock or consommé

1 cup (250 ml) light cream

½ cup (125 ml) slivered blanched almonds

1 tbsp (15 ml) butter

Salt and pepper to taste

½ cup (125 ml) buttered crumbs

Clean the head of the celery by first cutting off the leafy part, then trimming the root end. Do not separate the ribs, but wash under running water while opening the ribs to let the water run through.

Shake out as much of the water as possible. Then, holding the head of celery together with one hand, start cutting from the top into thin slices. Or slice each rib individually as they fall, the pieces will be shaped like little crescents. Blanch for 3 minutes; freshen. Drain thoroughly.

Beat together the eggs, stock or consommé, and the cream. Brown the slivered almonds in the butter over medium heat. Add these to the egg mixture. Add salt and pepper to taste.

Place the drained celery in a buttered casserole and pour the almond mixture on top. Sprinkle with the buttered crumbs. Bake at 350°F (180°C) for 30 minutes. Makes 4 servings.

Fennel

Fennel is a very aromatic plant with a bulbous base. It looks like a short, fat head of celery. The fleshy ribs, especially the bulbous part, are edible raw or cooked following any of the recipes given for celery. The feathery leaves can be used as an herb and the seeds as a spice. If you want more information, you will find it in the chapter on herbs and spices, Vol. I.

You will find superlative food in London at The Ivy Restaurant, with its dark wood panelling and its superior service. Scottish smoked salmon with a little terrine of wonderful potted baby shrimps; one spreads the shrimp mixture on top of the salmon. It's delicious. Another smoked salmon dish the Ivye serves is Smoked Salmon Celery. This is an elegant way to use ends of smoked salmon that cannot be cut into thin slices.

The Ivy smoked salmon celery

1 heart of green or Pascal celery

2 tbsp (30 ml) unsalted butter

¼ tsp (1 ml) curry powder

⅓ cup (80 ml) chicken consommé

Pepper to taste

¼ cup (60 ml) chopped smoked salmon

½ cup (125 ml) grated Swiss cheese

1 tsp (5 ml) butter

1 tsp (5 ml) flour

⅓ cup (80 ml) clam juice

Chopped parsley

Clean the celery and cut into thin crescent-shaped slices. There should be about 2 cups (500 ml) of this.

Melt the butter and stir in the curry powder. Mix for a second or two into the hot butter, then add the celery and stir over high heat until it is well coated with the butter. Add the consommé and pepper to taste, but no salt because the salmon is salty. Boil, uncovered, until the celery is semi-tender, usually 5 to 7 minutes. Strain, reserving the liquid. Place the celery in a well-buttered casserole. Stir the salmon into the celery. Sprinkle the cheese on top. Bake in a preheated 425°F (220°C) oven for 10 minutes.

Use the reserved cooking liquid to make a sauce to serve with the casserole. Melt the teaspoon of butter and add the flour; stir well. Add the reserved liquid and the clam juice. Stir until smooth, creamy and light. Season to taste. Add a bit of freshly chopped parsley. Makes 4 servings.

SEASONAL TREASURES

Today, most vegetables can be found in markets all year long, although they are more plentiful and cheaper during their natural seasons. Nothing can replace the flavour of a fresh vegetable in its own proper season. Out-of-season vegetables — frozen asparagus or hot-house tomatoes, for instance — are not like the seasonal vegetables in appearance, taste or texture.

Asparagus

A plant of the lily-of-the-valley family, asparagus comes with the first breath of spring and is considered a luxury. In France, asparagus is often served as an hors d'oeuvre. When cooked, it is drained and presented on a folded white napkin, with an individual bowl of hollandaise sauce into which it is dipped. On other occasions, asparagus usually is served as a separate course, to be savoured without distraction.

TO PREPARE: Snap off the tough lower portion of the stalk; hold the vegetable with both hands and bend gently to find the place where the tough portion ends. Even if you wish to have them all the same length for the sake of appearance, snap them first, then place the tips evenly together and cut the ends level with each other.

Don't discard the tough ends. Wash them and simmer in a small amount of water, covered, for 1 hour. Then strain the liquid and use it for sauces and soups.

Thoroughly rinse the trimmed asparagus under running cold water; sand often accumulates in the small scales. Do not let asparagus soak in water, however. When cleaned ahead of time, wrap the washed stalks in absorbent paper or cloth and refrigerate in the vegetable crisper until ready to use.

TO COOK: A few methods can be used. First, asparagus can be tied together in convenient bunches, or the stalks can be cooked loose. They can be cooked standing upright in a deep pan with a few inches of water in the bottom, but this usually discolours part of the stem.

The easiest way is pan-cooking. They will cook in 8 to 12 minutes, depending on their size and how tender you wish them to be.

When they are cut into 1- or 2-inch (2.5 to 5 cm) lengths, cook them by the stir-fry method. It won't take longer than 5 minutes. It is a good idea to cut them this way when 1 pound (500 gr) of asparagus must serve four as a vegetable dish.

When they are to be served cold or as part of a salad, cook them by the professional method of blanching and freshening.

TO SERVE: Melted butter and lemon juice or a hollandaise or *maltaise* sauce are the best.

Asparagus is also delicious topped with small bread croutons fried in butter and mixed with a grated hard-cooked egg.

To serve as an entrée or a luncheon dish, cook, then cool to room temperature. Pour French dressing on top and then sprinkle with grated hard-cooked eggs, capers and a dash of grated nutmeg.

The clever Roman chef Sabatini created this asparagus dish with a very special sauce. It makes a delightful luncheon entrée.

Asparagus Sabatini

3 lb (1.5 kg) fresh asparagus

⅔ cup (160 ml) heavy cream

¼ tsp (1 ml) grated nutmeg

3 tbsp (50 ml) melted butter

⅓ cup (80 ml) grated Parmesan cheese

Clean the asparagus and tie into 6 or 8 bunches. Blanch for 10 to 12 minutes. To make the sauce, whip the cream and add the rest of the ingredients. Drain the asparagus well, then place each bundle on a hot plate. Snip and discard the strings. Fan the stalks out so the points are at the edge of the plate. Pour sauce on the stalks, leaving the points uncovered. Makes 6 to 8 servings.

Corn

Before the white man came to North America, Indians were growing corn as their basic crop all over the continent. Perhaps it is because corn can be canned and frozen with little loss of flavour that it remains a constant staple in our diet.

The summer sweet corn on the cob must be garden fresh to be tender and moist; once picked, corn quickly loses its sweetness and moisture. Corn is at its very best when you can go into a garden, gather it fresh and cook and eat it immediately.

TO PREPARE: Remove husks and all shreds of silk; or remove outside leaves of the husks, separate the remaining leaves from the top, remove all shreds of silk, and then close the leaves again.

TO COOK: Even if you cook corn the moment after it is picked, as it should be cooked, you can very easily ruin it by overcooking. Use a large saucepan. Put enough water to cover the bottom, about 1 inch (2.5 cm) in a pot large enough to hold all the corn. Add 1 cup (250 ml) of milk and 1 tablespoon (15 ml) sugar. Above all, no salt. Bring to a boil, then place the corn in the pot. Cover tightly and steam for 8 to 10 minutes over medium heat. It is the steam that cooks the corn. **O——⚡** Cooking corn with some of the husk left on increases the flavour.

Leftover corn on the cob does not reheat well, but you can cut the kernels from the cobs and reheat them with a little milk and a piece of butter.

The corn kernels can be cut from the cob before cooking. Do this with a sharp knife. Sauté the kernels in a small amount of butter for a few minutes and serve. You can also heat the kernels in the top part of a double boiler with a few spoonfuls (15 to 50 ml) of milk or cream for 20 minutes.

Indian-style corn

This recipe comes from a Canadian trapper. Try it at your next brunch.

1 lb (500 gr) sausages or bacon

1 large onion, chopped

6 eggs

12 ears of corn and ½ cup (125 ml) light cream or 1 can (about 1 pound/500 gr) cream-style corn

Place the sausages or bacon in a cold frying pan without any fat. Brown over medium-low heat until done; do not overcook. Remove some of the fat as it accumulates. When the sausages or bacon are cooked, set aside in a warm place. Keep about ⅓ cup (80 ml) of the fat in the pan and pour off the rest. Add the onion and fry until golden brown, stirring often.

Beat the eggs lightly. If you use fresh corn cut from the cobs, cook in the cream for 8 minutes, then add to the eggs. If you are using canned corn, add it to the eggs.

Add the corn and eggs to the fried onion. Cut each sausage into 4 pieces, or crumble the bacon, and add to the eggs and corn. Then scramble the whole mixture together. Season and serve. Makes about 6 servings.

Cucumbers

Cucumbers belong to the large gourd family that includes melons and vegetable marrows.

TO PREPARE: Any recipe used to cook squash, gourds or zucchini can be used for cucumbers. They can be salted, drained and cooked; or simply cut into thick slices, blanched for 5 minutes, and freshened; or steam-baked. I think they are at their best when stir-fried.

Cucumbers can also be used uncooked for flavour and texture in the same way as celery.

They are a summer treat when sliced and fried in butter, especially when served with steak.

Eggplant

Eggplant belongs to the potato family. It is a colourful, beautiful vegetable. Eggplant varies from the size and length of cucumbers or to the size of pineapples. Choose an eggplant heavy for its size, with a fresh, shining, purple skin. They are available all year, but are at their best during the late summer and early fall.

TO PREPARE: Eggplant can be cooked whole, or peeled and sliced or cubed before cooking. Remove the leaves and stem end.

TO COOK: To bake unpeeled, whole or halved, wash and dry the eggplant. Cut lengthwise into halves. Cut the flesh side with deep crisscross gashes over the entire surface, then butter the top. Set the pieces on a pan and bake in a 350°F (180°C) oven for 30 minutes.

Another method of baking is to place the whole eggplant on a baking sheet and bake in a 400°F (200°C) oven for 1 hour, or until the eggplant has a collapsed appearance. Then remove the skin. Mash the flesh with butter, lots of chopped fresh parsley, and the juice of 1 lemon. Add salt and pepper to taste.

To broil eggplant, wash, but do not peel. Cut into round slices ½ an inch (1.25 cm) thick. Spread with soft butter on both sides. Broil 4 inches (10 cm) from the source of heat for 5 minutes on each side. It is necessary to turn it only once.

Slices of eggplant can also be baked. Place unpeeled slices on a generously buttered baking sheet. Butter the tops of the slices with soft butter and sprinkle with salt and pepper to taste. Bake in a preheated 400°F (200°C) oven for 15 to 20 minutes. Do not turn.

Spanish cucumbers

In winter, you can substitute zucchini for the cucumber. Serve with boiled rice and chops.

3 medium-sized cucumbers

3 tbsp (50 ml) salad oil

1 large onion, chopped

3 tomatoes, diced, or 1 tbsp (15 ml) tomato paste

½ cup (125 ml) chopped olives

2 tbsp (30 ml) chopped fresh dill or 1 tsp (5 ml) dill seeds

¼ cup (60 ml) chicken stock or consommé

Garlic powder to taste

Salt and pepper to taste

Pare and quarter the cucumbers. Remove the seeds and cut each quarter into 3 or 4 sticks.

Heat the oil in a frying pan and add the onion; fry until light brown here and there. Add the tomatoes or tomato paste, the olives, dill, stock or consommé, and the cucumbers. Stir gently until the mixture is boiling. Add garlic powder and salt and pepper to taste. Boil gently, uncovered, for about 10 minutes, or until the mixture forms a sauce around the cucumbers. Serve. Makes about 6 servings.

Finnish cucumber salad

Finnish cooks combine sugar and herbs with cucumbers to achieve an unusual flavour. This salad is a classic of their cuisine.

4 medium-sized cucumbers

1 tbsp (15 ml) minced fresh or dried dill

½ cup (125 ml) cider vinegar or white wine

½ cup (125 ml) water

3 tbsp (50 ml) sugar

1 tsp (5 ml) salt

2 tbsp (30 ml) salad oil

Peel the cucumbers and slice paper-thin. Arrange attractively in a fairly shallow glass dish or bowl. Sprinkle all over with the minced dill. Stir together the vinegar or wine, the water, sugar, salt and salad oil; pour over the cucumbers. Do not stir. Cover and refrigerate for at least 2 hours, if possible 4 hours, to allow the flavours to blend. Serve without stirring. Makes 6 to 8 servings.

Cucumber and yogurt salad

Yogurt and cucumber have a natural affinity. When cucumbers are to be served with fish, Greek cooks replace the yogurt with thick commercial sour cream. Both are equally good. I often serve this as a luncheon dish in a nest of cottage cheese.

4 medium-sized slender cucumbers

1 tsp (5 ml) salt

1 cup (250 ml) yogurt

1½ tsp (7 ml) cider vinegar

1 garlic clove, crushed

¼ tsp (1 ml) dill seeds

2 tbsp (30 ml) minced fresh mint

Peel the cucumbers. Cut lengthwise into quarters and slice very thin. Then sprinkle with the salt, toss, and set aside.

Blend together the yogurt, vinegar, garlic and dill seeds. Stir into the cucumbers when ready to serve. Adjust seasoning to suit your own taste. To serve, place in a glass salad bowl and top with the minced mint. Makes about 6 servings.

Peppers

The pepper family is a big one that includes many varieties of large and small pods of varying "degrees of pungency" and different shapes and colours. The strong peppers — cayenne, tabasco and chili — are used in hot sauces and in dishes that should have bite. They are very different from the sweet, gentle pimiento, the pepper used to stuff olives and make paprika. Peppers are a good source of Vitamin C and also contain some Vitamin A and many minerals.

The pepper used as a vegetable by itself is the big, bell-shaped, sweet green pepper, which makes a handsome container for other foods and so is often stuffed. As a salad vegetable it is highly esteemed, and rings of green pepper make a nice crispy garnish. Fried green peppers are delicious as an accompaniment to meat.

TO PREPARE: Slice off the stem ends of peppers; remove the core and white ribs. Rinse to eliminate the seeds. The trimmed vegetables can be left whole, or cut into any shape you wish.

TO COOK: The professional method is the best for a plain cooked pepper: Blanch for 20 minutes, then freshen.

Pimientos

The pimiento is a bright red thick-walled pepper. It is sold packed in cans or jars; the outer skin has been removed by roasting, in the way described for the Green-Pepper Appetizer. Pimientos have good nutritional value, like other peppers, and have only 7 calories. This is a good vegetable to know because it can be used in place of fresh red peppers, which are seasonal and expensive, and in place of tomatoes when you want a red garnish for winter foods. They come whole, sliced and sometimes chopped.

An open jar of pimientos will keep in the refrigerator with a bit of oil on top for a week to 10 days. Pimientos, frozen in their own juice, will keep for 6 to 8 months. They thaw very fast when needed, or can be added still frozen to a hot liquid.

This wonderful vegetable mixture comes from the French Riviera. Serve it cold as an entrée, or make a meal of it with hot crusty bread and a bottle of red wine. This recipe comes from an old French cookbook. I have not found one to equal it. Ratatouille will keep in perfect condition, covered and refrigerated, for 8 to 15 days.

Ratatouille niçoise

4 medium-sized tomatoes, peeled and sliced

3 green zucchini, unpeeled and sliced

1 medium-sized eggplant, peeled and diced

2 onions, sliced

2 garlic cloves, chopped fine

2 green peppers, cleaned and sliced

½ tsp (2 ml) sugar

¾ cup (200 ml) olive oil

Salt and pepper to taste

¼ tsp (1 ml) dried thyme

Juice of 1 lemon

First prepare all the vegetables and the garlic. Place them separately on a large platter. Sprinkle the sugar on the tomatoes.

Heat ½ cup (125 ml) of the oil in a heavy metal saucepan over high heat. Then add the vegetables in the following order: add the onions and brown lightly; add the eggplant and cook, stirring, for about 3 minutes, or until slightly softened; add the tomatoes and crush into the mixture with a wooden spoon, stirring and blending for another 3 minutes; add the zucchini, the garlic and the green peppers; stir until well mixed.

Then cook the whole over high heat for a few minutes, stirring most of the time. Season with salt and pepper to taste. Add the thyme. Then cook, uncovered, over low heat for about 1 hour, stirring once in a while. By that time the mixture should have the texture of a thick tomato sauce. Pour into a covered dish and refrigerate for 10 to 12 hours.

Before serving, stir in the remaining oil and the lemon juice. Makes 6 to 8 servings.

Tomatoes

The tomato was avoided for centuries because it belongs to the same family as nightshade. Only in this century has it become one of our most popular vegetables. Cooking with tomatoes, or just eating a fully ripe tomato, is something very special when this vegetable is in its peak season.

The tomato is another of those versatile vegetables that can turn up in dozens of different forms — transformed into a spicy red sauce for pasta, in a mild parsleyed scalloped English dish, broiled or baked, as a filling for a sandwich along with crisp lettuce and tangy mayonnaise, or in a hundred and one other guises.

At the height of their season, tomatoes are so plentiful we are almost staggered by their abundance. In the past, preserving the bounty for off-season meant endless canning, infinite processing, and an all-pervading, overpowering smell of steaming tomatoes throughout the house. Today we can enjoy them fresh when they are at their peak, then depend for the rest of the year on commercially canned tomatoes, or use fairly fresh but somewhat expensive out-of-season ones.

TO PREPARE: To peel tomatoes, place them in a bowl and pour boiling water over them. Let stand for 2 minutes, then drain off the water and place the tomatoes in a bowl of cold water. The peel then comes off easily. Start peeling from the blossom end.

To peel only 1 or 2 tomatoes, spear on the tip of a fork and hold over direct heat until the skin blisters here and there. Then peel.

To remove some of the acidity from tomatoes, remove the seeds by pressing the tomato gently in the hand, holding the cut side down. **0—⚷** When cooking tomatoes, always add 1 teaspoon (5 ml) sugar for each 4 tomatoes. It doesn't make them sweet, but brings out their flavour and colour. **0—⚷** Always keep ripe tomatoes refrigerated, but bring to room temperature when serving them raw. They have more flavour warm than cold.

Stuffed green peppers

This is a basic recipe for stuffed green peppers, which make a good luncheon dish. If you have no cooked meat, use minced raw meat; my favourite is lamb. Brown raw meat in butter before adding it to the other ingredients.

4 nicely shaped, squatty green peppers

Salt and pepper to taste

Savory or thyme or curry powder

1 cup (250 ml) cooked rice

1 cup (250 ml) ground cooked meat

1 tsp (5 ml) minced onion

Tomato sauce, mushroom soup, or gravy to moisten

Grated cheese

Cut the top off each pepper. Remove seeds. Place the peppers in a saucepan with ½ inch (1.25 cm) of boiling water. Cover tightly and steam for 5 minutes. Dust inside of peppers with salt and pepper and a little ground savory or thyme, or curry powder. Combine rice, cooked meat and onion, and enough sauce, soup or gravy to moisten the mixture. Fill the peppers with the meat mixture; top with cheese. Place in a pan with ½ inch (1.25 cm) of water on the bottom. Bake at 350°F (180°C) for 40 minutes. Serve with more of the sauce or gravy used to moisten the filling. Makes 4 servings.

Green-pepper appetizer

This delicious salad is very nice in the summer, served cold on a thick bed of sliced tomatoes. Use also as a dip with fingers of toasted French bread. Serve very cold with meat curry.

3 red or green peppers

Salt to taste

3 tbsp (50 ml) olive oil

½ cup (125 ml) yogurt

½ tsp (2 ml) curry powder

2 tbsp (30 ml) minced celery leaves

Roast the peppers over direct heat until the skins are blackened all over. Do this quickly, because the peppers themselves should not be really cooked. Turn them to roast evenly all over. Then wash off the skins under running cold water. Cut off the tops and remove cores and seeds. Slice the peppers into long shreds, sprinkle with salt, and pour the oil over them. Marinate 1 hour.

Put the peppers through a food chopper, or purée in a blender. Stir the purée into the yogurt along with the curry powder and fine-minced celery leaves. Makes about 1½ cups (375 ml) of salad or dip.

This soup is best made with sweet summer red tomatoes. A blender is a must for this recipe.

Finnish chilled tomato soup

4 medium-sized sweet red tomatoes

1 tsp (5 ml) sugar

2 cups (500 ml) cold buttermilk

¾ tsp (3 ml) salt

Fresh dill, minced

Chives, or minced green onions

Peel the tomatoes and cut into quarters. Place in a blender with the sugar. Cover and blend until smooth. Add the buttermilk and salt, and blend for 1 second; pour into a bowl. Add dill and chives or minced green onions to taste. Refrigerate for 1 hour. Serve in old-fashioned glasses with not buttered crackers and a pepper grinder. Makes 4 servings.

I have never tasted a better fresh tomato soup than this one, which was the delight of my childhood. My Aunt Amelia always used fresh basil to flavour the soup.

Aunt Amelia's tomato soup

24 medium-sized sweet red tomatoes

1 tbsp (15 ml) sugar

2 tbsp (30 ml) butter

1 onion, quartered

2 bay leaves

2 celery ribs with leaves

1 tsp (5 ml) minced fresh basil or crumbled dried basil

1 tsp (5 ml) salt

¼ tsp (1 ml) freshly ground pepper

3 tbsp (50 ml) minced fresh parsley

Juice of ½ a lemon

½ cup (125 ml) whipped cream

Cut the unpeeled tomatoes into quarters. Place in a heavy metal saucepan with the sugar, butter, onion, bay leaves, celery and basil. Cover and simmer over *low* heat for 30 minutes. Do not add water at any time. Pass through a food mill or a sieve. Put back in the saucepan and add the salt, pepper, parsley and lemon juice. Simmer for a few minutes. Adjust seasoning. Serve hot in cups, topped with a spoonful of whipped cream, slightly salted. Makes 8 or more servings.

Parmesan broiled tomatoes

Serve these tomatoes as a quick garnish with steak, hamburger or veal chops.

6 firm ripe tomatoes

Salt and pepper

Sugar

1 tbsp (15 ml) grated Parmesan cheese

1 tbsp (15 ml) butter

Halve tomatoes crosswise and sprinkle each half with salt, pepper and a good pinch of sugar. Top each with about ½ teaspoon (2 ml) Parmesan cheese and dot with ½ teaspoon (2 ml) butter. Broil at a distance of about 6 inches (15 cm) from the source of heat for 4 to 5 minutes. Makes 6 servings.

Variation: Cut tomatoes into 4 thick slices each. Sprinkle each slice with a little sugar and brush the tops with melted butter. Season with salt and a sprinkle of dried or ground basil. Put the slices under the broiler 4 inches (10 cm) from the source of heat and broil for 3 minutes. You can use this version with lamb or pork.

My husband's favourite baked tomatoes

Serve this dish for breakfast, lunch or light supper. It is wonderful in the morning with lots of crisp bacon and in the evening with a thick slice of broiled ham and chutney.

4 medium-sized tomatoes

Sugar to taste

½ cup (125 ml) sour cream

2 tbsp (30 ml) grated Cheddar cheese

½ tsp (2 ml) curry powder

Halve tomatoes crosswise. Squeeze a little to remove the juice and seeds that come out naturally. Sprinkle each half with a bit of sugar; use no salt or pepper.

Mix the sour cream, grated cheese, and curry powder until well blended. Cover the top of each tomato half with some of the mixture. Place tomatoes on a buttered pan and bake in a 350°F (180°C) oven for 15 to 20 minutes. Makes 4 servings.

This is a delicious salad to serve with an outdoor meal, and it takes only a few minutes to prepare.

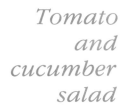

Tomato and cucumber salad

4 tomatoes, sliced

¼ cup (60 ml) salad oil

¼ cup (60 ml) cider or red-wine vinegar

1 tbsp (15 ml) chopped parsley

Fresh dill, minced or dried dill

3 green onions, chopped fine

1 small head of lettuce

2 cucumbers, peeled and sliced

Salt and pepper to taste.

Place the tomatoes in a bowl with the oil, vinegar, parsley, dill and green onions. Refrigerate for 1 to 2 hours. When ready to serve, shred the lettuce just as you would a cabbage, and add to the tomatoes with the cucumbers. Season with salt and pepper to taste. Toss lightly until well blended and serve. Makes 4 to 6 servings.

We treat some foods as vegetables although they are not true vegetables. Among these are mushrooms, which are fungi; chestnuts, which are nuts; bamboo shoots, which are the shoots of young trees; and water chestnuts, which are the fruit of a water plant.

Mushrooms

The mushroom is a flavourful food with great versatility.

A mushroom has no apparent leaves, blossoms or fruits. Indeed, it is not a true plant but a fungus. **0—** The mushroom itself is the fruit of the fungus and contains the spores or seeds.

Mushrooms come in all shapes and colours — some delicious, some deadly. Today, cultivated edible mushrooms are found in all supermarkets. If you want a bit of woodsy flavour with your cultivated fresh mushrooms, get an ounce or two of dried wild mushrooms, and add one or two, crushed, to the dish. These dried mushrooms come from all over the world — and they, too, are safe to eat. Dried mushrooms retain the unmistakable scent of their original habitat, a smell of the woods, the mountains or the fields.

Simply served, mushrooms are good for dieters because they are very low in calories.

Use mushrooms as soon as possible after buying them. Do not leave them exposed to sun or air. Refrigerate them, tightly shut in their container, as soon as you arrive home.

TO PREPARE: Cultivated fresh mushrooms need not be peeled. Cut off ¼ inch (6 mm) of the stem if it has turned brown. If it is white and clean, it does not have to be removed. Peeling the skin from the cap causes some loss of the finest flavour of the mushroom.

Never peel a mushroom that is to be broiled or pancooked, one that is to be cooked after slicing or one that is to be stuffed. Removing the skin weakens the structure of the mushroom. However, mushrooms can be peeled when they are to be used raw in a salad. But even then, it is not necessary to peel them if they are white and fresh.

Never throw away the mushroom stems or peelings. The stems can be used chopped in sauces, stuffings and soups. The peelings can be used to prepare a very tasty broth that will keep refrigerated for 2 weeks, or frozen for 6 months.

To wash mushrooms, place them in a colander and hold under warm, not hot, running water, tossing them about for 3 to 4 seconds. Then rinse them again under cold running water for about 2 seconds. Turn them onto absorbent paper and gently dry them. Too much washing causes dark browning of the mushrooms when cooking, just as energetic handling causes quick bruising. They are a delicate food and should be handled gently. Under no circumstances should they stand for any time after they are washed; wash them just before cooking, unless they are to be sautéed. For sautéing, wash them ahead and let them dry thoroughly.

Sautéed mushrooms

A perfect sautéed mushroom is delicious in both flavour and texture. These mushrooms make a perfect light lunch served on buttered toast with a dish of chutney and a green salad.

½ lb (250 gr) mushrooms

3 tbsp (50 ml) butter

Salt and freshly ground pepper to taste

Parsley or chives, minced

Clean the mushrooms, dry them thoroughly and cut them into thin slices.

Melt the butter in a heavy metal pan until it has a nutty brown colour. Add the mushrooms and cook, stirring constantly, over high heat for 2 to 3 minutes. Remove from the heat, add salt and pepper to taste. Sprinkle with parsley or chives or use tarragon or basil, dried or fresh instead. Serve as a side dish or on toast. Makes 2 servings.

Marinated mushrooms

You can vary this recipe to suit your purposes. In any version, it is delicious! The mushrooms are not cooked at all; the marinating mixture gives them a cooked texture.

¼ lb (125 gr) mushrooms

4 tbsp (60 ml) olive oil

2 tbsp (30 ml) cider vinegar or wine

½ tsp (2 ml) salt

⅛ tsp (0.5 ml) pepper

2 green onions, minced

Chop the stems and caps of the mushrooms very fine. Add the remaining ingredients. Mix together and let stand for 1 hour before using.

Here are some of the many ways these can be used:

O—🕱 Sprinkle them on salad greens instead of dressing; adjust seasoning; toss and serve.

O—🕱 Place on unbuttered rounds of French bread or toast; serve as appetizers.

O—🕱 Use as dressing for cold chicken, lobster or shrimp.

O—🕱 Add to the mixture 2 chopped hard-cooked eggs, 1 tablespoon (15 ml) capers, 1 minced pimiento; serve as a mushroom salad on lettuce leaves, or garnish with watercress.

O—🕱 Use as a filling for small sandwiches for afternoon tea.

Mushroom consommé

Make this from leftover mushroom stems and peelings. It will keep refrigerated for 2 weeks and frozen for 6 months. Use it to dilute canned cream of mushroom soup, or as the liquid in chicken or veal gravy, or to replace chicken stock or consommé in any mushroom recipe, or to make cream of mushroom soup.

To make the soup, make a cream sauce with 1 cup (250 ml) of the mushroom consommé and 1 cup (250 ml) light cream, then add a few sliced buttered mushrooms for garnish.

3 cups (750 ml) water
¼ tsp (1 ml) salt
1 small onion, halved
1 cup (250 ml) mushroom peelings or stems, or both.

Bring the water to a boil with the salt and onion. Add the mushroom peelings and stems. Cover and simmer for 30 minutes. Drain and set aside the liquid. Throw away the peels. Makes about 1½ cups (625 ml).

Note: Add 1 or 2 dried mushrooms of any type to the peelings and stems; it will greatly enhance the flavour. Or use the juice from canned mushrooms for part of the liquid instead of water.

This is another classic way to cook and serve mushrooms. A cup or two (250 to 500 ml) of diced cooked chicken, salmon, lobster or shrimp can be added to the sauce and served with rice or noodles for a whole meal.

Creamed mushrooms

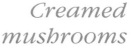

1 lb (500 gr) mushrooms

4 tbsp (60 ml) butter

1 garlic clove, minced

Salt and pepper to taste

½ cup (125 ml) flour

1 cup (250 ml) light cream

1 cup (250 ml) commercial sour cream

¼ tsp (1 ml) dried tarragon

¼ cup (60 ml) sherry (optional)

Parsley, for garnish

Wash the mushrooms and remove the stems from the caps. Leave the caps whole but mince the stems. Melt 3 tablespoons (50 ml) of the butter. Add the garlic. Brown the whole mushroom caps with the garlic over high heat, stirring constantly. Add the minced stems, brown quickly, and remove from the heat. Add salt and pepper to taste.

Melt the remaining butter in a saucepan. Add the flour and cream. Blend together thoroughly and cook over low heat, stirring, until the sauce is creamy. Add the sour cream and the tarragon. Then heat but do not boil.

Finally, add the browned mushrooms and the sherry. Simmer for a few minutes, but do not boil. Adjust seasoning. Serve with parsley sprigs, or sprinkled with minced parsley. Makes 4 servings.

Pickled mushrooms

Pickled mushrooms keep indefinitely under refrigeration. They can be served as an appetizer, as a condiment with fish or duck, or as a garnish to vegetables or a rice salad.

3 lb (1.5 kg) small button mushrooms

Cider vinegar

1 tsp (5 ml) salt

Salad oil

1 tbsp (15 ml) minced pickling spices or 1 tbsp (15 ml) sliced peeled fresh gingerroot

Rinse whole unpeeled mushrooms in a colander under warm, then cold water. Place in a saucepan and cover with half cider vinegar, half water; measure 1 cup (250 ml) of each, then add as needed. Add the salt. Boil for 15 minutes. Drain the cooking liquid into another pan. Cool the mushrooms.

Mix 1 cup (250 ml) cider vinegar with 1 cup (250 ml) salad oil and the spices. Pour the reserved cooking liquid into sterilized jars until they are one fourth filled. Add the cooled mushrooms, packing them down. If you are using gingerroot instead of pickling spices, put 1 slice in the top of each jar. Fill the jars to overflowing with the oil and vinegar mixture; do this with each jar placed on a plate. Cover and refrigerate.

Mushrooms Verona

This dish can be served as a main dish or as a vegetable with veal or lamb chops.

2 lb (1 kg) fresh spinach

2 tbsp (30 ml) butter

2 medium-sized onions, minced

¼ lb (125 gr) mushrooms, sliced thin

2 tbsp (30 ml) flour

¾ cup (200 ml) milk or chicken stock

⅛ tsp (0.5 ml) ground basil

Pinch of grated nutmeg

Salt and pepper to taste

1 cup (250 ml) small bread cubes

1 tbsp (15 ml) butter, melted

Place the washed spinach in a saucepan without any water. Cover and cook over medium-high heat for 3 to 4 minutes. Drain in a sieve, pressing out as much water as possible. Place in a buttered shallow casserole.

Melt the 2 tablespoons (30 ml) butter in a frying pan. Add the onions and mushrooms and cook over high heat, stirring constantly, for 3 to 4 minutes. Add the flour. Stir until well mixed, then add the milk or stock and cook, stirring, until smooth and creamy. Add the basil, nutmeg, and salt and pepper to taste. Pour over the spinach. Mix together the bread cubes and the melted butter and arrange them over the casserole. Bake in a 350°F (180°C) oven for 20 to 25 minutes. Serve hot. Makes 4 servings.

Chestnuts

Although chestnuts are not vegetables but nuts, they are often used with vegetables or meat. They can be found fresh in the late autumn and winter.

One pound (500 gr) of chestnuts in the shell contains 30 to 40 chestnuts, depending on their size. One pound (500 gr) will yield 2 to 2½ cups (500 to 625 ml) cooked and peeled.

TO COOK: With a small pointed knife, peel off a tiny strip of shell from the flat side of each chestnut, or make an incision there. Then place the nuts in a pan of cold water, bring to a fast rolling boil, and boil for 1 minute. Remove from water and strip off the hard shell and the bitter brown skin covering the chestnut. The hotter the nuts are, the more easily the skin comes off.

You can also place the uncooked nuts in a 400°F (200°C) oven for 20 minutes, then peel them. Or they can be cooked in a corn popper over the fire and eaten hot with melted butter. This is a great winter treat.

After shelling and peeling, the chestnuts should be cooked in liquid — water, bouillon, or milk, depending on how you plan to use them — for 10 to 20 minutes, or until tender. For a purée, they must be very tender. They can be puréed by mashing, like potatoes, or put through a sieve or food mill. Add butter, cream or sour cream. Chestnut purée is excellent with turkey or duck.

Another way to prepare these popular nuts is described in the recipe for Brussels Sprouts and Chestnuts.

Bamboo shoots

Bamboo shoots, the ivory-coloured young shoots of an Oriental plant are used as a vegetable. Delicate and crisp, they are a familiar ingredient of Oriental food. They can be purchased fresh at Oriental food shops and are readily available in canned form at all supermarkets. The best are packed in water rather than in brine. They come whole, in chunks, or sliced.

Always rinse canned shoots before using them. If they are not all used, place what remains in a glass jar and cover with water. Cap tightly and keep refrigerated. Change the water every day and they will keep for a few weeks.

TO COOK: Bamboo shoots can be added to any stirfried vegetable. They can replace celery, green peppers, green beans or carrots as a garnish or in a salad, and can be mixed with other vegetables.

1½ to 2 cups (325 to 500 ml) bamboo shoots

Salad oil

1 tbsp (15 ml) cornstarch

1 tsp (5 ml) sugar

½ cup (125 ml) water

(15 ml) soy sauce

Cut the bamboo shoots into matchsticks, the same as for French fried potatoes. Dry in paper towels. Place 1 inch (2.5 cm) of salad oil in a large frying pan and heat. Add the bamboo shoots and fry, stirring constantly, until they are a pale golden colour. Drain on absorbent paper.

Remove the used oil from the pan and heat 2 tablespoons (30 ml) of fresh salad oil. Blend the cornstarch, sugar and cold water. Place the bamboo shoots in the fresh hot oil and stir-fry just long enough to warm them. Add the soy sauce. Stir well and pour in the cornstarch mixture. Stir until thick. Serve at once. Makes 4 servings.

Stir-fried bamboo shoots

Water chestnuts

Water chestnuts add crisp texture and subtle flavour to Oriental cooking. This small nutlike fruit has an icy crunch, a moist and tender brittleness and a sweet and clear flavour.

You will find peeled whole water chestnuts at Oriental grocers, canned ones at your supermarket. Fresh water chestnuts have a tough brown skin that is peeled off before they are used. To store, cover fresh water chestnuts — and canned ones that have been opened —

with water, and refrigerate. Use fresh and canned water chestnuts interchangeably in recipes.

Try water chestnuts first in Chinese or Japanese preparations. Chop them along with pork, chicken or seafood, and with mushrooms and green onions, to make minced fillings for won ton and egg roll. Drop water chestnuts into soups and broths; slice or sliver them into meat, poultry and seafood specialties, and add them to crisp-cooked vegetables.

Rumaki

This is a famous hors d'oeuvre. Use your hibachi, barbecue or oven broiler.

½ lb (250 gr) chicken livers

¼ cup (60 ml) soy sauce

1 garlic clove, minced

1 5-oz (142 gr) can water chestnuts, drained

15 slices of bacon

Cut each chicken liver into 3 pieces. Marinate the chicken liver pieces in the soy sauce and garlic at room tempera-

ture for 3 hours, or in the refrigerator overnight.

Cut each water chestnut into 3 pieces. Cut the bacon slices into halves. Wrap a piece of water chestnut and a piece of chicken liver with a half-slice of bacon. Secure with a food pick. Place on a wire rack set over a shallow pan and bake in a hot oven, 425°F (220°C) or on a grill over charcoal. Cook, turning occasionally until the bacon is crisp, about 25 minutes. Makes about 30.

Chicken salad Oriental

Ginger adds a touch of the Orient to this favourite.

3 cups (750 ml) diced cooked chicken

1 cup (250 ml) diced celery

2 tbsp (30 ml) sliced green onions or shallots

1 5-oz (142 gr) can water chestnuts, drained

¾ cup (190 ml) commercial sour cream

1 tsp (5 ml) ground ginger

½ tsp (2 ml) salt

Dash of pepper

Salad greens

¼ cup (60 ml) slivered almonds, toasted

Combine the chicken, celery and onions. Slice the water chestnuts and add them. Chill. Blend sour cream, ginger, salt and pepper. Add to the chicken mixture and toss lightly. Serve on crisp greens. Sprinkle with toasted almonds. Makes 6 servings.

CHAPTER 14

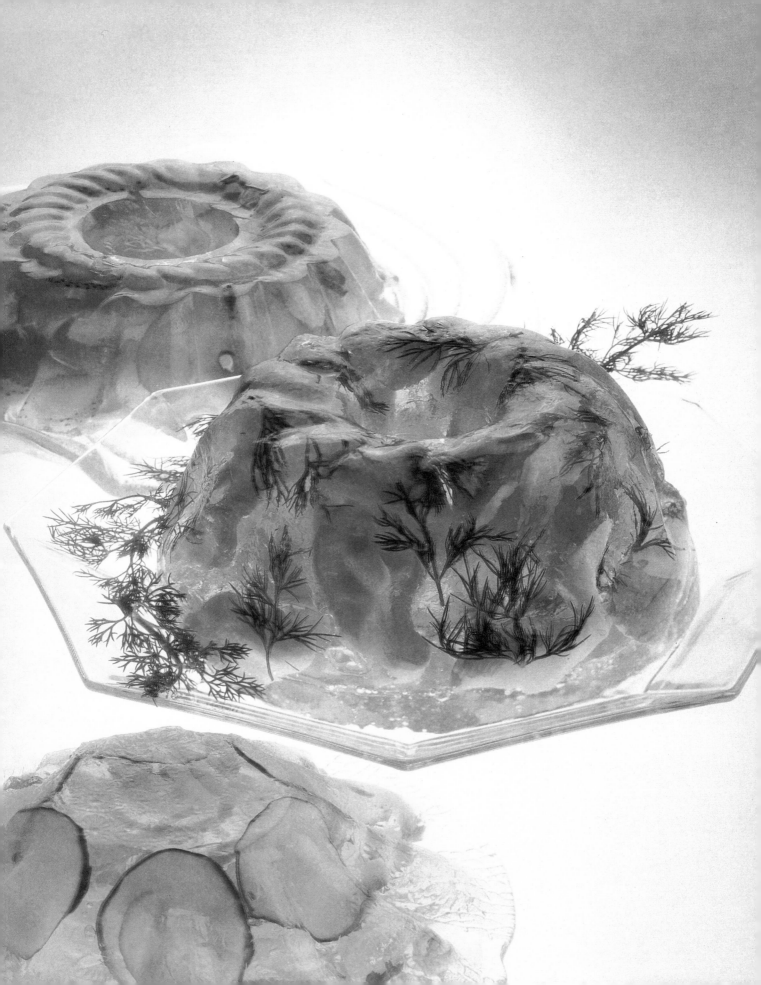

Aspics and jellied-base foods

A N ASPIC is a jelly. It can be flavoured and served by itself, or it can contain pieces of meat, poultry, game, fish, vegetables, fruits or a mixture of several foods. It can be a main course, an entrée, a salad course, a garnish or a dessert. Either freshly cooked or leftover food can be added to the gelatin. Sweet aspics or sweet gelatins are for desserts. An aspic has form, shape and sparkle. With aspic you can be inventive, playing with colour and flavour combinations, deciding what tastes and textures to bring together.

A mousse has whipped cream beaten into the gelatin when it is partly set.

A snow is a gelatin mixture that has egg whites, beaten until light and fluffy, added to it when the gelatin is partly set. This is put into a mold and refrigerated until set.

A chiffon is a gelatin mixture made with egg yolks, cooked and cooled, then mixed with beaten egg whites.

When a white sauce is added to a partly set gelatin mixture, it becomes a white *chaud-froid,* a jellied sauce to be spread on cold roast chicken, turkey, or ham, for a fancy buffet dish.

Once the basic method of making aspic jelly is understood, it is easy to transform a gelatin mixture into any of its variations.

Few people can spare the many hours of tedious work required to produce a tasty jelly out of calf's feet, calf's head, veal bones, fish bones or other gelatin-bearing foods. Happily, it is not necessary to do so, because you can achieve perfect success with high-quality unflavoured gelatin that can be kept in the kitchen cupboard all year round. Well-seasoned canned consommés can also be used instead of stock. Many liquids can be used and many can be combined. For example, a mixture of white wine and clam juice makes a delectable jelly to use on salmon, shrimp and sole. Red wine and tomato juice are ideal with pink slices of roast beef or lamb. Consommé and orange juice can be served with duck or game. And these are but a few of the many types of aspic you can make. Blended apple juice can replace wine, and lime or lemon juice will give the necessary zip.

WHAT MOLDS TO USE

Many utensils can serve as molds for gelatin dishes — custard cups, teacups, demitasses, muffin tins, large or individual ring molds, ice-cube trays, coffee cans, mixing bowls, baking pans, even paper cups. Metal is the easiest from which to unmold.

If a recipe calls for a 6-cup (1.5 L) ring mold and you do not have one, you can use a 6-cup (1.5 L) bowl or loaf pan, or even an 8-inch-square (20 cm x 20 cm) pan; once the mixture in the pan is set, cut the jelly into squares rather than unmolding it.

0—⚷ Professionals always rub molds with colourless, tasteless, sweet almond oil, which can be purchased at a drugstore. This enables you to unmold the aspic very easily and it adds a shiny film to the top of the aspic.

To unmold

Loosen the set aspic from the mold by following along the edge with the tip of a paring knife. For small molds this may be enough to loosen the jelly, which can be gently shaken out onto individual plates.

For a large mold, begin by running cold water over the dish you plan to use for serving the aspic. Place the dish face down on top of the mold and turn them over, holding them tightly together. Shake gently, holding the dish tightly to the mold. When the aspic settles onto the dish, carefully lift off the mold. **0—⚷** If the aspic is not centred on the serving dish, the cold water on the dish makes it easy to slide it into place. If you must touch the unmolded aspic, make sure to do it with wet hands.

If the aspic does not shake loose, it may be necessary to wrap the outside of the mold with a towel wrung out in hot water. Or the mold can be dipped into hot water for a few seconds, but do this with great care, because too long a dip will cause the jelly to melt. Then proceed to unmold as described.

ASPIC MATHEMATICS

One envelope of unflavoured gelatin equals about 1 tablespoon (15 ml), and it will set 1¾ to 2 cups (450 ml to 500 ml) of liquid.

Soften 1 envelope of gelatin by sprinkling it on ½ cup (125 ml) of whatever cold liquid is called for in the recipe. Let it stand for 5 minutes.

If a recipe calls for 1 tablespoon (15 ml) or more of sugar, it is not necessary to soften the gelatin in liquid. Just mix the gelatin with the sugar and then add the liquid.

When the gelatin has been softened in the liquid, place over very low heat and stir until it is dissolved. Remove from heat and add the remaining liquid called for in the recipe. Stir until well mixed, then pour into the mold.

An aspic gelatin will take 3 to 5 hours to set in the refrigerator.

0—⚷ Acid is important for gelatin dishes. Use fresh lemon or lime juice, or wine or cider vinegar. It helps to tenderize the gelatin. Use 2 tablespoons (30 ml) acid for 1 cup (250 ml) liquid; measure carefully, as too much acid can prevent setting.

0—⚷ To all commercial flavoured gelatin, add the juice of 1 orange, lemon or lime, counting it as part of the liquid required. It will give the aspic a most interesting flavour.

CHILLING ASPIC MIXTURES

When other ingredients are to be added to an aspic — meat, vegetables, fish or fruit — the basic jelly mixture must be chilled first. (And, of course, the ingredients you add must also be cold). Different degrees of chilling are used, depending on the type of gelatin mixture being prepared.

For simple aspic to be garnished, or for a chiffon mixture: Chill until the mixture pours from a spoon in an unbroken stream, or until chilled to the consistency of unbeaten egg white.

For whips and snows: Chill until the mixture dribbles unevenly from a spoon, or to a consistency thicker than unbeaten egg white.

For chaud-froid and whipped-cream mousse: Chill until the mixture is thick enough to mound slightly when dropped from a spoon.

To quick-chill a gelatin base: Set the container with the gelatin mixture in a bowl filled with ice cubes or crushed ice and stir until the gelatin mixture thickens to the desired consistency. A second method is to place the container in a freezer compartment for about 10 minutes. Stir occasionally so that it will chill evenly. The first method is preferred because the mixture chills more evenly and has a better texture.

If the mixture becomes too solid, you can remelt it over boiling water and chill it again to the required consistency.

To master aspic gelatin, practice with the following recipes, which illustrate various types of aspic. Then experiment with different liquids, ingredients and flavourings to suit your taste.

Basic aspic

This simple type of aspic is most professional looking when well done. Vary the liquid and the garnish and mold individually or make into one fancy mold. Use as entrée, main dish, or canapés.

1 envelope unflavoured gelatin

1 10½-oz (312 gr) can condensed beef or chicken broth, undiluted

½ cup (125 ml) Madeira, sherry or red wine or ¼ cup (60 ml) each of lemon juice and water

8 to 10 drops of hot-pepper sauce

Sweet almond oil

Spinkle the gelatin over 1 cup (250 ml) of the beef broth and let stand for 5 minutes to soften. Place over low heat and stir until gelatin is dissolved. Remove from heat and stir in remaining liquid and the pepper sauce. Stir until well blended. Oil a mold with sweet almond oil and pour in the mixture. Garnish to your taste and chill. Makes about 4 servings.

Jellied canapés

Make basic aspic. To make jellied canapés, rub an 8-inch-square (20 cm x 20 cm) pan with sweet almond oil and pour half the mixture into it. Chill in the refrigerator until almost firm; 20 to 30 minutes. Chill the rest of the mixture in another container until it is somewhat thickened but not set.

Slice or halve 6 hard-cooked eggs. Arrange the slices or halves 1 inch (2.5 cm) apart on top of the set jelly. Spoon on the remaining soft jelly, keeping eggs in place and well covered with aspic jelly. Chill until firm.

To serve, prepare 12 rounds of toasted bread. Spread with a savoury paste, such as liver or lobster. Cut the aspic with a round cookie cutter, to have a neat circle of set aspic around each egg; cut straight through to the bottom of the pan. Place the aspic rounds on the prepared toast rounds.

Chop the aspic remaining in the pan into small pieces with a knife, and use these shining bits to garnish the serving platter of canapés. Makes 12 canapés.

Tomato vegetable aspic

This recipe can serve as a pattern for any preparation that adds vegetable, fish or meat to gelatin base. Again, liquid and garnish can be varied in many ways.

1 envelope unflavoured gelatin

1 ¾ cups (450 ml) tomato juice

¼ tsp (1 ml) salt

½ tsp (2 ml) sugar

½ tsp (2 ml) crumbled dried basil or curry powder

Juice of 1 lemon

1 tsp (5 ml) Worcestershire sauce

Few drops of hot-pepper sauce

1 cup (250 ml) fine-shredded cabbage

½ cup (125 ml) diced celery

¼ cup (50 ml) diced green pepper

3 green onions, finely chopped

Sprinkle the gelatin on top of ½ cup (125 ml) of the tomato juice. Let stand for 5 minutes. Place over very low heat and stir until gelatin is dissolved. Remove from heat and stir in remaining tomato juice, the salt, sugar, basil or curry powder, lemon juice, Worcestershire sauce, and pepper sauce. Stir until well blended. Refrigerate until the mixture has the consistency of unbeaten egg white.

Then fold in the cabbage, celery, green pepper and green onions. The vegetables will stay suspended in the jelly because it is partly set. Turn the mixture into a well-oiled 3-cup (750 ml) mold. Chill until firm. Unmold and garnish to taste. Makes 4 servings.

Meat or fish aspic

Proceed in the same manner, substituting diced cooked meat or fish for some or all of the vegetables.

Concord grape whip

Whips can be made with many fruits. This is my favourite for flavour and texture.

1 tbsp (15 ml) unflavoured gelatin

1 ¾ cups (450 ml) grape juice

½ cup (125 ml) sugar

2 tbsp (30 ml) lemon juice

¾ cup (200 ml) evaporated milk or heavy cream, chilled

½ cup (125 ml) instant dry-milk powder

Soak the gelatin in ½ cup (125 ml) of the grape juice for 5 minutes. Dissolve over low heat. Add the sugar, lemon juice and remaining grape juice. Chill until the gelatin is half set.

Beat the chilled evaporated milk or heavy cream until stiff. Add the powdered milk to the whipped milk or cream and beat lightly. Beat the half-set jelly until foamy and fold in the beaten cream. Pour into a ring mold and refrigerate until set. Makes about 6 servings.

Chicken mousse

Any cooked meat or seafood can be used instead of chicken. An haute cuisine *recipe can be prepared with white Bordeaux, Rhine or Moselle wine, fresh-cooked lobster and diced raw mushrooms. Garnish the top with a few spoonfuls of caviar.*

1 envelope unflavoured gelatin

1½ cups (375 ml) chicken consommé or 1 cup (250 ml) dry white wine and ½ cup (125 ml) chicken consommé

1 small white onion, grated

¼ tsp (1 ml) crumbled dried tarragon

1 cup (250 ml) heavy cream

1½ cups (375 ml) diced cooked chicken

2 tbsp (30 ml) chopped celery

1 tbsp (15 ml) minced green or black olives

Sprinkle the gelatin on ½ cup (125 ml) of the chicken consommé. Let stand for 5 minutes. Place over low heat and stir until gelatin is dissolved. Then remove from heat and stir in the remaining chicken consommé, or wine and consommé, the grated onion, and the tarragon. Refrigerate until the mixture has the consistency of unbeaten egg white.

Then whip the cream and fold it into the gelatin mixture along with the chicken, celery and olives. Blend thoroughly. Turn into a well-oiled 4-cup (1 L) mold and refrigerate until firm. Unmold and garnish to taste. Makes 6 servings.

Chiffon aspic

Although a bit more cooking is involved in this type of aspic, it is easy to prepare. Fish and seafood are best for chiffon aspic. Use heavy or light cream instead of milk when a richer texture is desired.

1 envelope unflavoured gelatin

1¾ cup (450 ml) milk

2 eggs, separated

1 tsp (5 ml) salt

Pinch of white pepper

1 tsp (5 ml) prepared French mustard

2 tsp (10 ml) prepared horseradish

1 cup (250 ml) crabmeat, fresh, frozen or canned

Juice of 1 lemon

½ cup (125 ml) diced celery (optional)

2 to 4 tbsp (30 to 60 ml) finely chopped pimiento

Sprinkle the gelatin into ½ cup (125 ml) of the milk and let stand for 5 minutes. Beat the egg yolks and add the remaining milk and the salt and pepper. Place over low heat. When hot, add the softened gelatin and stir constantly over low heat until the gelatin is dissolved, about 5 minutes. Do not let the mixture boil. Chill to the consistency of unbeaten egg white.

In the meantime, combine in a bowl the remaining ingredients except the egg whites. Beat the egg whites until stiff but not dry. Thoroughly fold the crabmeat mixture and the beaten egg whites into the chilled jelly. Turn into a well-oiled 3-cup (750 ml) ring mold or individual molds. Chill until firm. Unmold and garnish to taste. Makes 4 servings.

Sweet aspic dessert

The method used for this kind of aspic is the same as that used for Tomato Vegetable Aspic.

Remember, when sugar is used with gelatin, you can omit softening the gelatin in cold liquid. Simply combine unflavoured gelatin with the sugar. 0—x However, there is one problem when using sugar with gelatin: more than 3 tablespoons (50 ml) of sugar to 1 cup (250 ml) of liquid will keep the gelatin from setting, so when you are experimenting and inventing your own combinations of ingredients, be sure to keep the proper proportion of sugar to liquid.

The liquid used can be varied infinitely — strong coffee, tea, fresh fruit juice, sweet wine, and so on. The liquid can be tinted by adding vegetable colouring.

As for the fruit, you can use what you like with this one precaution: If fresh or frozen pineapple is used, boil it in syrup for 2 minutes before adding it to the gelatin mixture, as fresh pineapple contains an enzyme that prevents gelatin from setting.

Orange and lemon snow aspic

Snows are sweet, light, fluffy aspics. They are used mostly for desserts, but they are very nice to serve as a garnish to fruit salads as well. You can vary the fruit juice called for. For instance, use 6 ounces (170 gr) of undiluted frozen concentrate and water, apple juice or fresh orange juice for the balance of the liquid.

1 envelope unflavoured gelatin

½ cup (125 ml) sugar

⅛ tsp (0.5 ml) salt

1½ cups (375 ml) orange juice

¼ cup (60 ml) lemon juice

2 unbeaten egg whites

Grated rinds of 1 orange and 1 lemon

Thoroughly mix the gelatin with the sugar and salt in a small saucepan. Add ½ cup (125 ml) of the orange juice. Place over low heat and stir constantly until gelatin is dissolved. Remove from heat and stir in the remaining orange juice and the lemon juice. Chill until slightly thicker than unbeaten egg white.

At that point, add the unbeaten egg whites and the grated rinds of the lemon and orange. Then beat the mixture with an electric beater until it foams up and begins to hold its shape. Spoon into a glass serving dish or into small molds, and chill until firm. Top with thawed berries of your choice, or a custard sauce made with the remaining egg yolks. Makes 8 servings.

Wine and cherry aspic

1 envelope unflavoured gelatin

2 to 4 tbsp (30 to 60 ml) sugar, to taste

Pinch of salt

1¾ cups (450 ml) white or red wine, sherry or port, fruit juice, or a mixture of any of these

Juice of ½ lime or 1 tbsp (15 ml) lemon juice

2 cups (500 ml) pitted black cherries, fresh or canned

Mix the gelatin, sugar and salt thoroughly. Add ½ cup (125 ml) of the chosen liquid and stir over low heat until the gelatin is dissolved. Add the remaining liquid and refrigerate the mixture until it has the consistency of unbeaten egg white. Then fold in the cherries. Turn into a well-oiled fancy 3-cup (750 ml) mold, or 6 individual molds, and refrigerate until firm. Makes 6 servings.

CHAPTER 15

Croquettes, fritters and doughnuts

TO FRY FOODS, you cook them in or with fat. There is quite a difference between sautéing, which uses only enough fat to keep the food from sticking to the pan, and deep-frying in which the food is completely immersed in a large quantity of fat in a deep pan or kettle. The most familiar deep-fried food is probably French-fried potatoes, and the method used to cook them is sometimes called French frying. Shallow-frying, or panfrying, uses fat ½ to 1 inch (1.25 to 2.5 cm) deep in a shallow pan — a frying pan.

For sautéing or panfrying, you can use oil, butter, margarine and all-purpose vegetable shortening because the foods cook quickly and the fats do not have time to break down and scorch, as they do for longer frying jobs.

In deep-frying, the fat is heated to a much higher temperature and kept there for a relatively long time. This eliminates butter, margarine, olive oil or any fat that smokes or burns at moderate heat, thus altering its flavour.

Almost any food-meat, poultry, fish, vegetables, fruits, pastries — can be cooked by frying, whether sautéing, panfrying or deep-frying. You will find directions for sautéing or panfrying meats, poultry and fish in the chapters that deal with those foods, and in the vegetable cooking method you will find information on sautéing, panfrying, deep-frying and French frying. In this chapter you will find some basic directions for deep-frying that you can apply to many different foods, and, in particular, information on frying coated foods and mixtures of foods.

PAN FOR DEEP-FRYING

The best utensil to use for deep-frying is a narrow deep pan or kettle with straight sides; it must be made of heavy metal. Or use an electric deep fryer with thermostatically controlled heat.

☛ For foods that expand, such as doughnuts, fill the pan only half full of fat. If there is too little fat, food will burn on the bottom. If there is too much fat, it may bubble over and catch on fire. ☛ If this should happen douse the flames with a heavy-sprinkling of baking soda. Do not use water.

FATS FOR DEEP-FRYING

The very best fat for good flavour and perfect frying is the suet from ribs and kidneys of beef. This has to be rendered over very low heat. Other meat fats, such as lamb fat, can be prepared in the same way.

Lard is pork fat that has already been rendered, but it is solid and must be melted before being used in order to gauge the correct amount. This added work is worthwhile because lard gives a sweet, delicate flavour and a non-greasy finish to food fried in it.

Vegetable oils give foods a glossy appearance. It is easy to gauge the needed quantity because they are liquid. Peanut oil is best. Many vegetable oils add no flavour of their own to foods, but some, such as sesame-seed oil, give a delicate flavour to foods fried in them.

Vegetable shortening is a vegetable oil that has been treated with hydrogen to make it solid at room temperature and to keep it from spoiling. This gives good results in deep-frying.

Bacon fat and chicken fat are excellent for shallow frying, but they do give foods a flavour of their own. They can be used for deep-frying when mixed with some of the other fats mentioned.

Whatever fat you choose, you must use one that can be heated to a high temperature without burning. Burning fat smokes and develops an unpleasant flavour that is transmitted to the food being cooked.

Storing used fat

Never allow used fat to remain in the fryer. Let it cool. Then, when trepid, strain the fat through a sieve lined with several layers of cheesecloth or a double layer of absorbent paper. I like to use a large coffee filter in its holder; this gives perfect clarification. This operation removes all foreign particles, such as bits of food, batter or coating, from the used fat.

Return the strained fat to a container for used fat and while it is still warm add 1 cup (250 ml) of fresh fat of the same kind. This freshens and prolongs the life of the frying fat. Store in a cool dark place or in the refrigerator.

Clarifying used fat

When fat gets dark and has an off-odour, this indicates that the fat, however well taken care of, is starting to break down. **0—⯎** To clarify what is left, strain the fat as explained before. Place it in a deep-frying utensil and add a few slices of raw potato. Bring the fat slowly to a boil. When it has bubbled gently for 1 minute, turn off the heat and remove

the potatoes. They will absorb all odours and flavours. Cool the fat, strain again, and store. Of course, this will not work with a fat that has become rancid. You can determine when a fat is rancid by its smell, which is quite unpleasant. When it reaches that point, discard it.

TEMPERATURES FOR FRYING

0—⯎ The secret of success in deep-frying is to heat the fat slowly over medium-low heat until it reaches the correct temperature; then try to maintain that temperature throughout the entire frying period. Fat that is not hot enough soaks into the food and the food overcooks before it browns. Fat that is too hot burns the food on the outside before the interior is well cooked.

A rule of thumb is that almost all foods will fry properly when the fat is at 365°F to 375°F (185°C to 190°C), but to be more specific:

Uncooked foods, such as doughnuts and fritters made of raw fish, etc., will cook best at 365° to 375°F (185° to 190°C)

Uncooked foods with a large water content, such as potatoes, onions, etc., will cook best at 380° to 390°F (192° to 197°C)

Cooked foods, such as croquettes which are made of chopped or ground cooked meat will cook best at 375° to 385°F (190° to 195°C)

The old-fashioned method of determining when the fat has reached the correct temperature is to brown a 1-inch (2.5 cm) cube of bread. The cube should be browned in 60 seconds if the fat is at 365° to 370°F (185° to 188°C). The bread you use for this must be 2 or 3 days old and dry. A frying thermometer is, of course, the most accurate guide.

COATINGS FOR FRIED FOODS

While it is possible to fry foods without a coating — potatoes for instance — this doesn't always result in the crisp golden morsels, cooked throughout but not greasy, that a good coating helps to achieve. The pieces of food can be rolled one at a time in flour or crumbs, or dipped into milk and then rolled in flour or crumbs. The Japanese dip their foods into a batter called *tempura* and the delicious shrimps prepared this way are a popular item in Japanese restaurants. The English use a mixture of egg, water and oil, with seasoning; so this kind of coating is called *à l'anglaise*. The foods are coated with bread crumbs after being dipped into the *anglaise* mixture.

Egg and crumb coating is particularly good because the egg cooks instantly upon contact with the heat of the fat and this seals in the juices of the food and seals out the fat. Also, the egg acts as an adhesive to hold the coating in place; in the case of mixtures such as croquettes, it helps to hold the pieces together.

To obtain a chef's result, prepare the food ahead of time, dip it into the egg and crumbs, then refrigerate it for 1 hour before frying. This allows the egg to dry and any excess liquid in the food to evaporate. The coating will then adhere better.

Basic method to coat food

1. For 1 to 2 pounds (500 gr to 1 kg) of food, beat 1 egg and 1 tablespoon (15 ml) cold water with a fork, only enough to blend the two. Add ½ teaspoon (2 ml) salt, ½ teaspoon (2 ml) paprika and ¼ teaspoon (1 ml) pepper.

2. Spread the coating material on a sheet of paper. This can be fine bread crumbs or cracker crumbs, cornmeal, instant potato powder or flour. Any of these can be combined, and part of the coating can be grated cheese. Use about 1½ cups (375 ml) of any of these, plain, combined, or with cheese added, for this amount of food.

3. Dip the prepared food into the coating material. Do this gently; you want only a light coating. Then dip the food into the egg mixture, then a second time into the coating material. Set the dipped pieces on a plate, one next to the other. Do not overlap or put one over the other. Refrigerate for at least 20 minutes, or when possible for 1 hour, then the food is ready to be deep-fried.

For an example of a batter coating for entrée or hors-d'oeuvre foods, see Batter-Fried Fish; for an example of a batter coating for dessert preparations, see Fruit Fritters. You will find both these basic recipes later in this chapter.

HOW TO FRY

Prepare the food and refrigerate for 1 hour if possible. Fill the frying kettle half full; the fat should be deep enough to allow the largest-size piece of food to be completely immersed. Slowly bring the fat to the correct temperature. When it has reached this point, add the food. The pieces can be added directly to the fat, or can be lowered into the fat in a frying basket. Be careful not to overcrowd the pan, because this lowers the temperature of the fat. Add only a few pieces at a time, and do it gently to prevent spattering. With doughnuts and fritters, overcrowding prevents expansion and makes for heaviness in the food.

Turn deep-fried foods only once. Use a slotted spoon; a fork or a pointed knife will cause a puncture in the crust and allow the hot fat to soak in.

Remove the finished foods from the fat with a slotted spoon — or lift out the frying basket — and drain on a double layer of absorbent paper placed on a baking sheet or on a thick layer of newspaper.

If additional fat is needed to keep the pan filled to the correct point, add the new fat to the pan when it does not contain food, and slowly bring the fat back to the correct temperature.

Croquettes,
basic method

¼ cup (50 ml) butter or other fat

½ cup (125 ml) flour

2 cups (500 ml) milk

1½ tsp (7 ml) salt

½ tsp (2 ml) pepper

¼ tsp (1 ml) ground thyme or basil or curry powder

Pinch of cayenne

3½ cups (875 ml) finely chopped chicken, meat or fish, cooked or well-drained canned

1 to 2 tbsp (15 to 30 ml) minced parsley

1 tbsp (15 ml) lemon juice

Minced onion to taste

Make a white sauce by mixing together the butter or other fat, flour and milk. You can make the sauce richer by substituting cream for some of the milk. Season with salt, pepper, ground thyme, basil or curry powder, and pinch of cayenne. When sauce is cooked, taste it to be sure it is well seasoned, as the flavour of the croquettes depends upon the sauce.

Add the finely chopped chicken, meat or fish. Add the minced parsley, lemon juice and a bit of minced onion, to taste. Blend thoroughly. Spread the mixture on a baking pan and pack it down well, to get rid of any air bubbles, by patting with the hands. Make the layer about 1 inch (2.5 cm) thick. Cover with waxed paper and refrigerate for 1 hour.

For perfect croquettes, cut the cold mixture with a round cookie cutter. Shape the remaining mixture into cones or sausage shapes; make them about the same thickness as the rounds, 1 inch (2.5 cm). Croquettes burst open when they are too thick or too big because steam forms in the middle.

Coat the rounds and cones with egg then with crumbs as described, fry in deep fat, and drain on paper. Makes about 12 croquettes.

To make 4 small croquettes, use ¼ cup (60 ml) milk, 1 tablespoon (15 ml) each of butter and flour, and seasoning to taste. Add ⅓ cup (80 ml) meat or fish, ½ teaspoon (2 ml) minced parsley and 1 teaspoon (5 ml) lemon juice.

Fish for fish and chips is probably the best-known batter-fried food. Small fish such as smelts can be used whole. Larger fish, such as cod, haddock or sole, can be cut into sticks or filleted.

1 cup (250 ml) all-purpose flour

½ tsp (2 ml) salt

Pinch of ground thyme

1 tbsp (15 ml) salad oil

1 egg, beaten

¾ cup (200 ml) milk

18 small whole smelts, cleaned, or 12 small fillets or 2 lbs (1 kg) fish sticks

1 lemon, halved

Salt and pepper

Flour for dipping

Peanut oil for deep-frying

Prepare the batter ahead of time. Mix flour, salt and thyme. Stir in the salad oil, egg and milk. Beat until thoroughly blended. Refrigerate for at least 1 hour before using.

About 1 hour before coating with batter, rub the fish with lemon, season with salt and pepper and set the pieces side by side on a plate. Do not overlap and do not cover. Refrigerate the fish to dry it and make the batter cling better.

When both the batter and fish have chilled for at least 1 hour, dip the fish into flour, then into the batter, until it is completely coated. Allow excess batter to drip off.

Heat the peanut oil to 360°F (184°C) on a frying thermometer and drop the fish in gently. Cook for 5 to 6 minutes, or until fish is richly browned and crisp. Drain on absorbent paper. Serve as soon as ready.

1 cup (250 ml) all-purpose flour

1 tsp (5 ml) baking powder

1 tbsp (15 ml) sugar

¼ tsp (1 ml) salt

2 eggs, separated

⅓ cup (80 ml) milk

1 tbsp (15 ml) melted butter

Fruit of your choice, thinly sliced

Mix and sift together the flour, baking powder, sugar and salt. Beat 2 egg yolks with the milk. Stir the liquid into the dry ingredients. Stir in the melted butter. Beat the egg whites stiff. Fold into the batter with care.

When ready to fry, add thinly sliced fruit of your choice — apples, peaches, pineapple, bananas, etc. Stir, then pour the mixture by spoonfuls into the deep fat heated to 365°F (185°C) on a frying thermometer. Fry, drain and serve.

The very best doughnuts I know

My daughter's doughnut recipe is easy to mix, roll and cook, and the doughnuts disappear so fast. Their proportions are just right, so they are never fat-soaked or heavy.

3 cups (750 ml) all-purpose flour

3½ tsp (17 ml) baking pwoder

1 tsp (5 ml) salt

½ tsp (2 ml) grated nutmeg

¼ tsp (1 ml) ground cinnamon

3 eggs

1 tsp (5 ml) vanilla extract

¾ cup (190 ml) sugar

3 tbsp (50 ml) soft butter or margarine

¾ cup (200 ml) milk

Sift together the flour, baking powder, salt, grated nutmeg and ground cinnamon.

Beat the eggs until light. Add vanilla extract and sugar. Beat until thick and pale yellow. Add the soft butter or margarine, and beat until well mixed.

Add the milk, alternately with the dry ingredients, to the creamed mixture. Remember, the lighter the doughnut dough, the better the doughnuts will be. Refrigerate the dough for 1 to 1½ hours, until hard enough to roll.

Sprinkle a generous amount of flour on a pastry board. Cut off a piece of dough. Keeping the board well floured, roll into a sheet ⅓ inch (8mm) thick. Cut with a floured doughnut cutter. Place the rounds on a baking sheet as you cut them.

Lift each round of dough with a wide spatula and carefully ease it into deep fat heated to 375°F (190°C) on a frying thermometer. Put only as many doughnuts into the fat as can be turned easily. Fry for about 3 minutes, until completely browned on both sides, turning only once. Lift from the fat with a long fork, picking up each doughnut through the hole. Drain on brown paper or paper toweling. Cool and roll in icing sugar to taste. Makes about 2 dozen.

Table of Contents

Métropole Litho Inc.
Printed in Canada